THE EVOLUTION OF THE SOUL

THE EVOLUTION OF THE SOUL

RICHARD SWINBURNE

CLARENDON PRESS · OXFORD

Oxford University Press, Walton Street, Oxford OX2 6DP
Oxford New York Toronto
Delhi Bombay Calcutta Madras Karachi
Kuala Lumpur Singapore Hong Kong Tokyo
Nairobi Dar es Salaam Cape Town
Melbourne Auckland
and associated companies in
Beirut Berlin Ibadan Nicosia

Oxford is a trade mark of Oxford University Press

Published in the United States
by Oxford University Press, New York

First published 1986
First issued in paperback 1987

British Library Cataloguing in Publication Data
Swinburne, Richard
The evolution of the soul.
1. Soul 2. Philosophy
I. Title
128'.1 B105.S6l
ISBN 0–19–824483–5 (pbk.)

Library of Congress Cataloging in Publication Data
Swinburne, Richard.
The evolution of the soul.
Includes index.
1. Soul—Addresses, essays, lectures. 2. Ethics—
Addresses, essays, lectures. 3. Thought and thinking—
Addresses, essays, lectures. I. Title.
BL290.S95 1986 128'.1 85–21690
ISBN 0–19–824483–5 (pbk.)

Set by Cambrian Typesetters
Printed in Great Britain
at the University Printing House, Oxford
by David Stanford
Printer to the University

PREFACE

THIS book is based on two series of Gifford Lectures, delivered at the University of Aberdeen in the Spring Terms of 1983 and 1984. I have not included in the book the material of a few lectures of the second series, dealing mainly with the moral responsibility of men for their actions, and the theological consequences thereof. I hope that this latter material will be published subsequently in a different context. I am most grateful to the University of Aberdeen for the honour which they paid me in inviting me to give the Gifford Lectures, and for the friendly hospitality and critical interest in my ideas which colleagues at Aberdeen showed to me during the two terms of lectures.

Earlier versions of various parts of this book have been delivered as shorter series of lectures, or as individual lectures at many other universities over a number of years; and the book has, I hope, benefited by the wealth of helpful criticism which I received on these occasions. Part of Chapter 14 was delivered, under the title 'The Structure of the Soul', as my Inaugural Lecture as Nolloth Professor of the Philosophy of the Christian Religion in the University of Oxford. Versions of certain parts of the book have received prior publication in various forms. My contribution to a book co-authored with Sydney Shoemaker, *Personal Identity* (Basil Blackwell, Oxford, 1984) was a fuller version of the ideas contained in Chapters 8 and 9 of the present book. Some passages of Chapter 7 are reprinted from my *Faith and Reason* (Clarendon Press, Oxford, 1981). Recent articles which are earlier or fuller versions of other material are: 'Are Mental Events Identical with Brain Events?', *American Philosophical Quarterly*, 1982, **19**, 173–81; and three articles being published in 1985–6, 'The Indeterminism of Human Actions' (in *Midwest Studies in Philosophy*, vol. 10), 'Thought' (in *Philosophical Studies*, © 1985 by D. Reidel Publishing Co.), and 'Desire' (in *Philosophy*). I am grateful to the publishers of the books and editors of the journals concerned for permission to reuse the various materials.

My writing of this book was greatly facilitated by the University of Keele giving me study leave from my position there as Professor of Philosophy for two terms of 1982–3; I am very grateful for the relief which was provided thereby from normal teaching and administrative duties.

CONTENTS

1. INTRODUCTION

MEN evolved from apes, and apes from more primitive animals, and the primitive animals evolved from the soup of inanimate atoms which consolidated to form the Earth some four thousand million years ago. Although there is much uncertainty about the exact stages and mechanisms involved, the fact of evolution is evident. Even more evident, to my mind, is the fact that what has evolved is different, radically and qualitatively, from that from which it has evolved. Rocks and rivers are not conscious; they do not have thoughts, sensations, and purposes; but men, and some animals, do have thoughts, sensations, and purposes. And having a thought or a sensation or a purpose is not just having some physico-chemical event occur inside one of greater complexity than the physico-chemical events which occur in rocks and rivers. It is not the same sort of thing at all. The mental life of thought, sensation, and purpose may be caused by physico-chemical events in the brain, but it is something quite different from those events: it is rich in inbuilt colour, smell, and meaning. The process of evolution so rearranged the atoms and molecules as to bring about creatures with a life of conscious experience, which is something altogether new in the history of the universe.

Once the thinker takes seriously this vast evident qualitative difference between inanimate things on the one hand, and animals and men on the other, two things will strike him about conscious experience. The first is the fairly evident fact that there is a continuity in experience. The person who has these experiences today has different experiences tomorrow, including ones in which he remembers the experiences of yesterday. This continuity of experience may indeed be caused by continuity of brain matter, but it is not the same thing as it. The second thing is the fairly evident fact that conscious experience is causally efficacious. Our thoughts and feelings are not just phenomena caused by goings-on in the brain; they cause other thoughts and feelings and they make a difference to the agent's behaviour. Apparently, people have trains of thoughts, and present thoughts are suggested by previous thoughts; and an agent acts in the world as he does because of his purposes which he seeks to fulfil.

These two further differences between inanimate things on one hand and animals and men on the other are not quite as evident as the fact of consciousness itself, and more argument is required to substantiate their existence: that will be provided in this book. The theme of the book is the nature and source of the differences between the inanimate objects which alone existed on the Earth at its formation, and the animals and men which have subsequently evolved. Part I will analyse the different facets of the mental life, enjoyed by animals as well as men—sensations, thoughts, purposes, desires, and beliefs. I shall argue, contrary to recent philosophical objectors, that evident appearance is not delusory—there really are mental events and states different from brain processes and observable public behaviour; and they really do make a difference to the organism's public behaviour. Part II will argue that we can only make sense of the continuity of this conscious life by supposing that there are two parts to a man (and to many another animal)—a body and a soul (or mind). The body is an ordinary material object, and so is that crucial part of it—the brain; but the latter is connected to a soul which is the essential part of a man, and which is the part which enjoys the mental life (i.e. which is the subject of sensation and thought and the originator of actions). The evolution of consciousness is the evolution of organisms with souls which are conscious and which interact with the body. The occurrence (though not the details) of the mental life of the soul is however dependent on physical processes in the brain—at any rate at present.

Part III will go on to consider the differences between the mental life of men and that of other animals. I shall describe two evident differences—that men have powers of complex and logically ordered thought and an awareness of moral goodness and obligation, lacking to animals. And I shall argue for the existence of two further differences, not immediately evident—that men have free will in the sense that their choices are not totally predetermined by their brain-states or anything else; and that a human soul has a structure or character which is formed in part through the brain to which it is connected, but which acquires some independence of that brain. No doubt the different facets of animal mental life appeared at different stages of evolutionary history—first perhaps there evolved animals who have sensations, then animals who have also purposes, desires, and beliefs, then animals who have, as well, conscious occurrent thoughts. And if evolution can produce animals with characteristics qualitatively different from those of inanimate things, it would not be surprising if it went on to produce men with substantial further qualitatively different characteristics from the higher animals. I shall argue that it has done so.

The physiologist studies the development of the first cell of each new human baby into a full-grown adult. The evolutionary biologist studies the forces which have formed the genetic structure of such a first cell. But relatively seldom do either of these scientists point out that their descriptions and explanations cover only the evolution of the physical characteristics of man, and that they give no account of the evolution of the most important characteristics of man—the characteristics of his conscious life, his feelings and desires, hopes and beliefs, those characteristics in virtue of his possession of which we treat men, and think that we ought to treat men, as totally different from machines. Most philosophers of the past four centuries have been well aware of the difference between the conscious life of a man and goings-on in his body, but their views have relatively seldom made any significant difference to the writing and teaching of biologists and physiologists.

Scientists have tended to regard the life of conscious experience as peripheral, not central to understanding man. But there is so much and so rich human experience, and experience which is apparently continuous and is causally efficacious, that this attitude will not do. His life of experience has to be taken seriously if we are to understand man. Scientific revolutions occur when data and coincidences previously regarded as unimportant are taken seriously and made the focal point of understanding. This book takes seriously the fact of human conscious experience, its continuity and its causal efficacy—and around these facts, hitherto regarded as peripheral, builds its understanding of man and his evolution. While I shall attempt to describe the differences between men and machines, I shall not be able fully to explain their origin; and indeed I shall produce an argument to show that it is most unlikely that anyone will ever be able fully to explain their origin in terms of a normal scientific explanation. The prospects for a fully explanatory super-science which embraces the mental world as well as the physical world are poor. But we must not fall into the trap of believing that that which we cannot explain (at any rate by a normal scientific pattern of explanation) does not exist. The conscious life evidently exists—that we have sensations and thoughts, feelings and hopes is the most evident thing that there is.

Each of the many issues which I discuss in this book is normally the subject of a book to itself. A philosopher will write a book on sensation, or on belief, or on moral awareness. I am conscious of my temerity in writing one book concerned with all the differences between man and the inanimate and the story of their evolution; and I am well aware of the inadequacy of the treatment which I give to many detailed issues. But I am also aware of the need for an overview of the whole field, and of the difficulty of making plausible a view on some of the issues which I discuss towards the end of the book (e.g. the freedom of the will) without also stating and justifying a view on the issues discussed earlier. Such is my excuse for treating so large a subject within the cover of one volume.

Some Technical Terms

So far I have described my subject matter in vague and ill-defined terms. It is time to introduce more precise technical terms.

My inquiry is into the nature and evolution of man. A man is a member of the human species (and my use of the short and convenient English word 'man' which is also often used to denote a male member of that species carries no implications about any superior status possessed by the males of the species). I also use the word 'person'. As I shall use this word, a person is anyone who has all the facets of consciousness which men possess, whether a member of the human species or not. Thus, creatures from another planet with a conscious life like ours would be persons, but not humans; so, too, would angels. If I am right in my view that there are significant differences between human consciousness and the consciousness possessed by other animals (e.g. that the latter can only have thoughts of very down-to-earth kinds), it will, however, follow that such animals are not persons. As I shall use the words, I shall make it a matter of definition that a 'man' has a human body, but, I shall argue in Chapter 8, it is not part of our current understanding of 'person' that a person has to have a body, let alone a human body; and I shall not impose that restriction on the notion of 'person'. I thus leave it open to argument whether the persons who are men can lose their bodies or acquire non-human bodies, and so cease to be men while continuing to be. I sometimes use the more general terms 'subject' (to refer to any one who has a mental life) and 'agent' (to refer to any one who performs intentional actions), which apply to persons and most animals. In future I shall use the word 'animal' in the narrower sense in which men are distinguished from animals, although, of course, in a wider sense man is a species of animal.

I follow normal philosophical usage in understanding by a 'substance' a component of the world which interacts causally with other components of the world and which has a history through time. Tables and chairs, stars and galaxies, cabbages and persons are substances. Substances have (monadic) properties—such as being square or yellow, or having a mass of 2 lbs. They also have polyadic properties, or relations to other substances, such as being taller than, or lying between. 'Taller than' is a relation which relates two substances; 'lying between' is a relation which relates three substances. (One object lies between a second object and a third object.) I shall understand by an 'event' the instantiation of a property (either a monadic property or a relation) in a particular substance or particular substances at particular times—such as this tie being now green, or having a rough surface; or John being taller than James last year; or Keele now lying between Birmingham and Manchester. Events are states of substances.

In philosophical terminology, I understand by 'events' token events, particular occurrences; as opposed to properties which are universals, in the sense that the same property can be instantiated in many different substances on many different occasions. My use of the word 'event' is not that of ordinary usage. Ordinarily we think of events as changes in the properties or relations of substances—such as an object changing from being red to being green, or changing from being on my left to being on my right. But a list of events in my sense—of the properties and relations possessed by substances at particular times—would allow one to deduce which events in the more normal sense had occurred to those substances. If you know that my tie was red at 10.00 a.m. and was green at 10.01 a.m., you can deduce that an event in the normal sense of its changing its colour occurred during the period 10.00–10.01.

Properties, and, more obviously, events may themselves have properties, including relations to other properties and events. One event may be related to another event by the relation of 'occurring before' it, and by the relation of 'causing' it.

It is a complicated task to give a precise definition of a material object, but for our purposes a rough characterization will suffice.[1] Rocks, tables, chairs, plants, houses, and similar inanimate things are material objects. So is anything which is part of a material object (e.g. an atom), or anything of which such material objects are themselves parts (e.g. a planet). A material object excludes all other material objects (apart from objects which are part of it, or of which it is part) from the space which it occupies. The human body, consisting of atoms, is thus a material object. And so too is man (indeed, he is the same material object as his body)—unless he has a part which is not a material object. All material objects are substances, but a crucial issue is whether there are substances other than material objects, things which interact with material objects, but which are not themselves material objects and perhaps do not even have spatial position.

Properties and events may be physical or mental. I understand by a 'physical property' one such that no one subject is necessarily better placed to know that it is instantiated than is any other subject. Physical properties are public; there is no privileged access to them. Thus having a mass of ten pounds, being eight feet tall, and being square are all physical properties. So too are the typical properties of neurones in the brain—being in such-and-such an electrical state or releasing a transmitter substance. Anyone who chooses can find out as surely as can anyone else whether something is eight feet tall, or in a certain electrical state. Physical events are those which involve the instantiation of physical properties. 'Mental properties', as I shall understand the term, are ones to which one subject has privileged access, which he is necessarily in a better position to know about than anyone else. Some philosophers, as we shall see, deny that there are any mental properties in this sense. But it does rather look at first sight as if properties, such as being in pain or having a red after-image, are mental, for any person in whom they are instantiated does seem necessarily to be better placed to know about them than does

---

[1] For a fuller account of what is a material object, see my *Space and Time*, second edition, Macmillan, London, 1981, pp. 13–16.

anyone else. For whatever ways you have of finding out whether I have a red after-image (e.g. by inspecting my brain-state or studying my behaviour) I can share; and I have an additional way of finding this out—by my own awareness of my own experience (an awareness which may or may not be fallible). So it *looks* as if there are mental properties, distinct from physical properties. 'Mental events' are events which involve the instantiation of mental properties (e.g. John being in pain at midday yesterday).

There are properties, and so events, which look to be mental on this definition, which can be analysed in terms of a physical component and a mental component. These properties and events we may call 'mixed' mental properties and events. Thus 'saying "hallo" ' is a mixed property, for my saying 'hallo' consists in my intentionally seeking to bring about the sound 'hallo' (a mental event) causing the occurrence of the sound 'hallo' (a physical event). It is the property of the instantiation of a certain mental property causing the instantiation of a certain physical property, which is possessed by the substances which are persons who say 'hallo'. (Or at least so it is, if there are, as there appear to be, mental properties; and if, as appears, their instantiation causes the instantiation of physical properties. These issues will be explored more fully in due course.) Those mental properties which cannot be analysed in part in terms of a physical component I term 'pure' mental properties. 'Being in pain' and 'desiring to eat' seem to be such pure mental properties. In talking henceforward of mental properties I shall understand thereby (unless I specify otherwise) pure mental properties; and I shall understand by mental events the instantiations of pure mental properties.

Three Views on the Mind/Body Problem

The technical terms which I have now introduced allow me to expound the crucial issue of the first two parts of the book in more rigorous terms. Their concern is with the mind/body problem, the problem of the relation between a man's conscious life of thought and sensation, and the physical events in and around his body. On this issue there are three main positions which have been taken in the history of thought.

The first position, which I shall call hard materialism, claims that the only substances are material objects, and persons (including men) are such substances. A person is the same thing as what is loosely called his body (and his brain is the same thing as his mind). The only events which occur, the only things that happen in the world, are physical events, viz. ones which consist in the instantiation of physical properties in material objects. There are no mental events in the sense in which I have analysed this notion; for there are no events distinct from physical events to which the subject has privileged access. My being in pain or having an after-image may seem to be mental events, but really they are not—according to the hard materialist. Hard materialists differ among themselves as to which physical events those apparently mental events are. One school holds that they are brain-events— my having a pain just is certain nerve fibres firing in a certain pattern; my having a certain belief just is the existence of a certain nerve circuit in the brain. In recent times this doctrine has been known as Mind-Brain Identity Theory. The other school of hard materialists holds that talk about apparent mental events is talk about the subject's actual or hypothetical public behaviour, what he does and what he would do in different circumstances. For me to have toothache is for me to hold my jaw, be bad-tempered, arrange a dental appointment, etc. all when my tooth is somewhat decayed; and if asked, to say that I have toothache; and if I bite something hard, to cry out. My having the mental event just is the occurrence of the public behaviour which, ordinarily, we would say, it causes. This doctrine is of course known as behaviourism.

In chapters 2 and 3 I shall be discussing the nature of sensations—pains, visual sensations, auditory sensations, and so on. I shall be arguing that they, at any rate, are mental events in my sense; and in subsequent chapters I shall claim that there are mental events of other kinds. My sensations are no doubt *caused by* brain-events, but they are not *themselves* brain-events. My having a red after-image or a pain or a smell of roast beef are real events. If science describes only firings of neurones in the brain, it has not told us everything that is going on. For it is a further fact about the world that there are pains and after-images, and science must state this fact and attempt to explain it. Likewise sensations are to be distinguished from the behaviour to which they typically give rise. For people have sensations to which they give no expression—pains which they conceal or dream-sensations which they report to no one—and, if the sensations give rise to behaviour, the subject is aware of the sensation as a separate event from the behaviour to which it gives rise. The life of conscious experience seems a reality ignored by hard materialism.

The second position on these issues I shall call soft materialism. (It is sometimes called attribute or property dualism.) Soft materialism agrees with hard materialism that the only substances are material objects, but it claims that some of these have mental properties which are distinct from physical properties. Persons are material objects; again, a person is the same thing as his body, and his brain is the same thing as his mind. But persons (and their brains) have, as well as physical properties, also mental properties, such as feeling tired and having a visual sensation of such and such a colour and shape, whereas most substances such as tables and chairs have only physical properties. Mental events—e.g. my having a pain now—are different from brain-events; they are not physical events. Brain-events cause mental events. (Neurones firing in certain patterns cause me to have a red after-image.) And also perhaps mental events cause brain-events. (My decision to move my arm causes the brain-events which cause my arm to move.)

Soft materialism has appealed to the many philosophers and psychologists who hold that the unity of the self is constituted by the unity of the body without denying the evident fact that men are conscious. The basic difficulty however with soft materialism, as with hard materialism, is that there seem to be more truths about the world than the doctrine says that there can be. Hard materialism says that you have told the whole story of the world when you have said which material objects exist and which physical properties they have. But, as we have seen, there is also the issue of which mental properties are instantiated. Soft materialism says that you have told the whole story of the world when you have said which material objects exist and which properties (mental and physical) they have. However, full information of this kind would still leave you ignorant of whether some person continued to live a conscious life or not. Knowledge of what happens to bodies and their parts will not show you for certain what happens to persons. I shall illustrate this in Chapter 8 with the example of brain transplants. As is well known, the human brain consists of two very similar hemispheres, each of which is capable of performing many of the functions of the other; and people can survive when they lose much of one of the hemispheres. Now suppose one brain hemisphere is taken out of my skull and transplanted into the empty skull of a body from which a brain has just been removed; and the transplant takes, and we have a living person with a life of conscious experiences. And suppose that the other hemisphere is transplanted into a different empty skull, and that transplant also takes; so that we now have two living persons, both with lives of conscious experiences. Which would be me? Clearly, both would behave like me and make my memory claims; for behaviour and speech depends, at any rate in part, on brain-states. But both persons would not be me. For if they were both identical with me they would be the same person as each other (if *a* is the same as *b*, and *b* is the same as *c*, then *a* is the same as *c*) and they are not. They now have different experiences and different lives. Maybe the person with my right brain hemisphere is me, and maybe the person with my left brain hemisphere is me, and maybe neither is me. We cannot be certain. The point, which I shall be developing at length, is that mere knowledge of what happens to bodies does not tell you what happens to persons. Hence there must be more to persons than bodies. I shall therefore be arguing that a man living on Earth is a substance which consists of two substances, his body and his soul. The body is a material body, but the soul is not a material object or anything like it. (It occupies no volume of space.) Body and soul are connected at present, in that events in the body affect events in the soul, and conversely. But the essential part of the man is his soul; a man consists of his soul together with whatever, if any, body is connected to it. Mental events which happen to the human being do so in virtue of happening to his soul; bodily events which happen to the human being do so in virtue of happening to his body. This is dualism, the position which I shall defend.

Dualism has, however, often been held, as by Plato and Descartes, in the extreme form of the doctrine that the soul has a natural immortality, i.e. that the soul has a nature such that it will continue to survive 'under its own steam' whatever happens to the body. I shall argue that, on the contrary, there can be no justified general account of the nature of the soul; all we can say is that under normal mundane conditions the functioning of the soul requires the functioning of the body. My form of dualism might be called 'soft dualism'.

Principles of Inductive Inference

For our knowledge of the mental life of others, of mental states which exist when no one is conscious of them, and of what causes what, we are often dependent on inductive inference. That is, we observe or experience certain events and these are evidence for the occurrence of other events which we do not observe or experience. They are evidence for the latter in that they make their occurrence more probable or likely than they would otherwise be (i.e. they confirm their occurrence), and sometimes they make them very probable indeed; and so the enquirer ought to believe. When are some events evidence for other events?

The first and most general principle of inductive inference is the *Principle of Credulity*: that in the absence of counter-evidence probably things are as they seem to be, 'seem to be', that is, in the epistemic sense. There is an important class of verbs for describing an agent's awareness of the world—the general verbs 'appears' and 'seems'; and verbs for special senses, 'looks', 'sounds', 'feels', 'smells', and 'tastes'. There are two crucially different senses of each of these verbs, distinguished by Chisholm, the comparative and the epistemic sense.[2] An object looks φ in the comparative sense to a subject *s* if it looks to *s* the way φ things normally look (i.e. its visual appearance is that normal for φ things); an object looks φ in the epistemic sense to *s* if (because of the way it looks in the comparative sense) *s* is inclined to believe that it is φ. By saying that *s* is *inclined* to believe that the object is φ, I mean that he will believe this in the absence of further evidence—e.g. what someone else tells him. The penny lying on the table viewed from an angle looks elliptical in the comparative sense (because it looks the way elliptical things normally look, viz. look when viewed from above), but it looks round in the epistemic sense to most of us—because (on the basis of the way it looks in the comparative sense) we are inclined to believe that it is round. Similarly for the other verbs. An object seems φ to *s* in the epistemic sense if (on the basis of the way it seems in the comparative way) *s* is inclined to believe that it is φ.

The principle of credulity states that if (in the epistemic sense) it

---

[2] See R. M. Chisholm, *Perceiving*, Cornell University Press, Ithaca, NY, 1957, ch. 4.

seems to you that you are seeing an orange, or opening a tin of peas, or whatever, then probably you are seeing an orange or opening a tin of peas, or whatever, unless you have good reason for supposing that you are subject to illusion: and so you ought to believe. Such good reason will be the conflict of what seems to you to be the case with other things which seem to you to be the case—e.g. it can't be an orange if you can put your hand through it; and if it seems to you that you have put your hand through it, that is reason for supposing that you are subject to illusion in supposing that you are seeing an orange.

Without this principle, there can be no knowledge at all. If you cannot suppose that things are as they seem to be unless some further evidence is brought forward—e.g. that in the past in certain respects things were as they seemed to be, the question will arise as to why you should suppose the latter evidence to be reliable. If 'it seems to be' is good enough reason in the latter case, it ought to be good enough reason to start with. And if 'it seems to be' is not good enough reason in the latter case, we are embarked on an infinite regress, and no claim to believe anything with justification will be correct. If the fact that something looks square is not good reason for supposing that it is square without it being shown that in the past things that looked square have usually proved to feel square, behave in a square-like way, etc., the question arises as to why we should believe that things were thus in the past, and the answer must be that it 'seems' to us that we so remember. And if seeming is a good reason for believing in the latter case, then looking is a good reason for believing to start with. It is a slogan of science that we should rely on 'the evidence of our senses', on 'experience'; the principle of credulity crystallizes this slogan more precisely.

We should not, however, believe that things are as they seem when there is counter-evidence—either that in a particular case we are subject to illusion, or that in a particular range of cases (e.g. where it seems to men that they see round corners, or backwards in time) human experience is unreliable. But this counter-evidence itself will arise from trusting experience, from discovering that where people report seeing round corners things are not (it seems epistemically) as they report. There is no avoiding ultimate reliance on the principle of credulity. The rational man is the credulous man—who trusts experience until it is found to mislead him—rather than the sceptic, who refuses to trust experience until it is found not to mislead him.

The principle of credulity that an individual ought to believe that things are as they seem to him is backed up by the *Principle of Testimony*: that individuals ought to believe the reports of others about how things seemed to them, and so (given the principle of credulity) that things were as they report—in the absence of counter-evidence. That is, other things being equal, the reports of others are probably true. Only if we assume that people normally tell the truth, will we ever understand what they are saying. The child learns to understand his parents, by finding some feature of his environment which is present when they utter some sentence (e.g. they say 'it is raining' when it is raining) and then, supposing that they are seeking to describe that feature truly, he comes to learn what that sentence means. But without using the principle of testimony he could not even understand what was said. Of course, 'other things' are not always 'equal'. We find by experience that certain persons, or persons in certain circumstances, are not to be trusted. But what the principle states is that we must assume trustworthiness in the absence of counter-evidence.

The principles of credulity and testimony give the enquirer a vast data base. From it he constructs his theories about how the world works—what there is in it and how it operates. But our data base is only a finite collection of data, a finite number of events which we reasonably believe to have occurred. One can construct an infinite number of different theories compatible with that collection of data, theories about unobservable substances and properties which bring about the observable events, theories about the laws of nature which determine which events bring about which other events. Choice among such theories is determined by the *Principle of Simplicity*. Among such theories we take the simplest one as that most likely to be true—or, more precisely, in a given field, we take as most likely to be true the simplest theory which fits best with other theories of neighbouring fields to produce the simplest set of theories of the world. The simplest theory is that which postulates few substances, few kinds of substances, mathematically simple properties of substances determining their mode of interaction with other substances (i.e. mathematically simple laws of nature). Faced with a set of identical footprints, we could postulate that each was caused by a different man wearing a qualitatively identical shoe, or we could postulate that all the footprints were caused by one man. The latter hypothesis being simple is more likely to be true. Faced with certain points on a graph, being measurements of the value of one variable for a given value of a different variable (and given no other background information of how these variables are likely to interact), we draw the simplest (i.e. normally the smoothest) curve through the data-points, and regard it as more likely that future measurements will lie on that curve than that they will lie on some other curve. The simplest theory provides the 'best' explanation of the data, that is, the explanation most likely to be the true explanation of why the data are as they are.

Indeed, so convinced are we that the simplest theory is that most likely to be true, that we are prepared to regard some of our initial data as slightly inaccurate and a few of them as wildly erroneous in order to get a simple theory of a field. We seek not the simplest curve which passes through all our data-points, but the simplest curve which passes close to most of our data-points. The enquirer regards as best supported by evidence that simplest theory of the field which has the consequence that almost all of the claims of observers about how things seem (epistemically) to them turn out to be (more or less) correct. Science is prepared to correct a few observational reports in the light of the simplest theory compatible with the vast majority of observational reports.

The principle of simplicity thus shows what is to be regarded as 'counter-evidence' to the operation of the principle of credulity. We should not believe that things are as they seem to be in cases when such a belief is in conflict with the simplest theory compatible with a vast number of data obtained by supposing in a vast number of other cases that things are as they seem to be.

Any belief which we reach through application of the principle of credulity is corrigible. Suppose a certain metal object viewed from a certain angle looks (in the epistemic sense) elliptical. I therefore come to believe that it is elliptical. But when I view it from several other angles it looks (in the epistemic sense) round and when I feel it it feels round. So I come to believe that when I perceive it on the latter occasions it is round. It is simpler to suppose that it has always remained of the same shape rather than suddenly changing shape (which would make it unlike other metal objects, which, use of the principle of credulity leads us to suppose, do not change shape suddenly). So I come to believe that it has always been round, and retract my original judgement that on a certain occasion it was elliptical. But my retraction arising from my use of the principle of simplicity, depends crucially also on my use of the principle of credulity on other occasions, and on the results produced by many uses of it outweighing the result produced by a single use. There is, I repeat, no other access to justified beliefs about the world except by means of the principle of credulity.

In attempting to understand the mental life of other men, we apply a principle which is a consequence of the principle of simplicity—the *Principle of Charity*. Other things being equal, we suppose that other men are like ourselves—in the mental (or apparently mental) life to which similar stimuli to their bodies give rise and in the mental (or apparently mental) life which is followed by similar bodily responses. I believe that the principle of charity follows from the principle of simplicity, since it is simpler to postulate that organisms in so many ways similar to ourselves have similar connections between mental and bodily states to the ones which exist in ourselves than to suppose different connections to exist in different men. My claim that the principle of charity does follow from the principle of simplicity may be disputed by those who claim that the justification for our belief in 'other minds'— that other men are not just robots but have a life of sensation, thought, etc.—is quite other than the justification for our belief in inductive extrapolation. I shall not argue the point here, as the issue of 'other minds' is a complex one.[3] I shall simply use the principle of charity and assume, as we all do, that the principle is correct (whether or not it is independent of the principle of simplicity). Without this principle we would have no justification for believing that other men are conscious beings like ourselves. But with this principle we can infer not merely that there are 'other minds' but that they are similar to our own in various ways.

Any theory constructed from data by the principle of simplicity may be false, and may be shown to be false by subsequent

[3] For development of the claim that we derive our knowledge of the mental life of others from putting forward a simple hypothesis about the mental life which predicts well observable behaviour which flows from it, see C. Chihara and J. A. Fodor, 'Operationalism and Ordinary Language', *American Philosophical Quarterly*, 1965, **2**, 281–95, reprinted in J. A. Fodor, *Representations*, Harvester, Brighton, 1981.

observation and experience, but the principle which science uses is that the simplest extrapolation from certain data is the one which (given those data alone) is most likely to be true; the one which, for the time being, we ought to believe.

The above principles of inductive inference will be used from time to time in subsequent argument. They are, I suggest, the basic principles used by science.

PART I

THE MENTAL LIFE

IF there is a mental life to which a subject of experience has privileged access, it is a rich and varied one. A man's mental events will include perceptions and sensations (of all the different senses), imaginings, memories and hopes, thoughts and feelings, dreams, desires, and beliefs. I shall however be claiming, by considering typical examples, that all other mental events are *qua* mental (i.e. in respect of the pure mental events which compose them), composed of elements of five kinds—sensations, thoughts, purposings, desires, and beliefs.

By sensations I mean experiences (other than beliefs) of the kind normally brought about by the senses, or ones similar thereto in experiential content, such as my experiencing the patterns of colour in my visual field, sensations of taste or smell, mild aches and pains, sensations of hot or cold in parts of my body; together with their pale imitations in my recalling memory images or my imagining imagined images. By thoughts I mean those datable conscious occurrences of particular thoughts, which can be expressed in the form of a proposition. Often these are thoughts which occur to a man, flit through his mind, or strike him without him in any way actively conjuring them up. It may occur to me— that today is Tuesday, or that this is a receptive audience, or that the weather is cold. I may, instead, on occasion actively bring about thoughts, maybe rehearsing a train of thoughts, to drum them home to myself, or hoping that some thought which I produce will spark off some new thought which solves all my problems. But thoughts are in the main uncaused by the subject.

By a man's purposings I mean his endeavourings to bring about some events, meaning so to do. Every human intentional action, everything which a man does meaning to do it, consists of the man bringing about some effect, or trying but failing to do so. Yet when the man brings about some effect, his active contribution may be just the same as when, unexpectedly, he tries but fails to bring about the effect. When I move my hand, I bring about the motion of my hand. Normally this action involves no effort and is entirely within my control. But on some occasion, I may find myself unexpectedly paralysed. My active contribution is the same as when I move my hand successfully, yet, because I fail, we say that what I did was to 'try' to move my hand. Normally we speak of 'trying' only when effort or failure is involved. Yet we do need a word which covers both the trying which involves effort or failure, and an agent's own intentional contribution to an action, when the performance is easy and successful. For this intentional contribution, for an agent's setting himself to bring about some effect (even when effort or failure is not involved) I will use the word 'purposing'.

A man's beliefs are his view of how the world is, his 'picture' or 'map' of how things are. A man's desires are his natural inclinations to do things, experience things or have things—what he feels naturally inclined to do or seek, and so what he will do or seek but for a belief that he ought to be doing something else or that the pursuit of some other goal would be more in his long-term interest.

Among these suggested five components of the mental life there are, I suggest further, some crucial distinctions. Desires and beliefs are continuing mental states; sensations, thoughts, and purposings are conscious episodes. I understand by a continuing mental state a state in which the subject may be for a long period of time, including while he is totally unconscious. I understand by a conscious episode a part of the subject's (total) state of consciousness at a particular time. The subject's state of consciousness is a state of which he must be to some extent aware while he is in it. A subject's state of consciousness is the state consisting of all his experiences and purposings at a given time.

A belief that Edinburgh lies to the north of London, and a desire for success in an examination or revenge on an enemy, last while their subject is asleep or thinking of other things. Sensations, thoughts, and purposings are by contrast conscious episodes. Thoughts and purposes would not exist unless the subject was to some extent aware of them. I could not have the thought that it is

John who is knocking at the door, nor could I sign my name intentionally, unless to some degree I was aware that I was having the thought or was purposing to sign my name. There are, however, degrees of awareness, and subjects can be only half-aware (subconsciously aware) of their thoughts and purposes. They can, I shall suggest, be totally unaware of particular sensations but only to the extent to which other conscious episodes hold their attention. A sensation would not be a sensation, a pain would not be a pain, if, in the absence of any other conscious episodes, the subject was totally unaware of its occurrence; nor would pains or after-images be sensations unless the subject could become aware of them, through reflecting on what he was experiencing.

Beliefs, desires, sensations, and thoughts are all passive events; purposings are active events. The former are passive in that they consist of some event happening to the subject, while purposings are active in that they consist of the subject intentionally doing something. Those conscious episodes which are passive, viz. sensations and thoughts, are experiences. Beliefs, desires, sensations, and thoughts are also, on the whole, involuntary, in that what happens to the subject is not something which he himself brings about. Beliefs, I shall be arguing, are always totally involuntary—we do not choose our beliefs; they come to us. (We can to some extent choose the topics about which we will have beliefs by choosing which topics to investigate; what we cannot choose is which beliefs we will have as a result of pursuing the investigation.) Desires, too, are things we find ourselves having; but here we can through assiduous cultivation change the pattern of our desires over time. Most sensations and thoughts which happen to us are not the result of choice; sensations assail our senses, and thoughts flit through our minds without being chosen. But we can, if we choose, produce sensations and thoughts at will—in the case of sensations by exposing our senses to the right stimuli or conjuring up a faint image of a sensation.

Thoughts and purposings and, less obviously, beliefs and desires are, I shall be arguing, intrinsically propositional, whereas sensations are not propositional at all. By the former being propositional I mean that they consist in an attitude to a state of affairs under a certain description, i.e. as described by one proposition but not as described by a logically equivalent proposition. (Two propositions are logically equivalent if of logical necessity whenever one is true the other is true and conversely. 'John is two years older than James' is logically equivalent to 'James is younger than John by the number of years which equals the positive square root of four'.) A thought, for example, is a thought that a certain proposition is true or may be true or ought to be true. A purposing is a purposing that a certain proposition be made true.

Even if p is logically equivalent to q, the thought that p is a different thought from the thought that q and the one may occur without the other occurring. A thought or purposing is the thought or purposing it is in virtue of the proposition which it contains. Many writers have used the words 'intentional' or 'intensional' to do the job for which I am using the word 'propositional' but these words have a variety of meanings; and I hope that less confusion will result from my usage. By saying that thoughts or whatever are intrinsically propositional, I mean that this propositional character does not belong to the thought in virtue of some context in which it occurs (as it might be said that the propositional character of some spoken sentence of English belongs to it in virtue of the linguistic conventions of our society which give it its meaning), but is intrinsic to the thought, whatever the context of its occurrence.[1]

---

[1] That 'many mental states and events' have the property of 'Intentionality', that is 'that property by which they are directed at or about or of objects and states of affairs in the world' is the thesis of J. R. Searle, *Intentionality*, Cambridge University Press, 1983 (see his p. 1). He claims (p. 26): 'it is not possible to give a logical analysis of the Intentionality of the mental in terms of simpler notions, since Intentionality is, so to speak, a ground floor property of the mind, not a logically complex feature built up by combining simpler elements.'

2. SENSATIONS

I begin my analysis of these events which, if men have a mental life distinct from their public physical life, are the basic constituents of that life, with sensations. In so doing, I shall distinguish sensations from their causes and effects in the world outside a man's body, including a man's public behaviour. In the next chapter I shall argue that sensations are events distinct from events inside a man's body; and so I shall be able to conclude that since they are neither extra- nor intra-bodily physical events, they are not physical events at all; they are mental events (i.e. such that the subject has privileged access to them; he can know about them more surely than can anyone else). I shall not prejudge that conclusion in this chapter.

The Nature of Sensations

I understand by a sensation simply an experience of a non-propositional, non-appetitive character. (For these terms, see further below.) We are normally aware of our sensations, and so we believe that we are having them while we are having them. Normally, while a person is having an after-image, he is aware of having it. But, for reasons which I shall give later, I am not making it a matter of definition that a subject must be aware of a sensation while he has it. I shall argue only that he must be aware of some of the conscious episodes which he is currently having. A sensation can however only escape a subject's notice through being swamped, as it were, by other sensations, thoughts, and purposings. Also, I suggest, one thing which is involved in a sensation being part of a state of consciousness is that (whether or not with privileged access) a subject must be able to be aware of any current sensation if he chooses to consider which sensations he is having. An after-image wouldn't be an experience, a sensation, or an after-image if the subject was unable to become aware that he was currently having it.

Like all experiences, sensations are passive in the sense that they happen to the subject, they are experienced by him; they do not consist of his bringing something about. But although they do not *consist* of the subject bringing something about, they are subject to different degrees of voluntary control. Which mental images I have is often to a considerable degree up to me; and many of the sensations which are caused in me by the outside world are ones which I can shut off (e.g. by closing my eyes). Pains, however, by contrast are often unavoidable. Sensations are non-propositional in the sense that they do not consist in an attitude to a state of affairs under a description. They may occur without being conceptualized by the subject. This can be seen by the fact that to the extent that some proposition describes a sensation, any logically equivalent proposition will do so equally correctly. A pattern of dots in a subject's visual field described as four rows of three dots, may be described equally correctly as three columns of four dots, or as a pattern of dots in the shape of a rectangle with one side of two-thirds the length of the other. The subject may know that some of these descriptions apply to his sensation, and not know that others do, but he will not think of any one of these descriptions as in any way picking out the essence of the sensation in a way that the others do not. Sensations, as I am understanding the term, are non-appetitive, that is do not involve any element of desire. I thus distinguish the sensory component of a sweet taste from the desire to continue to enjoy it.

Paradigm cases of sensations exemplifying this definition include the experiencings of patterns of colour (when the subject has no belief that they correspond to anything in the outside world), such as the having of after-images, eidetic memory images, lines in the visual field symptomatic of migraine, images had by the drink- or drug-addict; the hearing of noises 'in the head', smelling a smell of roses, or tasting a taste of honey (where the subject does not believe that there are roses or honey present). It seems fairly evident (although I shall argue for this briefly later) that one element in perception is very similar to, and sometimes indistinguishable from, the above sensations, and hence also to be termed sensation. Experiencing of the patterns of colour which the subject does not believe to be the surfaces of public objects is very similar to experiencing patterns of colour which the subject does believe to be the surfaces of public objects; tasting a taste of honey when you do not believe that there is honey in your mouth is very like tasting a taste of honey when you do have this belief—except that in the latter cases there is something else mental present, the belief. Other examples of sensations are feeling bodily sensations, such as pains, itches, tickles, heat, and cold *minus* any desire which accompanies them. Experiences of certain kinds are so regularly accompanied by the desire that the experience cease, that we tend to make it part of the concept of an experience of those kinds that the subject desire not to have it. In one sense of 'pain', a pain would not be a pain unless it was unpleasant, i.e. the subject desired not to have it. But one can distinguish between the sensation and the desire in all of these cases. One can see the distinction in the case of pain by noting that a normal pain is a more acute feeling of a kind which would not be unpleasant in a very mild degree.[1] The mildest of pricks or aches is not unpleasant. Note also that when those suffering acute pain are subjected to the brain operation of prefrontal leucotomy, they sometimes report that although the 'pain' is still there, it is no longer unpleasant.[2]

Into the class of sensations come also the faint and blurred schematic copies of sensations of the central kinds which I have discussed, in the form of memory images (when memory comes to one via images) and the intentionally imaged diagrams or patterns of the imagination. Such is the class of the sensory. My examples of sensations should elucidate the sense of 'experience' in which sensations are experiences.

A person having a sensation is an event of a substance (the person) being characterized by a monadic property. My having a red image is my having a property (having-a-red-image). It is not my having a relation (experiencing) to some second substance (a red image). Although we are not tempted to analyse the having of certain kinds of sensations in this way—no one would suppose that

[1] See R. M. Hare, 'Pain and Evil', *Proceedings of the Aristotelian Society*, Supplementary Volume, 1964, **38**, 91–106. Reprinted in (ed.) J. Feinberg, *Moral Concepts*, Oxford University Press, London, 1969. And for full-length development of the distinction between the sensation of pain and any other elements involved with what we normally call 'pain'; the fact that some sensations other than pains are unpleasant; and the fact that although many sensations are pleasurable (i.e. we desire to have them), there is no sensation of pleasure corresponding to the sensation of pain, see R. Trigg, *Pain and Emotion*, Clarendon Press, Oxford, 1970.

[2] Not all cases of the lessening of concern for 'pain' resulting from pre-frontal leucotomy are to be given the interpretation that the 'pain' i.e. the sensation, has remained at the same intensity while the desire to be rid of it has declined. For different interpretations of different cases, see Trigg, op. cit., ch. 7.

having a headache was experiencing a thing—we are so tempted in other cases. Having a visual image, and especially an eidetic image (i.e. the very detailed image of an object, say the page of a book, which some people retain after looking away from the object), is more naturally thought of as experiencing a thing, a 'sense-datum'. The image seems something external to ourselves which we inspect. Although it is important to bring out that some sensations have this character of being an experience of something apparently external, it is equally important to emphasize that there is in fact no external substance to which we are related when we have such sensations. For if a sense-datum were a substance, it would have to be capable of independent existence—of existing unsensed and then being sensed now by you, and now by me. But if a sense-datum were in this way a public thing, it would be no more a component of sensation than my desk is a component of the visual sensation to which it gives rise when I look at it. One way of making the point that having a sensation is being characterized by a monadic property is what is known as the 'adverbial'[3] account of sensation, which recommends that the property of having a red image should be characterized less misleadingly as the property of 'being appeared to redly'.

The Description of Sensations

Our language is a public language, used in the first place, as Wittgenstein reminded us, for talking, not about our private mental life but about material objects and their properties and interactions—about sticks and stones and plants and animals being square or round or hitting each other. How is it that this public language can be used for talking about sensations? Individual sensations can be picked out by their temporal relations (e.g. before and after) to other events, including evident public events. We can pick out a sensation as 'that event which happened to a subject between my sticking a pin in him and his crying out', or

---

[3] For a well-known exposition of adverbial materialism, see J. W. Cornman, *Materialism and Sensations*, Yale University Press, New Haven and London, 1971, especially chapters 6 and 7, which set out the difficulties of postulating sense-data (or 'sensa' as he calls them) and the advantages of the adverbial account. For a careful account of just how such properties as 'being appeared to redly' (or 'sensing redly') are to be understood, and how they are related logically to each other, see M. Tye, 'The Adverbial Approach to visual Experience', *Philosophical Review*, 1984, **93**, 195–225.

'that event which happened to him when he looked in this direction and when I spoke to him'. Sensations being experiences of which their subjects can become aware and are normally aware, the subject then most naturally interprets talk of 'that event' as referring to the sensations.

One evident fact about many sensations is that they are caused by physical events in and around our bodies, which occur immediately before them—e.g. the pain is caused by my arm being pricked with a pin—and that this happens by those physical events causing brain-events (by transmission of nerve impulses) and the brain-events causing the sensations. Stimuli are causes of sensations. We can therefore identify a sensation more precisely, among those which happen at some time as the one caused by a certain cause. Many sensations also are often followed by typical responses—pain by the subject crying out, a red sensation by an English speaker when asked to name the colour of his sensation replying 'red'. But whether those responses are, as they appear to be, the effects of the sensation is an issue which will require further discussion. For it may be that the brain-event which causes the sensation also causes the response. Perhaps it is not the pain itself, but the brain-event which causes the pain, which also causes me to cry out.

Using the principle of charity (see p. 15), we assume, that in the absence of counter-evidence, when we ourselves have a sensation of a certain kind caused by a cause of a certain kind and often leading to our making (voluntarily or involuntarily) a response of a certain kind, others who are stimulated by a similar cause and/or give a similar response have a sensation similar to ours. Burning gives rise to a certain sensation in me and the sensation leads (in the absence of strong self-control) to certain typical responses including crying out; so, when we see some one else crying out after he has been burnt, we assume that he has had a similar sensation to ourselves. Similarity of stimulus suffices for us to assume similarity of sensation, without being backed up by similarity of response, and conversely, other things being equal. We assume that those who look at grass have colour sensations similar to ours when we look at grass.

Among the responses which men make to sensations are the response of saying that a sensation caused by a certain object is similar to sensations caused by similar objects and by certain other objects. We can then (given our general assumption) assume that the sensations concerned are the same in different men and give a name to that property which the sensations share. Objects vibrating 256 times per second, though differing in many other ways (e.g. in whether what is vibrating is a string or an air column) give rise to sounds which many men judge as similar to each other and which in virtue of that respect in which they are similar (to be called pitch), they call middle C.

Tea (Indian, Ceylonese, or Chinese) is judged by many men to give rise to somewhat similar sensations in each; we assume that the sensations in different men are the same, and we call the property which they share 'the taste of tea'. Once we have learnt to pick out and describe kinds of sensations in terms of their typical causes, we can then recognize and describe sensations of the same kind as those caused in a certain way but which are not themselves caused in that way. I can have a red image when not looking at a red object; and a burning pain when nothing is burning me; and I can learn to recognize and describe them as such.

As we saw earlier, having a visual sensation is a matter of experiencing something seemingly external to ourselves, viz. a pattern of colour, which forms our 'visual field'. Grass, leaves in springtime, and gooseberries all give rise in most of us to visual sensations similar to each other in a certain respect, and distinct from the sensations similar to each other in an analogous respect (colour) produced by other groups of objects (e.g. distinct from the sensations produced by ripe strawberries, ripe raspberries, and London buses). We then assume that most of us who group together objects producing colour sensations in similar ways have, on viewing a given object, similar sensations to each other, and we may call the sensation produced (in those of us who do so group objects) by grass, etc., green, and the sensation produced by strawberries, etc., red.[4] An object is then said to be (e.g.) green if it produces a green sensation in most observers under normal

---

[4] There is a difference between the sense in which the sensation is (e.g.) green and the sense in which the physical object is green, and it may be useful to draw attention to that difference by some notation—e.g. that proposed by Peacocke (C. Peacocke, *Sense and Content*, Clarendon Press, Oxford, 1983, p. 20). Peacocke (op. cit., chs. 1 and 2) distinguishes between the sensory and the representational (i.e. inclination to believe) elements in perception along similar lines to those which I shall follow, but uses examples of different kinds from those which I use later.

conditions. An object looks green in the comparative sense if it produces a green sensation which, because it is a visual sensation, comes to us as something external forming the surface of the object. (See p. 11 for explanation of the comparative and epistemic senses of verbs such as 'looks'.) But an object which looks green in the comparative sense need not look green in the epistemic sense—for example, if we know that the lighting is odd, we may have no inclination to believe that the object is green.

The description of sensations occurring in perception is often done by describing how the objects perceived appear, e.g. look or feel, in the comparative sense. For to say that the object looks green in the comparative sense is to say that it causes a green sensation. This way of describing sensations is thus, as with the earlier simpler examples, a way of describing sensations by the similarity to other sensations having a certain cause.

Sensations come to us as similar to certain sensations in some respects and to different sensations in other respects, and we develop names for any respect which many people recognize as such. We give a name to any similarity, which many people recognize by classifying sensations caused in a certain way together. Other people who do not have any inclination to group sensations in the same way do not recognize that sort of respect.

We come, further, to develop a vocabulary which picks out different kinds of respect in which sensations which we recognize as different from each other, nevertheless resemble each other. Honey, jam, and sugar, although tasting in many respects different from each other taste similar to many men in a certain respect; we give the name of 'sweet' to that respect. We learn to describe the tastes of overlapping groups of objects as 'pungent', 'bitter', 'sour', 'strong', etc. The development of a vocabulary which describes different properties of sensations, then allows us to describe a sensation different from any which we have had before, by describing it as characterized by a number of properties which we had never found to be exemplified together before—e.g. as 'like honey, but very bitter' or 'purplish green'.

We assume that other people's sensations are like our own—in the absence of counter-evidence. The counter-evidence will be that they respond to stimuli in a different way from ourselves, and the difference of response suggests a different sensation intervening between stimulus and response. Among primitive responses are seeking and avoiding. If most people when burnt avoid the flame, but one person goes on seeking it, that suggests (in absence of other evidence) that he, unlike the rest of us, likes the sensation which burning causes in him, and that, in turn, suggests (in the absence of other evidence) that it is a different sensation from the one we have.[5] Crucial among more sophisticated responses are how we classify objects together in the respect that they cause similar sensations, and how we describe them. If one person classifies blue and red objects as having the same colour (shown by his inability to recognize a figure of red dots set in a field of blue dots—the standard test for colour blindness), then either the blue objects or the red objects (or both) look (in the comparative sense) differently to him from the way they do to most of us. Likewise if a person refuses to call the taste caused by jam 'sweet', although he applies 'sweet' to sensations caused by other objects in the same way as do most people, that shows that either jam or most other objects causing sensations normally called 'sweet', taste differently to him from how they do to other people.[6] The simplest supposition in such cases, in the absence of other evidence, is to suppose minimum divergence—e.g. to suppose in the latter case that jam alone causes in the cited subject a different sensation from the sensation caused by it in other people; while other objects which produce in other people the sensation which they describe as 'sweet' produces in our subject the same sensation as in them.

In supposing that the same stimulus causes the same sensation (the basic initial assumption, open to correction in the light of the response to it), we normally only know the stimulus to or around the body (the peripheral stimulus) which triggers off a chain of

[5] The evidence of this response (this continuing to seek the sensation) would need to be weighed against any evidence of other responses (e.g. the description he gives of it) in determining whether he has a different sensation from the rest of us, or whether he has the same sensation as the rest of us, but likes it. His describing it as similar to and similar in similar ways to sensations which he and we dislike would suggest that the sensation caused in him by burning is the same as that caused in the rest of us.

[6] The argument of the last two sentences assumes that people notice differences and similarities between their sensations. I shall suggest later that that is not always so. However, when I have shown by the end of Chapter 3 that sensations are mental events, it will follow that subjects are in a better position to know about the nature of their sensations than is any outsider. Hence it will follow that we ought to take a subject's word about the similarities and dissimilarities between his sensations, even if he may sometimes be in error about them.

internal causes, impulses along peripheral nerves leading to brain-events. We do not know which brain-event is the immediate cause of the sensation. But assuming that humans have similar nervous systems and brains to each other (an assumption which can be, and in general is, borne out by experimental work on the brain), we suppose that the same peripheral stimulus brings about the same immediate cause. To the extent to which we discover that that is not so, we must drop our assumption that the same peripheral stimulus causes the same sensation. For we only take the peripheral stimulus as evidence of the sensation in virtue of our belief that it shows that the same peripheral stimulus brings about the same immediate cause of the sensation. If we discover that some peripheral stimuli cause different brain-events, that takes away our grounds for supposing the sensations caused indirectly by the peripheral stimuli to be the same. To the extent to which the construction and wiring of a brain is seen to be different from that of the normal human brain, to that extent we have reason to doubt whether the sensations associated with it are similar to ours. It is for this reason that inference from public events to the sensations of creatures with different sense-organs and physiology from ourselves is a very speculative business.

The lower mammals are sensitive to various olfactory differences to which we are also sensitive, but their brains are constructed so differently that there is not much reason for supposing that raw meat smells the same to them as to us. And when we come to animals very different indeed from ourselves, it may well be that although their bodies react to different features of the environment, that does not betoken their having any sensations at all. Ants and spiders may well be programmed to react to chemical features of their environment in certain ways, without these features causing any sensations. They may simply react unfeelingly.

Knowledge of Sensations

In discussing our vocabulary for describing sensations, I have inevitably also been discussing the extent of our knowledge of the sensations of others; and while I have assumed that we can know quite a bit about the sensations of fellow humans, it should be apparent that any particular knowledge claims we make about the sensations of others, e.g. that some individual now has a headache, or a green after-image, is fallible. You may be subjected to burning, and you may scream out. But on this occasion perhaps you felt nothing and cried out only in order to deceive the spectators. It is unlikely that normal causal links between peripheral stimulus and brain-event, brain-event and sensation have broken down; but it is possible, and if the normal response takes place, no one would know that the normal sensations had not occurred—except the subject himself.

One way in which a subject's sensations could be very different from that of others is if, relative to them, he has an inverted colour-spectrum. Ripe strawberries, and raspberries, tomatoes, and British mail boxes, and other objects normally called 'red' would then look to him the way the sea and the sky and other objects normally called 'blue' look to others, and conversely; and to the extent to which there is a tinge of red in an object, to that extent it would look to the subject the way objects normally called 'blue' look to others and conversely. Such a subject will group objects as similarily coloured in the same way as others do, and he will describe their colours with the same words as others do; yet he will call objects 'red' in virtue of their producing in him a sensation which others call 'blue', and conversely. The subject's public behaviour would give to others entirely mistaken beliefs about the nature of his sensations; and if the construction and wiring of his brain was similar to those of other men, we would be utterly unable to discover our error.

Is our knowledge of our own sensations infallible? We may misremember our past sensations. But is our knowledge of our present sensations infallible?

A subject may easily have a false belief about the nature of his present sensation, arising from false beliefs about the nature of things beyond the present sensation, e.g. false beliefs about past sensations. In order to describe his sensations a subject must use words which apply to them in virtue of their similarities to sensations with certain standard causes. I may believe (and say to myself and others) that I have a red star in my visual field, meaning thereby that I have a star in my visual field of the colour of sensations typically produced by ripe strawberries, English mail boxes, and London buses. That belief could be mistaken, if I misremember the colour of the sensations caused by such standard objects. So, more generally, a subject can have false beliefs about his present sensations, when those beliefs depend for their correctness on true beliefs about absent things, that is, normally absent sensations. But can a subject have false beliefs about his sensations, whose falsity does not arise in this way from mistaken beliefs about things beyond his present experience?

Suppose that the subject's relevant beliefs about things beyond present experience are all correct. His beliefs, for example, about the sensations caused by ripe strawberries, etc. and so his belief about what it is to be red, are all correct. Can he still have false beliefs about the nature of his present sensations? My answer is Yes; there is no infallible knowledge of sensations. I shall approach that answer gradually, making first some preliminary points.

Sensations often have parts or aspects of which the subject is totally unaware, and so may have no belief that they have those parts or aspects; although he can, by paying attention, become aware of them, and so acquire such a belief. Thus I may have an eidetic image of a page of a book, yet not be aware of the words on the tenth line, and so have no belief about what those words are. Or I may have a tune running through my mind, without being aware of what the tenth note is. Or, to take a much discussed example, I may have an image of a striped tiger without having noticed how many stripes it has.

One reaction to these examples is to deny that there is any more content to the sensation than the subject is currently aware of. On this view, the image of the tiger is simply a blurred image, like a blurred photograph which gives a stripey impression without depicting a definite number of stripes. There may indeed be such images. But some images are not like that; they have features of which the subject is unaware. My reason for saying that is that, if asked, a subject can often report features of his images of which he was previously unaware, e.g. the exact number of stripes possessed by the image of the tiger, without the image appearing in any way to change.[7] If you make it a matter of definition that necessarily a sensation has only those features of which the subject is currently aware, you deprive yourself of the vocabulary which would enable you to do justice to this feature of experience.[8]

[7] For a child who had an eidetic image of a cat with a striped tail counting the number of stripes on the tail, see R. N. Haber, 'Eidetic Images', *Scientific American*, 1969, **220** No. 4, 36–44; see p. 39.

[8] The striped tiger and analogous examples have often been used as arguments against the claim that there are mental images. For, the argument goes, if there was

So, through ignorance of the details of my sensations, I may fail to have true beliefs about them. I may even have false beliefs which I express to myself in thought and to others in spoken words. (A belief expressed by the subject to himelf in thought I shall later term a 'judgement'.) For when asked, I may pay too quick attention to my image of the tiger or the line on the page, and miscount the stripes or misread the line. My beliefs about parts or aspects of my sensations are open to correction, and so are not infallible.

But what about whole sensations? Again, a subject may have sensations of which he is at the time unaware, e.g. because he is distracted by something else which is going on in consciousness. Just as we may by paying attention discover some part of an apparently unchanging sensation, of which previously we were unaware, so we may discover some apparently unchanging sensation of which previously we were unaware—a toothache or a noise which we did not notice before our attention was drawn to it. By the principle of credulity (see p. 11), since it subsequently seems that previously we had a sensation when we were not aware of it, probably we did and we ought so to believe in the absence of counter-evidence.

But could I have a false belief which I express to myself, that I am having some whole sensation when I am not, or conversely— having a red visual image, or tasting a taste of honey? If I can have self-expressed false beliefs about parts of sensations, why cannot I

a mental image of a striped tiger, it would have a definite number of stripes; yet, how can it, if the subject who is imagining it, cannot tell us how many stripes it has? One way out of this difficulty which I have taken, is to deny that subjects need to know all the details of their images. Another way, which I am happy to take with respect to some such examples, is to allow images of stripiness which are not images of a definite number of stripes (with analogous ways out of the difficulty for examples of other kinds). For the difficulty, and these and other ways out of it, see J. A. Fodor, *The Language of Thought,* Harvard Univeristy Press, Cambridge, Mass., 1979, pp. 187–95.

For yet another example justifying the claim that sensations may have features other than ones of which the subject is currently aware, consider this one from Sibley. 'When asked how the distant mountains look today, I may, after looking at them, give my opinion that they look bluish. But if asked to look again to see whether I am not mistaken, through inattention, prior expection, etc., and whether today they do not look greyish rather than bluish, I may look again and agree.'—F. N. Sibley, 'Analysing Seeing', in (ed.) F. N. Sibley, *Perception*, Methuen, London, 1971. (I omit an 'n' subscript, whose meaning is explained in his paper, from Sibley's first 'looks' as irrelevant to the point being made.)

have self-expressed false beliefs about whole sensations (given, as I am assuming, the correctness of my relevant beliefs about things beyond present experiences)? The difference between part and whole of sensation is one of degree. Yet it is hard to think of a plausible case of a false belief about a whole sensation. My answer to why, although we cannot have infallible knowledge of our sensations, there are no plausible cases in which we have false self-expressed beliefs about whole sensations is that, *qua* conscious episodes, sensations are, as it were, naked before the subject; nothing stands between him and them in all their detail. The only way in which he can go wrong in his beliefs about them is if he fails to notice what 'stares him in the face'. The more what 'stares him in the face' occupies his state of consciousness (the less other sensations or parts thereof, thoughts, or purposings, there are) the less likely he is to make a mistake about it. Hence false self-expressed belief about whole sensations is much less likely than false belief about parts of sensations. The sensation is however one thing, and belief about it another; and quickness or built-in bias of judgement can lead to error, even with whole sensations.

The philosophical tradition which insists on making it a matter of definition that a sensation is as it seems (epistemically) to be and so a subject has infallible knowledge of the character of his sensations; confuses the occurences of sensations with the occurrence of judgements (that is, naturally occurring thoughts which express beliefs) about them. I shall argue in Chapter 4, that we cannot be mistaken about our thoughts—if I have the thought that my sensation is blue, necessarily I know that I have that thought. The reason for philosophers insisting that we must have incorrigible knowledge of our sensations was an epistemological one; they wanted to have something we could be certain about, some foundation for knowledge. But if there is a foundation for knowledge they looked for it in the wrong place. They reasonably claimed that although I could not be certain that there was a table in front of me, I could be certain that it looked as if there was a table in front of me. They then wrongly supposed that 'it looks as if there is a table in front of me' was in this case a description of my visual sensations. It is only in the epistemic sense of 'looks' (in which to say how something 'looks' is to say what I am inclined to believe about it, and so when in the absence of further evidence I make a judgement about it, what judgement I make) that I can be certain that 'it looks as if there is a table in front of me'. But 'looks' needs to be used in the comparative sense if this sentence is to describe my sensation. For then it would describe, not what I am inclined to believe on the basis of my sensations, but what the character of the sensation is, viz. that it is the kind of sensation you normally get by looking at a table. And it is possible that I could be mistaken about that.

The Role of Sensations in Perception

I claimed earlier that sensations are an important element in perception; that perception normally involves visual, auditory, etc. sensations, as well as a further element—the acquisition of a belief. To defend that view, I need to consider at a little length that rival account of perception which analyses perception simply as the acquisition of belief, and denies that there is any further sensory element involved. The 'cognitive' theory of perception was set out carefully by David Armstrong in his *A Materialist Theory of Mind*.[9] Armstrong accepts the causal theory of perception, according to which to perceive that a is ϕ (believing that one does), is for a's being ϕ to cause the subject to have the experience of it seeming to him that a is ϕ; and to perceive a (believing that one does), is for a to cause the subject to have the experience of it seeming to him that a is present. For me to perceive the table (believing that I do), is for the table to cause me to have the experience of it seeming to me that there is a table present. Armstrong interprets the 'seems' in the epistemic sense, and so reads the causal theory as saying simply that to perceive that a is ϕ (believing that one does), is for a being ϕ to cause the subject to believe that a is ϕ. Armstrong then goes on to analyse the having of sensations other than those involved in perception (e.g. the having of 'non-veridical' sensations) in terms of *inclinations* to believe. If I 'perceive' the dagger before me, but do not believe that it is a real dagger, then my 'perceiving' is simply acquiring an inclination to believe, i.e. coming to be in a state where I would believe that there was a dagger in front of me but for stronger contrary evidence and so a stronger contrary belief. And similarily for having other sensations.

The trouble with this cognitive account of perception is that it

[9] Routledge and Kegan Paul, London, 1968.

cannot account adequately for the differences between the senses. There is a difference between seeing that the table is round and feeling that it is round, hearing the man walk and seeing the man walk. In both cases I perceive, and so am caused to hold a belief by the object perceived—that the table is round or that the man is walking. But there is a difference. Wherein does it consists? According to Armstrong,[10] it consists in the sense-organs by which I acquire the information. To see a table is to have a belief that the table is present caused via the operation of my eyes; to feel the table is to have a belief that the table is present caused by the operation of my hands.

However, this latter analysis is mistaken. It *may* in fact be the case that in perception people only have visual sensations as a result of the operation of their eyes. But one is saying something very different when one claims to have visual sensations, from when one says that one has beliefs or even sensations caused by the operation of one's eyes. For suppose we operate on a man and connect his optic nerves to the parts of the brain normally connected to the auditory nerves coming from the ears, in such a way that when he looks at a red object he hears a high note, when he looks at a blue object he hears a low note, and when he looks at a typical multicoloured array of objects he hears a sound as of a large orchestra. He would then be able to acquire beliefs (true and justified) about the colours of objects, by the operation of his eyes. But the character of his sensations which mediate these beliefs would be entirely different from the character of our sensations which mediate our beliefs about colours—which difference we may naturally express by saying that he has no visual sensations, whereas we do. Although he acquires beliefs about them by the operation of his eyes, he does not *see* the colours.[11]

Also, there have been claims from time to time that people can see by means other than their eyes, e.g. through the skin of their fingertips. Such claims seem comprehensible, even if false; and if they are comprehensible, what they would seem to be saying is that men's fingers can operate in such a way as to cause them to have the kind of experience which we normally get by looking at

[10] Op. cit., pp. 211 ff.
[11] In his paper 'Some Remarks about the Senses' (in (ed.) R. J. Butler, *Analytical Philosophy* (first ser.), Blackwell, Oxford, 1962), H. P. Grice reached this conclusion—that the different character of the experiences involved was a necessary part of the distinction between the senses.

things with our eyes. In that case the character of the resultant experiences would not be merely a necessary part but would be the whole of the distinction between the senses. So it would seem that normal perception by means of one of the five senses involves two mental components, sensations as well as beliefs. Unless we admit this, we cannot account for the differences between the senses.

The fact that normally perception involves both the acquisition of belief and having sensations, can be further brought out by drawing attention to certain acquisitions of belief about the environment which are not mediated by sensations. These beliefs are caused by the environment and are normally true; and so the acquisition of such beliefs seems to have all the characteristics of perception except the involvement therein of sensations. The best-known example of such beliefs are those which we acquire about the position of our limbs when we are not looking at them or otherwise perceiving them by means of the five senses. Put your hand behind your back. You acquire a belief (indeed, a strong and well-justified belief) about whether the palm is facing upward or downward. But you have no sensations. You may say that you do, and some psychologists will tell you that you have 'kinaesthetic sensations'. But I do not think that most people do have any sensations in my sense, as you will see by asking yourself whether you experience anything over and above an inclination to believe. The difference between 'kinaesthetic sensations' and other sensations such as visual sensations is just this, that there is something left over in the case of 'looks round', 'feels round', etc. when you take away the inclination to believe, but nothing left over in the case of 'feels palm upward' when you take away the inclination to believe.

Another example, which is discussed by J. J. Gibson is that of the blind man who comes to believe that there is a wall in front of him without (to quote Gibson) 'realizing what sense has been stimulated'. In the kind of case discussed he does in fact acquire this belief through auditory echo detection, but he does not know what causes the belief; and is unaware of the 'visual, auditory, or other quality of the input'. Gibson summarizes this case by saying 'in short there can be sensationless perception, but not informationless perception.'[12] An alternative way of describing the

---

[12] J. J. Gibson, *The Senses Considered as Perceptual Systems*, Houghton, Boston, 1966, p. 2. Quoted in Fodor, *The Language of Thought*, p. 49.

situation (if you count sensation as part of the essence of perception) would be that there can be acquisition of belief without perception.

Another modern example is provided by the phenomenon of 'blindsight'. Some patients who suffer brain damage in certain parts of their visual cortex deny that they see anything in corresponding parts of their visual field—e.g. they deny that they see a spot of light which stimulates the right side of their two eyes, and thereby their right visual cortex. They can, however, tell you more or less exactly where that spot of light is with such regularity that we must describe them as knowing (and hence truly believing) that it has such and such a location. The damage to their cortex allows the visual stimuli still to cause beliefs, but no longer to cause sensations.[13]

Perception indeed involves the acquisition of belief, but this acquisition is normally accompanied by sensations of different kinds, visual, auditory, or whatever.[14] So also the having of sensations other than those involved in perception is to be distinguished from any inclination to belief, which may normally accompany them.

What, in that case, is the relation of the sensation to the belief (or inclination to belief) which normally accompanies it? There are obviously regular correlations between the sensations and the accompanying beliefs. For different background beliefs (i.e. different beliefs about the surrounding circumstances and different expectations as to what will be seen on the given occasion), different sensations are connected with different beliefs about physical objects in our environment. Thus, given a background belief that the light is daylight, an object's causing me to have a red visual sensation (i.e. it looking red in the comparative sense) will

---

[13] For one such case, see M. D. Sanders *et al.*, '*Blindsight*: vision in a field defect', *Lancet*, 20 Apr. 1974, 707 f. For a fuller survey and a detailed account of one case, see L. Weiskrantz, 'Varieties of Residual Experience', *Quarterly Journal of Experimental Psychology*, 1980, **32**, 365–86.

[14] Peacocke (op. cit., p. 45) claims that it is 'plausible' that it is a necessary truth that 'every experience has sensational properties'. If any sudden acquisition of belief about the environment is to count as an experience, the supposed truth is false. Similarly, in *The Subjective View* (Clarendon Press, Oxford, 1983), Colin McGinn defends the thesis that we cannot perceive objects at all except as characterized by secondary qualities—viz. as coloured, noisy, warm, etc. But again, given the reasonably wide understanding of perception with which McGinn seems to operate, that seems false.

go together with the belief that the object is red. And for a background belief that an object is viewed perpendicularly, its looking round (in the comparative sense) goes together with the belief that it is round. But there are two possible explanations of these correlations, (given the background beliefs)—either the sensations cause the beliefs, or the two have a common cause.[15] Those who wish to downplay the role of the mental will take the latter alternative—and it is the doctrine known as epiphenomenalism that, although there are sensations which are mental events, they are mere epiphenomena i.e. mere effects, not causes (as it were, mere shadows of brain processes which make no difference to anything else). We shall see strong reason later for holding that sensations are often causally efficacious, but phenomena such as blindsight do show that beliefs about physical events can be caused by stimulation of sense-organs without any sensations forming part of the causal chain. This suggests that when sensations do occur in perception they may sometimes, perhaps often, be mere epiphenomena.

But in that case, if sensations do not necessarily cause perceptual beliefs, a supporter of Armstrong will naturally enquire,[16] what is their role in perception? The answer is that there is a twofold connection. First, on any particular occasion, a man may justify his perceptual beliefs by reference to his sensations; and secondly and more importantly, sensations are necessary if many of our perceptual beliefs are to have content.

First, justification. Any initial belief of mine about my perceptions, any belief that I have seen, heard, felt, etc., anything, is of course open to challenge. If I claim to have seen a pink elephant or a round hole, I can be asked what grounds I have for supposing that it is pink or round, and one way in which I can provide justification is by describing the character of the sensations which the seen object caused. 'It looked a sort of dark red in a green light, and only pink things look that sort of dark red in a green light'; or 'it looked slightly elliptical when I looked at it from an angle, and only round things look slightly elliptical when looked at from that angle'. We can use our acquired knowledge of the kinds

---

[15] It cannot be simply that (given the background beliefs) the beliefs cause the sensations, since something else other than the beliefs determines whether the sensations are auditory, visual, or whatever.

[16] See Armstrong, op. cit., pp. 217 f.

of sensation which objects of different kinds cause, to justify our perceptual beliefs.[17] This is not to say that we often justify our perceptual beliefs in this way, but we can do so, and it does provide a justification for them.

Secondly, content. Our beliefs are beliefs that objects are red or square, hard or soft, etc. How is it that we understand what it is for an object to possess these properties? Many of the properties we ascribe to objects are secondary qualities, such as being red, hard, salty, etc; and secondary qualities are defined by the sensations which they cause in most circumstances in normal observers. As we have seen, for an object to be red is for it to cause red sensations in most circumstances in normal observers. A subject would not understand a belief that an object was red, and so could not acquire such a belief through perception, unless red objects normally caused in him red sensations. The same goes for beliefs about the possession by objects of any secondary quality—that noises are loud, or fish is salty. Although the primary qualities of objects—their having a certain size, shape, velocity—are not defined in terms of the sensations which they cause, it is clear that many of our beliefs about the world would not be ours, if we had no sensations to give content to them.

Sensations have Effects

Although the sensations which occur in perceptual experiences may often play no causal role in giving subjects the requisite perceptual beliefs, nevertheless, sensations must often be causally efficacious, i.e. have effects. They cannot all be mere epiphenomena for the following reason. I have beliefs, not only about the physical world but about my sensations themselves—that they have such and such a shape, or colour or taste, and beliefs on some occasion that I am then having a sensation. If sensations are purely epiphenomenal, these beliefs will not be caused by the sensations but by brain-states. Take an extreme case. I have an eidetic image of a tiger. You ask me to count the stripes; I do; superficially I am inspecting the image and adjusting my belief by what, in a none-too-metaphorical sense, stares me in the face. But if epiphenomenalism is true, my belief about the number of stripes will be something caused in no way by the sensation with its particular

[17] On this point and for other arguments in defence of sensory images, see E. Wright, 'Inspecting Images', *Philosophy*, 1983, **58**, 57–72.

properties, but by some brain-state. And what goes for me, goes for everyone else as well. But if that is so, everyone's belief that there are sensations will be totally without justification. For my primary grounds for believing that there are sensations is that they stare me in the face, i.e. that I have many particular beliefs with respect to many particular occasions that I then had sensations, and that these beliefs arose from 'confrontation' with sensations. My grounds are grounds in virtue of my belief that these particular beliefs were caused by sensations and would not otherwise have occurred (just as my belief that I see a table involves the belief that my belief that there is a table present was formed in part by the table, viz. by light rays from the table impinging on my eyes, and that I would not otherwise have had that belief). If sensations are causally inefficacious, I cannot have these grounds for my belief that there are sensations. My other grounds for believing that there are sensations arise from the reports of others about their sensations; but if sensations are causally inefficacious, these too will be worthless.

But since it is as evident as anything can be that I have sensations (that I am aware of pains and noises and patterns of colour, whether or not they depend on anything in the physical world), and so that my belief that there are sensations is a rational one, sensations must be causally efficacious. They cause my beliefs that I have sensations, and (equally evidently) thereby they cause me on occasion to make public statements about my sensations. Epiphenomenalism is false.

That the reports of subjects about their images are caused by inspection of and so reaction to those images, receives further support from recent empirical work in psychology. S. M. Kosslyn and his associates have performed a considerable number of experiments in which subjects were asked to store information in image-form (e.g. to hold in memory some image of a diagram). The speed at which, and the accuracy with which, they derived information from such an image was what you would expect if what is going on is similar to the subject visually inspecting a public diagram, i.e. if he is scanning a mental picture with a mental eye, and reporting what he detects there.[18] Thus subjects who focus on

---

[18] See S. M. Kosslyn, *Image and Mind*, Harvard University Press, Cambridge, Mass., 1980, Ch. 3; and S. M. Kosslyn and J. R. Pomerantz, 'Imagery, Propositions and the Form of Internal Representations' reprinted in (ed.) N. Block, *Readings in*

a certain part of the image take longer to report details of a region of the image spatially distant from the point of focus than to report details of a closer region; they have more difficulty in reporting details which are small in their image than those which are large in their image. If image inspecting is like seeing, all of this is to be expected.

But then what affects what subjects believe and say about their images of diagrams is the image-sensations themselves, not mere beliefs about the diagrams stored in non-imaged from—for it is the sizes and distances of parts of the imaged diagrams which affects what and how they report. So, again, sensations are not mere epiphenomena; they causally affect the subjects' reports. In Chapters 4 and 5 we shall find different kinds of reason for believing that thoughts and purposes also are causally efficacious, in addition to the *general* reason which applies to thoughts and purposes as well as to sensations, that otherwise we would have no justified knowledge of them.

The Distinctness of Sensations

So then sensations differ from the beliefs with which they are associated. For the reasons given earlier they differ also from the desires to which they give rise. A hot pain in the toe and a cold pain in the toe are both such that we desire them to cease, but they differ from each other in the quality of the sensation. Two distinct patterns of auditory sensations may be equally pleasant, and so on. More obviously, sensations are distinct from thoughts, and from purposings. My having a yellow sensation is distinct from my thought that I am having a yellow sensation; if it was not, the thought would have no content; there would be nothing about which it was making a claim. And a sensation is a passive event, something that happens to an agent, not his trying to do something—and so not a purposing.

Philosophy of Psychology, Methuen, London, 1981, vol. 2. It must be granted to many recent critics of Kosslyn's interpretation of his data that there are interpretations of those data, according to which subject's reports are not descriptions of picture-like images. It is just that those data are explained most simply on the supposition that they are such interpretations, and so that interpretation is probably correct.

For criticism of Kosslyn's interpretation of his data, see: Z. W. Pylyshyn 'Imagery and Artificial Intelligence' reprinted in (ed.) N. Block, op. cit., and N. Block, 'Mental Pictures and Cognitive Science', *Philosophical Review*, 1983, **92**, 499–541.

Once the distinctness of sensations from mental events of other kinds, and especially from beliefs and desires, is recognized, the temptation to give a behaviourist account of sensations should vanish. By a behaviourist account of some apparently mental event I mean an analysis of it in terms of the public behaviour which follows certain stimuli. In *The Concept of Mind* Gilbert Ryle discussed the concept of intelligence.[19] He argued that to say that some man is intelligent might seem to be ascribing to him some very private mental property. But when we think about it, we realize that to say that a man is intelligent is to say that he answers difficult questions quickly, usually gets the answers right, draws our attention to problems which we had not noticed, avoids courses of conduct which will prevent him from obtaining his goals (courses which most of us would not notice were unsatisfactory). And so on. In all these ways a man's being intelligent is a matter of how he does behave publicly ('answers', 'draws attention', 'avoids'); and how he would behave if circumstances were different (not merely does he get right the answers to actual questions; but we have reason to suppose that this is no accident, because he would have got right the answers to different questions, if they had been put). There is some initial plausibility in such a behaviourist account of intelligence. There is also some initial plausibility in a behaviourist account of belief. Is not to believe that John is my friend to 'act as if' he is my friend?

I do not believe that a behaviourist account of belief will work, and I will give my reasons in a later chapter. I am not even very sympathetic to a behaviourist account of intelligence. But behaviourist accounts of these mental concepts have more plausibility than a behaviourist account of sensations. Ryle, notoriously, did not give one in *The Concept of Mind*.

Armstrong's attempt to get rid of sensations had as its first move his attempt, which I have argued to be unsuccessful, to show that sensations are really acquisitions of belief or inclinations to acquire a belief. Armstrong then went on to argue that beliefs are simply states of brain apt to produce certain kinds of behaviour in certain circumstances. His is not quite a behaviourist theory because it equates beliefs with the brain-states which produce certain

[19] G. Ryle, *The Concept of Mind*, Hutchinson, London, 1949, pp. 42–50.

behaviour rather than with the behaviour itself. But the difference is not a very great one. However, once it is clear that sensations are distinct from beliefs, this kind of approach cannot even get started, and the initial implausibility of a behaviourist account of sensations stands apparent.

On a behaviourist account, for a subject to have a red image would be for him to react publicly in the sort of way in which people react to ripe strawberries and tomatoes, British pillar boxes and labour party badges, viz. to say that he has an image of the same colour as they, if he is asked and if he has the purpose of telling the truth. But of course he may not have the purpose of telling the truth on this matter (a fact which may not be revealed by his public behaviour) and so his red image may not affect his behaviour at all. And even if it does, maybe he has, relative to others, an inverted colour-sensation spectrum, of the kind which we considered earlier, and what he calls 'red' looks to others the way blue things look to him, and conversely. I argued earlier that this sort of thing is not empirically very likely, but it could happen, and if it did, the subject's public behaviour would be exactly the same as if his colour-sensation spectrum was normal, for he would classify objects in the same way. Or again maybe the subject is a robot without any sensations at all, but programmed to react publicly to light-waves in the same way as those who do have sensations. There is more to having a sensation than public behaviour of the kind normally caused by stimuli from objects of certain kinds.

These are old points and, I hope, obvious points. They are only likely to be obscured if you come to think that sensations are the same as beliefs, which you may begin to do if you think that they are incorrigible foundations of knowledge. That is why I have devoted quite a lot of his chapter to distinguishing between sensations and beliefs.

Hard materialism, to repeat, is the doctrine that there are no mental events (the instantiation of mental properties, ones to which the subject has privileged access) but that all talk about events which are apparently mental, such as sensations, is really talk about physical events. There are two forms of hard materialism—behaviourism which claims that talk about apparent mental events is really talk about public behaviour; and mind/brain identity theory which claims that talk about apparent mental events is really talk about brain-events. I have argued in this chapter that behaviourism is false because it cannot deal with sensations. In the next chapter I shall argue that mind/brain identity theory is false, because it, too, cannot deal with sensations.

3. SENSATIONS AND BRAIN-EVENTS

I argued in the last chapter that sensations are distinct from public behaviour. A man's having a red image or feeling a pain is not his behaving in certain public ways under certain public circumstances. I now wish to argue in this chapter that sensations are distinct from brain-events. The brain consists mainly of billions of nerve-cells, neurones, which transmit to neighbouring neurones electrical charge by 'firing', that is undergoing a sudden change of electric potential which is transmitted across the gap between the neurones by a chemical transmitter. I shall argue that goings-on in his brain may cause and may be caused by a man's sensations, but they are not the same as them. Just as the ignition of a fuse is distinct from the explosion which it causes, so, I shall be arguing, firings of neurones are distinct from the visual sensations or pains which they cause.

Mind/brain identity theory claims otherwise. It claims that every sensation (and every other apparently mental event) is really identical to some brain-event. The last twenty five years has seen an explosion of philosophical writing elaborating and defending mind/brain identity theory, and there are many subtly different variants of the theory.[1] I shall not discuss the different variants in detail; but hope that the arguments which I shall marshal will be conclusive in showing that (whatever might be the case with beliefs, desires, or other apparently mental events), sensations are not brain-events.

For the purpose of assessing identity theory, I shall allow the identity theorist a crucial assumption—that persons are simply material objects; that there is no more stuff to persons than the

[1] Beginning with the famous papers by U. T. Place in 1959 and J. J. C. Smart in 1962. These early papers and subsequent important papers arguing for and against identity theory published over the next decade are contained, among other places, in (ed.) C. V. Borst, *The Mind/Brain Identity Theory*, MacMillan, London, 1970. The best known fuller-length defences of identity theory (other than those which I shall discuss in detail later) are D. M. Armstrong, *A Materialist Theory of Mind*, Routledge and Kegan Paul, London, 1968, and D. Dennett, *Brainstorms*, Harvester, Brighton, 1979.

matter of which they are made. It is an assumption which I shall see reason later in the book to reject, but it is one which identity theory inevitably makes. Events (see Chapter 1) consist in the instantiation of properties in substances. Physical events consist in the instantiation of physical properties. A physical property is one such that no one person is necessarily better placed to know that it is instantiated than is any other person. Brain-events, as discussed by identity theorists, are supposed to be physical events.

The question of whether sensations are identical with brain-events, then boils down to the question whether the instantiation of sensory properties (e.g. having a red image) in the material object which is a person is a different event from the instantiation of any physical brain property (e.g. having certain groups of neurones, let us call them C-fibres, fire) in that person. Just as a disc being round is a different event from its being red, and a jelly being transparent is a different event from it being circular or tasty, is my having a red image or a headache a different event from any brain-state? Are these are connected events, or just one?

Identity theory draws our attention to the fact that the same event can be described in different ways—my writing Chapter 3 of *The Evolution of the Soul* and Richard Swinburne writing the chapter about identity theory in the book of his Gifford Lectures. Identity theory claims that that is how it is with my being in pain and my having certain specified nerves fire;[2] the same event is described in two different ways.

In order to discuss properly whether sensations are brain-events, I shall need to consider first the very general question of when two events are the same, or rather of when an event described in one way is the same event as an event described in another way. And in order to discuss that question, I need to discuss a prior question—when are two properties the same, when do two words '*P*' and '*Q*' pick out the same property?

The Criteria of Property Identity

A property may be picked out either by a name or a description. The distinction between naming and describing is illustrated most

---

[2] Having certain nerves fire is a monadic property of me, because it is not a relation between myself and some distinct substances, but the characterization of a part of me (those nerve fibres) by a property—the substance, myself, has the property of having a certain part have a certain property.

easily in connection with substances. A substance, such as myself, may be named (e.g. 'Richard Swinburne'), or described (e.g. 'The Professor of Philosophy of Religion at Oxford'). The difference between naming and describing is that names are, in Kripke's terminology, rigid designators—that is, they pick out a certain substance, whatever happens to it, however its properties change. Whereas a description only picks out a certain substance while it has certain properties—'Richard Swinburne' applies to me, whether or not I lose my appointment at Oxford; 'The Professor of Philosophy of Religion at Oxford' only applies so long as I retain my appointment. Likewise, properties may be picked out by words which apply to that property, whatever happens in the world (viz. whatever substances that property characterizes or ceases to characterize); or they may be picked out by descriptions, which pick out a property by its properties, e.g. by which substances it characterizes. 'Blue' picks out the property of blueness, whether or not anything is blue and whatever is blue. Whereas 'the colour of the sky' in the sense of 'that colour-property which is possessed by the sky' is a description of the colour blue.

When '*P*' and '*Q*' are both names of properties, the strongest theory of property identity is that these words pick out the same property if, and only if, they mean the same, if to say that a substance is '*P*' means the same as to say that it is '*Q*'. By this criterion the property which the English call being 'green' is the same property as the property which the French call being 'vert'. That this is a sufficient condition of property identity all would agree, but whether it is a necessary one is open to dispute. A more liberal position is that *P* and *Q* are the same property if, and only if, the claim that an object has '*P*' (where '*P*' is the name of the first property) is logically equivalent to the claim that it has '*Q*' (where '*Q*' is the name of the second property). By this criterion, being triangular will be the same property as being trilateral. (I understand by a triangle a closed plane rectilinear figure with three angles, and by a trilateral a closed plane rectilinear figure with three sides. Necessarily, any triangle is a trilateral, and conversely.) And being the sum of five and seven will be the same property as being the sum of eight and four.[3] There maybe some

---

[3] In his 'The Identity of Properties', *American Philosophical Quarterly*, 1974, **11**, 257–75, Peter Achinstein has this condition as a necessary condition of property identity. It is his condition V that (x) N $(x$ has $P = x$ has $Q)$. Achinstein adds a

support in ordinary language for this criterion, but ordinary
language gives quite a lot of support too to the view that this
criterion is too liberal. For example, a proof that a certain
trilateral necessarily is triangular would seem to be a proof that a
certain object necessarily has a property additional to being
trilateral, viz. being triangular.

The two theories can be filled out in an obvious way to deal with
the case where '*P*' or '*Q*' are descriptions of a property. If '*P*' is the
name of a property and '*Q*' is a description of a property as that
property which has the property *S*, then '*P*' and '*Q*' pick out the
same property if, and only if, the property named by '*P*' is the only
property which has the property *S*. If '*P*' and '*Q*' are both
descriptions of properties, '*P*' being that property which has the
property *R*, and '*Q*' being that property which has the property *S*,
the two properties picked out by '*P*' and '*Q*' are the same if, and
only if, the only property which has *R* has *S* and conversely.

Let me illustrate. 'The colour of the sky' and 'Amanda's
favourite colour' may both be used as descriptions of the colour
blue. Then 'blue is the colour of the sky' is true, because the colour
named by the word 'blue', viz. the colour blue, is the only property
which has the property of being the colour of the sky. 'The colour
of the sky is Amanda's favourite colour' is true because one and
only one property, viz. the property blue, has the two properties of
being the colour of the sky and being Amanda's favourite colour.

Note, however, that an expression such as 'the colour of the sky'
or 'Amanda's favourite colour' may be used either (as normally
and as in my examples) as the description of a property or as the
name of a property, viz. the property of being of the same colour
as the sky or of being the colour best loved by Amanda. If these
expressions are taken as names, then 'blue is the colour of the sky'
is false—for the property of being blue is not the same property as
the property of being of the same colour as the sky. For a thing
could come to have one property and lack the other—the sky
might change colour and then forget-me-nots would have one
property but lack the other.

So then, on the criteria discussed so far given that '*P*' and '*Q*' are

second condition, which is the condition that to be identical two properties must
have the same causal potentialities. He argues that these are necessary conditions
of property identity, and speculates that, probably, they are jointly sufficient
conditions also.

names of properties, they have to mean the same or at least be logically equivalent if they are to pick out the same property (qualifications being added for when '*P*' and '*Q*' are descriptions). However, a much more liberal criterion for property identity has been suggested in recent writing. The basic idea here is that properties are the same if their possession by objects has the same effect on the world. We ought, it is claimed, to use the discoveries of science as to what properties there are (not just appeal to our current vocabulary), and the only properties which play any role in science are those which make a difference to the world. More formally, on this view, two properties are identfcal if, and only if, they have the same causal potentialites. *P* will be the same property as *Q*, if, for any other properties and circumstances adding *P* to an object *a* with certain other properties in certain circumstances makes it have just the same causal influence on things as does adding *Q* to that object with those properties in those circumstances, and conversely. Thus it might be on this definition that being green is the same property as reflecting light of such and such wavelength—an object possessing the former will have the same heat absorption, have the same effect on observers, etc.[4] as an object possessing the latter. The difficulty here, however, is that not all properties can be just causal potentialities. Maybe a plate being brittle or hard is just a matter of the effects which are likely to follow, e.g. that it will be easily broken, or resist pressure. But not all properties could be nothing but causal potentialities. For if a casual potentiality is just the potentiality to produce an effect, and effects are events and so instantiations of properties, then properties are just potentialities to produce instantiations of properties which are just potentialities to produce instantiations of properties, and so *ad infinitum*. All causal potentialities and so all properties would then be the same, because they would all be simply potentialities to produce effects which consisted simply in potentialities to produce effects, etc. So

---

[4] For a statement of the same causal potentiality criterion of property identity see S. Shoemaker 'Properties, Causation and Projectibility', in (ed.) L. J. Cohen and M. Hesse, *Applications of Inductive Logic*, Clarendon Press, Oxford, 1980. In his two-volume work *Universals and Scientific Realism*, Cambridge University Press, 1978, D. M. Armstrong claims that if two properties have the same causal potentialities, we have every reason to suppose that they are identical, but he is careful not to claim that their having the same causal potentialities entails their identity. See his vol. ii, *A Theory of Universals*, p. 45.

some properties, at any rate, must have natures which include components other than causal potentialities. These other components however could differ while the potentialities remained the same, and in that case we would have different properties with the same causal potentialities. To be identical properties must have their other components identical as well. I conclude that the identity of properties cannot consist solely in the identity of their causal potentialities.

Similar difficulties face an alternative theory that properties are the same if they have the same causal liabilities. Two properties P and Q have the same causal liabilities if whatever events bring about the instantiation of P also bring about the instantiation of Q, and conversely. Again, however, there has to be more to some properties than their causal liabilities (what brings them about)— for again you would have the infinite regress which would have the consequence that no property was distinct from any other property. Similar objections would apply to a theory which held that properties are the same if, and only if, they have both the same causal potentialities and the same causal liabilities. There is more to being a certain property than having certain causes and effects.

I conclude that these more liberal scientific accounts of property identity are incoherent, and the pressures are on us to revert to the more logical accounts sketched earlier, accounts which have their roots in ordinary usage. These accounts have a crucial point— which is this. The story of certain substances is the story of now one property (or relation) now a different property (or relation) being instantiated in those substances. When you have listed all the properties which are at different times instantiated in the different substances, you have told the story of those substances. So we need to distinguish as different properties all those which need to be mentioned in a full story, such that if the history of those substances was in any way different, different instantiations of properties would have taken place. Hence if there is no logical inconsistency in P being instantiated in a certain substance without Q being instantiated in that substance, we need a criterion of property identity which makes them distinct properties. Properties are the same only if it is logically necessary that when the one is instantiated, the other be instantiated, and conversely. So our criterion must be that of the logical equivalence of their names, or stronger (synonymy of names).

On either of the two logical accounts, sensory properties (the properties possessed by a subject who has a sensation, such as being in pain or having a red image) are not, I suggest, the same as brain properties (such as having C-fibres fire). Certainly if 'having a red image' and 'having C-fibres fire' are the names of properties, the properties named are not the same. To 'have a red image' does not mean the same as to 'have one's C-fibres fire' or some other brain property, nor is having the one property logically equivalent to having the other; any connection between them is an empirical, scientifically discoverable, connection of fact, not a connection of logic. There are two separate properties, perhaps such that whenever the one is instantiated, the other is instantiated—they go together; but they are two distinct properties which go together.

Some sensory properties are picked out by description rather than by name. As we saw in Chapter 2, we pick out the taste of honey as that taste which is normally caused by honey. But again the property of which this is a description is a taste sensation, to which we could give a name; and to say that a person has that taste sensation does not mean the same as and is not logically equivalent to any statement about his brain. And even if 'having a red image' were shorthand for a description of a property—e.g. 'that sensory property which is instantiated in a man when he looks at ripe tomatoes and strawberries, British pillar boxes, etc,' that property is a particular sensory property; and not the same property as having one's C-fibres fire. I conclude that sensory properties are different from brain properties.

The Criteria of Event Identity

So much for properties. The history of the world, as we have noted, is the story of the instantiation of different properties in different substances at different times. The instantiation of a property in a substance at a time is an event, and the history of substances is the succession of events. I believe that it follows that sensations, the instantiations in persons of sensory properties, are different events from brain-events, the instantiation in persons of brain properties. This does, however, need to be argued for— since, as we have seen, there may be quite different descriptions of the same event. The identity theorist may allow that being in pain and having certain neurones fire are different properties, but still claim that their instantiation in me at noon today is the same event. We need now to develop our theory of event identity to deal with this suggestion.

An event is the event it is because of the substance or substances involved, the time of instantiation, and the property which is instantiated. The same substance may be picked out in different ways (e.g. by a name or a description, and so may the same moment of time. So, too, may the property involved ('green' or 'the colour of grass'). This suggests the following theory of the event identity: two events, S, being P, *at* t_1, is the same event as S_2 being P_2 at t_2 if, and only if, $S_1 = S_2$, $t_1 = t_2$, and $P_1 = P_2$—viz. the substances, times,[5] properties involved must be the same even if they are picked out by names or descriptions with different meanings.[6] That is a plausible theory, and has been defended in a number of articles by Jaegwon Kim.[7] It then follows that the tree in my garden being green today is the same event as the tree on the other side of Mr. Jones, my neighbour's, fence being the colour of grass on Tuesday of this week, because the same substances, times, and properties are involved, although picked out by different expressions.

However, Kim's theory cannot be quite the full story—for is not my marrying my wife the same event as my saying 'I will', even though the two properties 'marrying' and 'saying "I will" ' are not the same; and is not Brutus killing Caesar the same event as Brutus stabbing Caesar, although killing is not the same property as stabbing?

Kim's theory is fine, with one qualification to which I will come in a moment, for events given what I may call intrinsic descriptions— described as what they are in themselves, quite apart from their causes, effects, or what they are in view of the circumstances of

---

[5] In insisting on identity of times, I am concerned only with the criteria for the identity of actual events. An event cannot be the same as an event which occurred at a different time. However we do seem to allow that an event might have happened at a time other than the time at which it did happen. My birth could have happened earlier than it did. However I do not need to produce criteria for the identity of an actual event with a possible event.

[6] I phrase this and other theories of event identity so that they deal only with monadic properties of substances, and not with relations. However, the amendments needed to take account of relations are obvious ones.

[7] J. Kim, 'On the Psycho-physical identity theory', *American Philosophical Quarterly*, 1966, **3**, 227–35; R. Brandt and J. Kim, 'The Logic of Identity Theory', *Journal of Philosophy*, 1967, **64**, 515–37; J. Kim, 'Events and their Descriptions: Some Considerations' in (ed.) N. Rescher, *Essays in Honour of Carl G. Hempel*, Reidel, Dordrecht, 1969.

their occurrence. Thus 'Brutus stabbing Caesar' describes the event in terms which do not look beyond the event itself. But that event so picked out occurred in certain circumstances, and had certain causes and effects. And instead of describing it by its intrinsic nature, we can rather describe it as the event which did occur in those circumstances, or have those causes, or those effects. Because the effect of Brutus stabbing Caesar was Caesar's dying, we can describe the event as Brutus killing Caesar. Because the event of my saying 'I will', given where I said it and in whose presence and given the conventions of my society, constituted taking in marriage, we can describe the event as just that—taking in marriage. So two extrinsic descriptions pick out the same event if they both pick out an event with the same intrinsic description. An extrinsic description picks out an event with a certain intrinsic description if the latter event satisfies the former description in virtue of its causes, effects, and circumstances of occurrence.

Finally, one qualification on Kim's theory, as a theory of intrinsic descriptions. One description may be fuller than another in describing the property in more intrinsic detail. S_1 being P_1 at t_1 is the same event as S_2 being P_2 at t_2, where both descriptions are intrinsic descriptions even if $P_1 \neq P_2$ so long as P_2 is a determinate of the determinable P_1 (i.e. it is a particular way of being P_1) and where $S_1 = S_2$ and $t_1 = t_2$. Thus, if I move slowly, my moving at noon is the same event as my moving slowly at noon. If the ball is lilac green, the ball being green is the same event as the ball being lilac green.[8]

Mind/Brain Identity Theories

Given the theory of event identity which I have just outlined, it

---

[8] The relation between intrinsic and extrinsic descriptions, and intrinsic and fuller intrinsic descriptions of an event is like the relation of level-generation which Goldman described, which holds between actions. (See A. I. Goldman, *A Theory of Human Action*, Prentice-Hall, Englewood Cliffs, N J, 1970, ch. 2.) One action A level-generates another action A^1 if by doing A, a subject does A^1. Thus by stabbing Caesar, Brutus kills Caesar. Actions are a sub-class of events. Goldman distinguished four kinds of level-generation: causal generation, conventional generation, simple generation, and generation by augmentation. An action level-generated in one of the first three ways is in my terminology an action given an extrinsic description; an action generated by augmentation is one given a fuller description (in the way described above). For a more detailed use of Goldman's terminology to provide a theory of event identity, see my 'Are Mental Events Identical with Brain Events?', *American Philosophical Quarterly*, 1982, **19**, 173–81.

follows that my having a red image in my visual field at noon cannot be the same event as some brain-event such as my C-fibres firing at noon. The substances and times (me and noon) involved are the same, but the properties are, as we saw earlier, different. Both descriptions seem to be intrinsic descriptions. The events are described in terms of what they are in themselves, not in terms of what they are in virtue of their surroundings. My having my C-fibres fire is not a matter of the event having certain causes or effects or certain conventions being operative in any society. The same goes, I suggest, for my having a red image yet 'having C-fibres fire' is not 'having a red image' described in more detail or more fully. I conclude that the two events are different events.

The identity theorist may attempt to deny this conclusion by claiming that to describe an event as a sensation, the instantiation of a sensory property, and more generally to describe an event in apparently mental terms, is to give an extrinsic description of it, to describe it in terms of its causes or effects. This claim was first made by J. J. C. Smart in 1959[9] giving his 'topic-neutral' account of the sensory, and in more recent years it has been the hallmark of the form of identity theory known as functionalism. Functionalism is the doctrine that apparent mental events are the particular events which they are (this sensation, that belief, or that desire) in virtue of the causes which normally bring them about and the effects which normally follow them, i.e. in my terminology, sensory or other apparently mental properties are properties of having a certain pattern of causes and/or effects. Thus, according to Smart: 'When a person says, "I see a yellowish-orange after-image", he is saying something like this: "There is something going on which is like what is going on when I have my eyes open, am awake, and there is an orange illuminated in good light in front of me, that is, when I really see an orange" '.[10] To have an orange image is to have instantiated in you whatever property is caused to be instantiated in people when they look at oranges. Again, according to the functionalist, to be in pain is to have instantiated in you whatever property is normally caused to be instantiated by bodily damage and gives rise to inclinations to withdraw the damaged part from the cause of the damage, cry out, etc.

[9] 'Sensations and Brain Processes', *Philosophical Review*, 1959, **68**, 141–56. Reprinted in many collections including Borst, op. cit.
[10] Borst, p. 60.

(Inclinations are to be understood in terms of what the subject would do, unless other properties are instantiated in him—such as courage, of which a similar functionalist account can be given.)[11]

So, say Smart and the functionalists, in describing an event in sensory terms, we describe it in terms of its causes and effects (or normal causes and effects), and so in my terminology we give it an extrinsic description. Science tells us which event it is which has, or has normally, those causes and effects—it is a brain-event. There is a kind of brain-event normally caused in us when we look at oranges; we therefore call such an event an orange image; when one such event occurs after the subject looks hard at and then away from some bright object, it is (in virtue of its normal causes and actual circumstances) an orange after-image. There is an event caused in me by sticking a pin in me, which leads to my crying out. It is a pain because of its causes and effects, and science could tell us which event it is which has those causes and effects—a particular brain-event.

The functionalist draws our attention to the fact that bodily malfunction may cause to be instantiated in different kinds of organism different brain or other bodily properties, which in turn cause the subject to cry out. The same stimulus and response may be connected by a different intervening bodily process. Pains may be events of different kinds of different organisms; they may be brain-events of this kind in humans, and of that kind in cats, and very different electrochemical events in Martians. But, say the functionalists, they are always going to be brain- or other bodily events—we have good reason to believe that science will so discover.

However, functionalism is totally unsatisfactory. One major difficulty is that an attempt to identify sensations as those events which have such and such causes and effects ignore the point that

---

[11] For functionalism see, e.g. H. Putnam, 'Minds and Machines', 'The Mental Life of Some Machines', and 'The Nature of Mental States', in his *Mind, Language and Reality*, Philosophical Papers, vol. 2, Cambridge University Press, 1975. He writes: 'I propose the hypothesis that pain, or the state of being in pain, is a functional state of a whole organism' (p. 433), and he concludes that such identification 'is to be tentatively accepted as a theory which leads to both fruitful predictions and fruitful *questions*, and which serves to discourage fruitless and empirically senseless questions, where by "empirically senseless" I mean "senseless" not merely from the standpoint of verification but from the standpoint of what there in fact *is*.' (p. 440).

'*the* cause of *x*' (where *x* is an individual event) hardly ever picks out a particular event (unless further guidance is provided explicitly or by the context), for the reason that *x* will normally have been brought into being by a chain of events, each of which is *a* cause of *x*. What causes the present position of the planets? Their position and that of the sun one minute ago; and so does their position and that of the sun two minutes ago (by causing their position and that of the sun one minute ago). And so on. A similar point goes for 'the effect of *x*'. There is no one effect in me of my looking at an orange object; there is a chain of effects caused in me. There is no one effect of sticking a pin in me which causes me to cry out; there is a whole chain of events between the two. To which of such events are we referring by the words 'orange image' and 'pain'? The answer is obvious. It is the sensory event, the experience. If we cannot distinguish a sensation from other effects of stimuli and causes of responses in us in some non-functionalist way (i.e. in virtue of their having some intrinsic description), we cannot give a functionalist account of sensations.

However, functionalism is still wrong in its major assumption. Sensations are not sensations of a certain kind in virtue of being the causes or effects of certain responses or stimuli, even if we specify them as the *sensory* causes or effects. Although we pick out and learn to talk about sensations of different kinds by describing them as the sensory causes or effects of certain public stimuli and responses (in the way analysed in the last chapter), we do not *mean* by a sensation of a certain kind the sensory cause or effect of stimuli and responses. For sensory properties are not causal properties. In referring to the sensory property of 'having that taste caused by tea', we are normally describing the property (and in so doing, picking it out by some non-essential characteristic), we are not naming the property. Having a red image may be having that sensory property which is in fact instantiated in a man when he looks at ripe tomatoes, etc.; it is not having whatever sensory property is instantiated in a man when he looks at ripe tomatoes, etc. For in another world ripe tomatoes might be yellow, and so might ripe strawberries, etc. We may identify having a red image by its being the property which is in fact caused in us when we look at certain things, but note that it is a contingent matter that it is so instantiated on these occasions.

I conclude that my having a red image at noon and my having C-fibres fire at noon are both events described intrinsically. The properties involved are different, and are not determinates of the same determinable. Hence the events are different. Certainly the one may be the cause of the other—my C-fibres firing may be the cause of my having a red image; and in that case the former may be redescribed as the event which caused my red-imaging. My C-fibres firing may be my causing red-imaging, but it is not red-imaging itself.

For the sake of completeness, I must discuss very briefly a theory of event-identity different from the one which I have put forward, which is now very popular. It is a theory similar to the 'causal potentiality' and 'causal liability' theories of property identity. This theory states that two events are the same if, and only if, they have the same causes and effects.[12] This theory is different from the similar-looking theory of property identity, for events are actual particular occurrences and properties are universals which may be instantiated in many different circumstances. Indeed, unlike the similar property theory, it seems to me true—if taken in a very restricted sense. Suppose that there are two events E_1 and E_2, both of which have C as their cause and F as their sole effect. Now clearly E_1 and E_2 can be distinct events if they have the same cause. Likewise they can still be distinct if by each causing F is meant only that each in the circumstances was sufficient for the occurrence of F, for F might then be over-determined—each event separately might have caused it (and would therefore also have done so in the absence of the other). This theory is plausible only if overdetermination is ruled out. But to say the latter is to say that there is only one event which is a sufficient cause for the occurrence of F. We have already said that E_1 and E_2 are both sufficient causes of F—so necessarily they must be the same event.

However, this theory is of no use as a criterion for determining whether or not two events E_1 and E_2 are identical, for it is circular. It can only be applied, given a prior assumption that E_1 and E_2 are identical, or alternatively that they are distinct. For suppose that E_1 and E_2 both occur caused by C, and are followed by F. Then, by

---

[12] See for example D. Davidson 'The Individuation of Events' in (ed.) N. Rescher, *Essays in Honor of Carl G. Hempel*, Reidel, Dordrecht, 1969, p. 231. For Davidson's argument in 'Mental Events' to show that mental events are identical with physical events, see note (1) to p. 268.

the suggested criterion, they are identical if each is sufficient for F and there is no overdetermination. But if E_1 and E_2 are each sufficient for F, necessarily there will be overdetermination if E_1 and E_2 are distinct events but not if they are the same event. So we need a further criterion for determining whether they are the same event, e.g. the one which I have put forward.[13]

It might be thought that my arguments prove too much. Is not much of science marked by discovery of identities which the arguments of this chapter would rule out? Not so. Science has discovered many identities of substances—water with H_2O, light with electromagnetic radiation, etc.; but the arguments of this chapter do not concern substance identity. Science has also discovered some property identities—e.g. a gas giving a certain temperature with it consisting of molecules having a certain mean kinetic energy; and some event-identities—e.g. a certain flash of lightning with a certain electrical discharge. But these are not ruled out by my arguments. Consider the property identity. What does one mean when one says of a gas that it has such and such a temperature? Perhaps, today, one is not saying anything more than that its molecules have a certain mean kinetic energy. In that case, the cited identity is a necessary one, on the strongest criterion of property identity. Maybe two centuries ago, one was saying that it had a certain quantity of calorific fluid. But according to modern science that property cannot be identical with its consisting of molecules having a certain mean kinetic energy, for the reason that that property is never instantiated, as there is no calorific fluid. Maybe four centuries ago, one was saying that the gas felt to be a certain degree of heat. But that property is not identical at all with it consisting of molecules having a certain mean kinetic energy. The former property is a matter of the effect of the gas on human observers. The instantiation of one property may cause the instantiation of the other property but they are not the same property. But in making the claim in fairly recent years that 'temperature is mean kinetic energy', what I think scientists were saying is that the something, they knew not what but called

---

[13] In *Holistic Explanation*, Clarendon Press, Oxford, 1979, pp. 134 f., Christopher Peacocke in effect appeals to this theory to attempt to show the identity of mental and brain-events. He seems to me, however, to beg a crucial factual question in assuming that each of his events is sufficient for the effect, and also the crucial logical issue in assuming as well the absence of overdetermination.

'temperature' which was measured by thermometers and in general accounted for the thermodynamic behaviour of gases, was in fact mean kinetic energy. That is, 'temperature' was not a name, but the definite description of a property. Temperature meant 'the property which has the property of causing the thermodynamic behaviour of gases'. To equate that with mean kinetic energy is to put 'temperature is mean kinetic energy' in the same category as 'blue is the colour of the sky' (in the sense in which the latter is true). As we have seen, my arguments do not rule out such identities. But no such analysis can be given of having a red after-image or of having one's C-fibres fire. For one does *not* mean by my having a red after-image my having some property which *causes* me to have some sensation.[14]

Similar points apply to the event-identity—'this flash of lightning is such-and-such an electrical discharge'. What is meant by 'lightning'? If the event of lightning is the event of the sky suddenly appearing bright, then this event is a different event from the electrical discharge. The former is the effect which the electrical discharge has on observers. There is no identity here. But if lightning is not the event of the sky lighting up but 'the event (whatever it is) which causes the sky to light up', then the lightning is indeed an electrical discharge of a certain kind. But again we cannot construe 'my having a red after-image is my C-fibres firing' on these lines, because we do not mean by 'my having a red after-image' the event which causes a certain sensation, but the sensation itself.

The possibility of normal scientific identification of public properties and events gives no encouragement to the philosopher seeking to identify apparent mental properties and events with brain properties and events.

We reached this conclusion by an analysis of our normal criteria for the identity of properties and events, which have the consequence that no scientific discoveries about causes and correlations could upset the distinction between a man's experiences and what goes on in his brain. It may be objected that these criteria are those of an out-of-date world-view and that we need

---

[14] Kripke has a somewhat similar argument with respect to the similar sentence 'heat is the motion of molecules'. See his 'Identity and Necessity' in (ed.) M. K. Munitz, *Identity and Individuation*, New York University Press, 1971, pp. 158–61.

different criteria of property and event-identity for a new scientific age. But the whole function of science is to explain what happens, and all that these criteria seek to do is to distinguish as different events the different things that happen. They do not dictate to science how it shall explain, but only attempt to distinguish from each other the different things which need explaining. And science needs to explain both why certain things happen in the brain and why people have certain experiences. If it was able only to explain one of these things, there would be something occurring in the world which it had failed to explain. It is natural to call that something an event, and to use our ordinary criteria for event-identity and difference which bring out the evident fact that there are two separate things happening which require scientific explanation. Science must start from the data of experience, and these include sensations. And if it finds some of these too difficult to explain in terms of current theories, it should openly acknowledge this fact; not pretend that what it cannot explain does not exist.

Hard materialism claimed that apparent mental events such as sensations were really physical events. The behaviourist variant of hard materialism claimed that sensations were really just matters of public behaviour. I argued in the last chapter that behaviourism was false. In this chapter I have examined the alternative, mind/brain identity theory, variant of hard materialism which claims that sensations are brain-events; and developed a theory of event-identity which has the consequence that mind/brain identity theory is false. Both variants of hard materialism fail; and no one has ever suggested anything else physical beside public behaviour and brain-events which might constitute a man's sensations. Hard materialism fails, since there really are some events, viz. sensations, which are not physical events. That sensations are mental events, events about which the subject is necessarily in a better position to know than is anyone else, is indeed initially very plausible, as we saw in Chapter 1. For whatever ways an outsider has of finding out about my sensations I could use too (I could examine the evidence of stimulus and response), and yet I have a further way—by my experience of the sensation. Only under pressure of behaviourist or identity theory arguments is anyone likely to abandon this position, and we have now seen that those arguments do not work. Having argued for the mental nature of sensations at some length in these two chapters and reached the conclusion that sensations are mental events, there will not be the same need for such lengthy arguments to show the mental nature of thoughts, purposings, desires, and beliefs. Brief arguments about these will, however, be given.

4. THOUGHTS

Different Senses of 'Thought'

IN dealing with the components of the mental life, I come next to thoughts. In ordinary language the word 'thought' is used in a variety of connected senses, and I had better begin by clarifying that sense of 'thought' in which in this chapter I am concerned with thoughts. In my sense, thoughts are the occurrent thoughts which, like sensations, occur to a subject at some particular moment of time. But, unlike sensations they are propositional. They consist in an attitude to a state of affairs, described in a certain way, that it is so or may be or ought to be so. They are normally accompanied in the subject by sensations—e.g. the auditory sensations caused by oneself or others speaking, or the images of such sensations which are the vehicle of our private thoughts. They are, however, I shall argue later, distinct from the sensations which are their normal accompaniments.

Thoughts may be indicative, imperative, or interrogative in form. Some indicative thoughts (i.e. thoughts that so-and-so is the case) come to the subject as expressions of his belief; other indicative thoughts come as mere possibilities which the thinker entertains, or as the believed or imagined content of the utterances of others. Those which come to the subject as expressions of his belief, I shall follow philosophical tradition in calling 'judgements'. They are the thoughts which strike a subject, which he sees as 'welling up' in him as his comment on the world—such as, for example, the thought that today is Monday, that I ought to be in London now, that it is my wife's birthday, or that Labour is going to win the next election. That it is a judgement of his is part of the content of the subject's thought, it is the force of the proposition which constitutes the thought, of which the subject will be aware in having the thought. But if, by contrast, you say to me the words 'Today is Monday', that may cause me (if I understand English) to have the occurrent thought that today is Monday, without that thought being a judgement of mine.

One who understands English and one who does not may have the same auditory sensations on hearing an English sentence, but in the former a thought is caused, which the subject believes to be the proposition expressed by the English sentence. The English sentence may, however, be highly ambiguous, or the subject may misunderstand it; nevertheless the subject knows which thought he is having. Occurrent thoughts may also be brought about in a subject by him saying something to himself, or as the content of a public communication. In saying something publicly, I have the thought of what I intend to convey. If I say to you 'The book is on the shelf', and I understand the words which I utter to have a certain meaning, then I have that thought. The public sentence may be highly ambiguous, but I know what I mean, which thought I am producing.

We must distinguish occurrent thought of any of these kinds, first from the thought in which a man may be said to think this or that—that the Earth is flat, or that five is the cube-root of thirty-five—even while he is totally unconscious. In that sense 'thought' is a synonym of 'belief'. 'He thinks that John is his brother' is synonymous with 'he believes that John is his brother', and describes a state in which a man may be when he has no relevant occurrent thoughts. I deal with belief in Chapter 7. Occurrent thoughts which are judgements convey beliefs, but the beliefs exist even when there are no thoughts occurring which express them.

Secondly, occurrent thought is to be distinguished from that 'thought' which characterizes a public performance.[1] When we say of someone 'He thinks about what he is doing', we may mean only that he does what he does intelligently. His attention is on his job, and he performs those actions which secure his ends without unwanted consequences. When we say that some man thinks what he is doing when he is gardening, we may mean only that he doesn't tread on garden plants, uproots weeds rather than garden plants, waters what is dry, and fertilizes what is barren. We are describing the successful character of his public performance, not goings-on additional to that, such as occurrent thoughts.

Thirdly, we must distinguish occurrent thought which is passive, from the active process of thinking, which is the process of actively bringing about occurrent thought. Active thought may be of three

[1] Which G. Ryle drew so prominently to our attention in *The Concept of Mind*, London, 1949.

kinds. First there is the case where an agent produces in himself a thought as a by-product of attempting to communicate it to others in speech or writing. Secondly, there is the case where an agent, thinking privately, repeats to himself some familiar thought or train of thoughts. I may say to myself—on purpose, to remind myself, to drum the thought home—that today is Monday, or there is no money left in the bank. Or I may run through the steps of a familiar argument in order to keep it in mind for when I try to lecture on the subject without notes. Such thought is a matter of an agent intentionally bringing about the occurrence of the occurrent passive thoughts (i.e. purposing to bring them about and succeeding in so doing).

Since, as we shall see, occurrent thoughts are normally mediated by sensations, in the case of thoughts not expressed publicly imaged (usually auditory) sensations of words which express the thought, active thought will normally involve the bringing about of such (imaged) sensations. But note that, neither aloud nor to myelf, could I intentionally bring about an unfamiliar or new thought; for I can only intentionally bring about that which I know how to bring about and so that with which I am already familiar. Thoughts have to occur to a person unexpectedly, before he can rehearse them actively.

The third kind of active thought is when an agent intentionally thinks about some subject or problem, normally privately, for a certain period of time. He may choose or decide to think about philosophy for half an hour. He may think about how to spend the summer or about the solution to an equation—because he chooses or sets himself to do these things. What is going on here is that he is intentionally bringing about certain passive thoughts (in the way described above), normally by saying to himself certain things, or conjuring up certain images, in the hope that there will occur to him new and unexpected thoughts in the right subject area (e.g. philosophy), or thoughts which provide answers to the questions which concern him (e.g. how to spend the summer). The way to think about how to spend the summer is to ask yourself such questions as 'How do my friends spend the summer?', 'Where have I spent earlier summers?', etc. in hope that some of the answers (e.g. 'John goes to Italy') will spark off a thought which you do not actively bring about, but which is brought about by some process over which you have no control (e.g. 'I ought to go to Italy') which constitutes a solution of your problem. I conclude that active thought (of these three kinds) is analysable in terms of other more basic constituents of the mental life—purpose or intention, which I shall discuss in the next chapter, and occurrent thought.

Knowledge of our Thoughts

Occurrent thoughts (however caused) are, I claim, mental events. If others have means of discovering my thoughts (by investigating my brain-states or behaviour), I could use the same methods—and yet I could know better than they what I was thinking because I was doing the thinking and so have an additional means of discovering my thoughts. A man has privileged access to his thoughts. All the arguments against the claim that thoughts are mental events, of the kind which we considered in the last two chapters endeavouring to show that really sensations were physical events (i.e. behavioural or brain-events) would have no more success in endeavouring to show that really thoughts were physical events. Thought is not reducible to behaviour, for there could be a robot which had no thoughts (or thoughts very different from mine), and yet behaved in exactly the same way as myself. Nor are thoughts the same as brain-events. The properties involved ('thinking that today is Tuesday' and 'having one's C-fibres fire') are different properties, and their instantiations in some person at some time constitute different events by the criteria of event-identity, which I set out in Chapter 3.

While there may be more to a subject's sensations than he is aware of, there is no more to his thoughts than he is aware of (although of course he may be more acutely aware of some thoughts than of others; they may be more to the forefront of his awareness than the others). There seems no content to the suggestion, that just as a man might re-examine an image to discover details of it of which he was totally unaware at the time (see p. 31), so he might re-examine his thoughts to discover such details. If I have a thought that today is Tuesday, but, although I believe it to be true and to be entailed by today being Tuesday, I was not aware of it occurring to me that today is the third day of the week, then I did not have the latter thought. It belongs to the very nature of a thought that the subject is aware of it. Although ·conscious episodes stand, as it were, naked before the subject (see pp. 32 f.), they only count as thoughts (as opposed to e.g. auditory images of words) to the extent to which the subject is aware of them and is aware of them as having meaning; their being thought is the subject being aware of them as having meaning. In consequence our beliefs about our current thoughts (that so-and-so is what I am thinking) unlike our beliefs about our sensations, are infallible. For only in so far as we are aware of them and so have beliefs about their content, are they our thoughts at all.

This claim that the subject's beliefs about the content of his thoughts are necessarily true, needs however to be guarded by two qualifications. The first is that, although necessarily a subject who has the thought that p, believes that he has the thought that p, he may refuse to admit it—publicly or even to himself. He may refuse to let the judgement 'I have the thought that p' occur; if he allowed his judgements about the content of his thoughts to occur, that would be the judgement which did occur. But the belief that he has the thought that p may be a belief which the agent refuses to admit to himself and thus represses from consciousness.[2]

The second qualification to the claim that a subject's beliefs about the content of his thoughts are necessarily true, is that any descriptions which he may give of them in any language to himself or others, while attempting to describe them correctly, which depends for its correctness as a description on anything outside the thought itself, may be a wrong description. In particular any description in some language which depends on the subject's beliefs about the sense or reference of words, or force of sentences, in that language may be mistaken. I may attempt to report my thought that John is distinguished by using the words 'John is notorious'. This description of my thought depends for its correctness on my belief that 'notorious' means 'distinguished'; my belief is false, and so I have misdescribed my thought. But I do not have a mistaken belief about the content of my thought; I did not have the thought that John is notorious, and I did not believe that I did. I had the thought that John is distinguished. I may even have had the thought that John is correctly described as 'notorious'. I am not in error in my beliefs that I had those thoughts.

Any description of a thought which depends for its correctness on the subject's beliefs about the reference of his referring expressions may also be mistaken, if these beliefs are false. Having the thought that the shimmering lake before me is beautiful, I may describe that thought as the thought 'that water is beautiful'. This description depends for its correctness on my belief that 'that water' refers to the shimmering lake in front of me. But it doesn't if the lake is not a lake of water. But again I do not have a mistaken belief about the content of my thought. I do not have the thought that that water is beautiful, and I do not believe that I do. For the very reason why I could not be having that thought—that there is no water in front of me and so 'that water' refers to nothing—also prevents me from having the belief that I have the thought that that water is beautiful. The thought which I have is the thought that the lake is beautiful. I may even have the thought that there is water in front of me which is beautiful. If I have those thoughts I am not in error in my beliefs that I have those thoughts.

That others can put the content of my thought into words better than I can does not show that my belief about its content is fallible. The point is that given the requisite true beliefs about things outside my thought, I can choose to give a description of my thought which cannot be in error; whereas given the same requisite beliefs, clearly the outsider cannot. When I acquire a true belief about who John is, and what 'is', 'notorious', and 'distinguished' mean, beliefs about matters quite outside my thought (that is, their truth conditions have nothing to do with my thought), then I can, if I choose, give a description of my thought—as the thought that 'John is distinguished' which cannot be in error. I recognize the redescription of my thought which I make when I acquire new requisite beliefs about things outside the thought, as just that—a redescription of what I knew already. I do not see myself as coming to know better what thought I had (in the way that—see p. 31—carefully examining my sensation might show me something unnoticed about it), only as coming to know better how to express that thought in language.[3]

[3] H. Putnam (*Reason, Truth and History*, Cambridge University Press, 1981, chs. 1 and 2) brings out well that what a thinker can truly be said to believe depends on what there is in the world and how it is related to ourselves, as well as what is going on 'in the thinker's mind'. Putnam uses 'believe' and 'think' interchangeably, but he would, I believe, regard this thesis as applying both to what I am calling 'thought' and to what I am calling 'belief', and that seems right. He suggests the introduction of Husserl's device of 'bracketing' in order to distinguish the truly mental element of thought, which is my concern in this chapter and Chapter 7: 'If we "bracket" the belief that there is a glass of water on the table, then what we

Our knowledge of the thoughts of others, like our knowledge of our sensations, is dependent on fallible inference from their public behaviour, and depends on the principle of charity used in Chapter 2 with respect to sensations, that probably (in the absence of counter-evidence) other men have the same thoughts as we do when they receive the same stimuli and/or make the same responses. We soon learn that they will only give the same responses to spoken or written words as we would, when they have learnt the language involved. But in so far as they know the language, we have reason to suppose that they have the same thoughts as we would when they hear or read words, or when they utter or write them.[4] Thoughts not involved in communication do not occur under circumstances as easy in practice to predict, as do sensations. The testimony of others about their thoughts as evidence of their beliefs about those thoughts (on the assumption that they are like ourselves in generally seeking to communicate true information) is a crucial source of information about their private thoughts. Also, there are kinds of behaviour which our own experience and the testimony of others suggest to be explicable only by the occurrence of a thought, which was a conclusion of a train of thoughts—men do not set about achieving important long term goals without giving consideration to the worthwhileness of the goal; or seek unfamiliar and distant goals without working out how to do so. And, as I noted earlier, the acquisition of a surprising belief is normally accompanied by the thought that that is how things are. Frequently, too, certain movements and gestures are best explained by their having been caused by a sudden and unexpected thought.

ascribe to John is simply the *mental* state of an actual or possible person who believes that there is a glass of water on the table (in the full "unbracketed" ordinary sense) . . . We still say that he has the *bracketed belief* that (there is a glass of water on the table). In effect the device of bracketing subtracts entailments from the ordinary belief locution (all entailments that refer to the external world, or what is external to the thinker's mind)'—op. cit., p. 28. Similarly Dennett describes a subject's 'notional attitude' as the element of belief which remains constant in different surroundings. See D. Dennett, 'Beyond Belief', in (ed.) A. Woodfield, *Thought and Object*, Clarendon Press, Oxford, 1982, e.g. pp. 80 f.

[4] Quine's thesis of 'the indeterminacy of translation' is often read as casting doubt on whether men do understand sentences of their language in the same way as each other. See W. V. O. Quine, *Word and Object*, MIT Press, Cambridge, Mass., 1960, ch. 2; and 'On the Reasons for Indeterminacy of Translation', *Journal of Philosophy*, 1970, **67**, 178–83. My argument from the principle of charity suggests that probably they do so understand them.

We are only justified in ascribing to organisms who do not have a language such thoughts as provide a simple explanation of their behaviour, or which we would expect to occur in them in view of some similarity to ourselves. In other animals as well as ourselves we might expect the acquisition through perception of a surprising belief to be accompanied by the thought that that is how things are. And there are other occasions too on which animal behaviour is best explained by supposing that an animal is struck by a certain thought—e.g. because a look on the animal's face similar to the look which humans have when they have suddenly reached an unexpected conclusion is followed by conduct evincing a belief which follows from earlier beliefs of the animal. But the thoughts which we need to ascribe to animals in these circumstances concern very down-to-earth matters—how to get a banana, say. And, as we cast our minds back in time, we recall that the sophistication of our thought grew with the sophistication of our language; and that leads us to infer that without language our thoughts would be pretty simple.

Thought of any sophistication requires the learning of language through participation in a language-using community. I shall show in more detail in Chapter 11 how language made possible the having of certain kinds of sophisticated thought, which were not previously possible for animals.

Thoughts being propositional in character, must be expressible by some language or other. In contrast to the case of sensations, there will be a sentence which expresses a given thought, while even a logically equivalent sentence will not express just that thought. But any given language may be inadequate for expressing some thought. Human language, for example, is often too fine grained to express any animal thought. We may try to express the thought had by a dog, by the sentence 'My master has returned', and yet the dog may not think of the one who has returned as his 'master' in anything like the human sense of one who 'owns' him, which seems to be a legal concept too subtle for the dog to grasp. Still, clearly, some sentences get closer to expressing some animal thought than do others.

Thoughts are Unanalysable Mental Events

I have urged that thoughts are mental events, and that they are distinct from beliefs. They are obviously distinct from purposings and desires—to have a thought that so-and-so is the case is neither to attempt nor to desire to do anything.

Further, I contend, thoughts are not analysable in terms of sensations—whether auditory or visual sensations of publicly uttered words or images of such sensations. I shall develop this point mainly by considering the thoughts which occur to a man privately; the same points could be made with respect to thoughts had in understanding public speech or writing. Certainly when a man has such a thought, he often has auditory images of many of the words which would occur in a sentence which expressed the thought. When I have the thought that some President is dead, auditory images of the word 'President' and 'dead' flit through my mind. So it is natural to suggest an analysis of thought in terms of sensation—that having a thought consists in the occurrence of sensations or sensory images (normally auditory or visual) of words of a sentence which expresses that thought. For me to have thought that 'the President is dead' is for the words 'the President is dead' to 'flit through my mind'. I argue that this is neither sufficient nor necessary if I am to have thought in question.

Most importantly, it is not sufficient. To start with, the words which flit through my mind may be words of a language which I do not understand. I may have liked certain sounds of a foreign language, and they may occur to me again without my having the least idea what they mean and so without their occurrence constituting the occurrence to me of a thought. How often must the words of the Latin mass have passed through the mind of pious Roman Catholics of old (when the mass was said throughout the world in Latin) without those words being the vehicle of any thought. Let us suppose the restriction is added that the words be of a language which I understand. There are then three harder difficulties. First, it is not enough for me to know English for the occurrence to me of the words 'the President is dead' to express a thought of mine that some President is dead. They, too, may be the words of a song which pass through my mind without being the vehicle of a thought. A man is usually careful not to say aloud words which he does not mean (for fear of what his hearers might think), but he may say to himself much that he does not mean. Secondly, even given that the words which occur to a subject are words of a sentence which he understands as expressing a thought, the words may often not be enough to determine the meaning of the sentence. In particular they may be quite inadequate to determine the intended referent (for reasons which have nothing to do with mistaken beliefs about surrounding circumstance—see earlier). I speak of 'the President', but which President—of the USA, or of China, or of my local history society? The sentence does not fully capture the thought, for in having the thought I know of which President I am thinking, but the sentence does not make that clear.

And, finally, even given that we can determine which proposition the words express, we still do not know the force of that proposition, viz. whether the words express a judgement of the subject or whether he is recalling some past conversation or imagining some future one in which another person says something to him and which he understands in a certain way, but which in no way represents his own current belief. Imagined conversation is different from one's own judgements. 'The President is dead' may be words which I recall someone saying to me in the autumn of 1963 after the assassination of President Kennedy. Or they may even be words which I recall myself uttering on some previous occasion. And yet the subject knows whether he is making a judgement or merely imagining a past conversation; but the pattern of his sensations does not show this.

So which thought he is having is not determined by the pattern of the subject's sensations. Something else beside the words is necessary for the thought. Let us see if it can be supplied without making thoughts special unanalysable events.

There are two possible such theories in terms of actual context and in terms of hypothetical context. Let us take actual context first. I understand by the actual context of his imaged words the surrounding pattern of a subject's mental events, and of the physical events in the world around him—e.g. who is talking to him, what words they have been saying and which words he utters in response to them, and the longer-term pattern of his conversational habits. The suggestion then goes that what determines whether the words 'the President is dead' are meant as opposed to being just the words of a song would be factors such as whether I have previously been talking to somebody about 'the President' or had a picture in my mind of (say) President Reagan; or, by contrast, whether 'the President is dead' were the words of a song known to me and whether I was often in the habit of repeating to myself words of songs. What determines that the intended reference is (say) to Harold Jones, president of the local history society, is whether I have a picture of him in my mind when I imagine the words. What determines whether the words were a judgement of mine, as opposed to words which I was imagining someone saying, was whether I had visual images of someone out of whose mouth I seemed to hear the words coming.

It should be apparent that this kind of analysis will not work. Often there is no context to a man's thought. Thoughts flash through my mind when I have been thinking of nothing before—men often wake up suddenly with a nagging thought—'he's dead'. And before my subsequent train of thought could show who 'he' is, the thinker may be distracted by the crockery being dropped downstairs. But just as much as one's own thoughts there may flash through one's mind the utterances of others, or conversations one would like to have had. And again the sequence may be too short for any context to show whether they are one's own judgements or not.

Thought is often so casual and irrational that the context could not show which (if any) thought is expressed by the words of which one has images. We do not always think in paragraphs. Sudden thoughts strike us and then our attention is diverted to something else. I am walking along thinking of nothing in particular, having only the sensations involved in perception of my surroundings. The words flash through my mind: 'You are old'. Before more words can flash through my mind, my attention is diverted by catching sight of a colleague. There are many different interpretations which could be given to the words. They might be the beginning of 'You are old, Father William'. They might be part of an imaginary conversation with an elderly colleague. And so on. But the crucial point is that I know what is the interpretation of the words, and the surroundings do not dictate the interpretation.

Nor can visual images of faces determine the reference of referring expressions. I often imagine people saying things or refer to them without having visual images of them. Or if I do have visual images, the images are so vague that in themselves they could be images of almost anybody; what determines of whom they are intended images is not something in themselves but the way I construe them (i.e. the role they play in my thought). The thought determines of whom the image is an image; the image does not determine of whom the thought is a thought.

The context of public conversations normally determines the public meaning of public sentences. But the public meaning of a public sentence is a very different thing from the private meaning (the way it is understood by a subject) of a sentence, whether uttered aloud or to oneself. A sentence, expressed aloud, only has a public meaning to the extent to which it sets up similar clear thoughts in hearers who have learnt the language in question. There are various context-dependent devices which determine the reference, sense, and force of public utterances and so ensure that this happens despite any unclarity of sense or reference in the words uttered taken by themselves. I can pick out objects which it may be difficult to describe, by means of indexical expressions— i.e. expressions such as 'I', 'he, 'this', 'over there', 'now', 'here', whose reference is determined not just by what is said but by the context in which it is said (e.g. the reference of 'you' depends on which person I am talking to and the reference of 'over there' depends on the direction in which I am pointing). The context will include the previous sentences uttered by a speaker or the person to whom he was talking. The claim made by 'what you just said is false' will depend on what you just said; and the reference of 'the President' will depend on which President we had previously been discussing.

The public meaning of a sentence is a public matter and there are public criteria for determining what it is. But the private meaning of words which a subject utters to himself or finds occurring to him is not a public matter; the meaning of the words, and so his thought, is whatever the subject supposes it to be; and the fact that other people would understand those words differently if they were said aloud is quite irrelevant. Likewise, the private thought had by a speaker or hearer of a public sentence may be a perfectly clear one, even though the public sentence lacks a clear meaning. Thought is a matter of private meaning, the way the sentence—said aloud or to onself—is understood by the thinker— not a matter of the conventions which determine what is its public meaning and how others might understand it if it is used in communication.[5]

---

[5] That language is a device for expressing publicly, intentional states (such as beliefs and thoughts) which may exist independently of language is a major theme

It may be suggested that it is not the actual context, but the hypothetical context—how I would have filled the words out if I had sought to tell someone else the thoughts that I had, or how the sequence of words would have continued if my attention had not been diverted. Having a thought would thus be (in part) a dispositional property—like fragility or malleability. I do not think that any such dispositional account of thought will work. For although it may be the case that if I have a certain thought, I must have a certain disposition, and conversely, the description of the disposition already presupposes the thought to be a separate thing from itself and so cannot be what having the thought consists in. In this sense, the account of thought in terms of having a disposition will be viciously circular.

Accounts in which the disposition is a matter of how a subject would behave publicly in various circumstances, e.g. what he would say publicly if asked whether his thought was so and so are either false, or (in the above sense) viciously circular. If we say: my thought was a thought that p if, only if, when asked if p was my thought, I would say 'Yes', this analysis is false. For I might not wish my thought to be public, and so tell a lie. I might be an inveterate liar and the lie might come naturally and spontaneously out of my mouth. If we say: my thought was a thought that p if, and only if, when asked if p was my thought, and I was seeking to tell the truth, I would say 'Yes', the analysis, though plausible, is viciously circular. For 'seeking to tell the truth' is not seeking in general to tell the truth, but seeking to provide a true answer to the question. But how can I possibly seek to provide a true answer to the question, unless there is already an answer which is true, and whose truth does not depend on how I respond to the question? The description of the disposition already presupposes that thoughts exist prior to and independently of the disposition to manifest them in this way.

If, alternatively, we seek to analyse having a thought in terms of the hypothetical private context, that is how the sequence of imaged words would have continued under different circumstances, we run into a similar problem. Most accounts are obviously false. The words occur to me: 'You are old'. The suggestion is made that

of J. R. Searle, *Intentionality*. He claims (p. 27): 'An utterance can have Intentionality, just as a belief has Intentionality, but whereas the Intentionality of the belief is *intrinsic* the Intentionality of the utterance is derived.'

they constitute the thought that I myself am old if, and only if, if my attention is not diverted to something in the outside world (e.g. I catch sight of my colleague), they are followed by thoughts about such matters as my hair being grey, my children growing up, etc., the account is false. I may have the thought that I am old, casually, without brooding on it; I may not mind. If, alternatively, the suggestion is made that the words constitute the thought that I am myself old if, and only if, when I continue to have thoughts but not thoughts about anything else, then I will have thoughts about such matters as my hair being grey, my children growing up, etc., the use of the words 'anything else' makes the account viciously circular. For the account presupposes that there is an independent criterion of what I was thinking about originally. The account cannot be applied unless we can determine by some independent means when the subject of my thought changes; but we cannot do that unless we can determine what I was thinking about in the first place—which was what the account was seeking to elucidate. And, further, both suggested analyses presuppose that we can determine by some independent means what I am thinking about subsequently.

Thus, to give an example against the second analysis (that the words uttered to myself 'You are old' constitute the thought that I am myself old, if, and only if, when I continue to have thoughts, but not thoughts about anything else, then I have thoughts about such matters as my hair being grey, etc.)—the words occur to me 'You are old', and they are followed after a short pause by the words 'grey headed'. Now *if* I continued to think about the same subject, and *if* the words 'grey headed' constituted the thought that I was myself grey headed, then indeed my original words constituted the thought that I was myself old. But the analysis presupposes an independent criterion of my continuing to think about the same subject, and which thought is constituted by the words 'grey headed'. The latter words may have constituted the thought about some colleague that he was grey headed. I may have been thinking about him all the time, or I may have changed from thinking about me to thinking about him.

I suggest that all analyses in terms of how my imaged words or other sensations would have continued under different circumstances suffer from similar deficiences. This applies not merely to thoughts which occur to a man by himself, unpredictably; but to those caused through conversation. That I understand your words is not a matter of how I do respond to them in present circumstances, or would respond to them under other circumstances. Although my responses (of public behaviour or private sensations) are strong evidence of how I understand your words, they are not conclusive evidence. I may have misunderstood you and then conceal my misunderstanding by pretending that I understood you differently. And the thought which I intend to convey by my words may be other than my words understood by the normal conventions of society do convey. And whether that is so is not shown conclusively by the pattern of my public behaviour (or even of my private sensations). I may look at Jones, and say 'You are a fool', intending thereby to convey the thought that Brown is a fool. Then, coming to believe that more harm would be done by insulting Brown than by insulting Jones, I may pretend that I meant to refer to Jones all along.

And not merely are the auditory or visual sensations of the words of a sentence of a language known to the subject not a sufficient condition for the expression of a thought; they are not even a necessary condition. For, first and crucially, if a thought is expressed in words, the thought may be expressed in far fewer words than are needed for a grammatical sentence. The word 'old' alone said to myself may serve to express the thought that I am old. Secondly, it does seem very plausible to suppose that having thoughts is not confined to language-users. There are cases of those who learn to use words late in life yet report having thoughts earlier.[6] And we saw earlier the grounds for attributing thoughts to animals who do not have a language. Animal thoughts might be mediated, instead of by images of words, by picture images[7] of the objects and properties thought about. (But its expression in picture images would not be sufficient for the occurrence of a thought—any more than is its expression in images of words, and for just the same reasons.)

These considerations so far bring out that there is more in the way of occurrent events to a thought than words or images or other sensations which mediate it, and that we do not need much in the way of the latter. Do we need imaged words or other sensations at all as the vehicle of thought? I *suggest* that we do not; a man can

[6] See Wittgenstein's doubts about such a case reported by William James—*Philosophical Investigations*, § 342.

[7] For a detailed defence of the possibility of thinking in images, see H. H. Price, *Thinking and Experience*, Hutchinson, London, 1953, especially chs. 8 and 9.

have a thought without either picture images or words to express it. Since clearly thought goes far beyond the vague sensory content which goes with it, there seems no good philosophical argument to show that it needs the latter at all. In favour of this, I present two further empirical considerations. First, there is the familiar phenomenon of having an idea for which even if we try we cannot find anything like the right words; later the words come, which we recognize as capturing the thought. Secondly, there is the work of the Wurzburg school of psychologists in the first decade of this century who got subjects to introspect carefully and report the thoughts which they had and what went on mentally when they had these thoughts. (Often they were asked to report on the thoughts which they had between being given some question and making some reply.[8]) Subjects continually reported that thoughts came unmediated by sensations. True, reports of introspection are very suspect, liable to be over-influenced by the philosophical prejudices of the subject or investigator. Nevertheless, there is a wealth of empirical testimony to 'imageless thought', which the trend of my argument suggests to be logically possible.

I have in effect been arguing for the past few pages that not merely are thoughts propositional but they are so intrinsically. The thought being the thought it is is not a matter of the context in which it occurs, but is intrinsic to the content of the thought (though descriptions can be given of that content, whose significance depends on the surrounding context). But if thoughts are occurrent mental events distinct from images of words or other sensations which normally accompany them, we need an account of why many, perhaps most, thoughts are accompanied by sensations (normally, in men, sensory images of words); and an account of why, although there can be thoughts which a man does not express in words, it is a little odd to suppose that he has thoughts, which he would totally be unable to express in words, albeit imperfectly. It would be a little odd to suppose some New Guinea Tribesman to have the thought captured in Einstein's equation, $E = mc^2$, when he could not even do simple arithmetic in spoken or written symbols. So what is the connection between talk and thought?

It is, I suggest, this. As we are exposed to language, we hear

---

[8] For a description of their work in this field, see G. Humphrey, *Thinking*, Methuen, London, 1951, ch. 2.

public sentences uttered by others, the meaning of which is determined by public conventions; and we ourselves come to utter strings of public noises. We are corrected in our usage by others, helped to utter grammatically well-formed sentences appropriate to their circumstances, instead of randomly assorted noises. We also learn appropriate responses to the public sentences uttered by others. As we learn appropriate utterances and responses, the auditory sensations caused by hearing public sentences come to be connected with thoughts which are the propositional content of the public sentences, as determined by the public conventions which give them meaning. The brain-event caused by hearing a public sentence, which causes the auditory sensations, causes another brain-event which causes the thought. The process of learning a language is the process whereby having auditory sensations (e.g. of the words 'the cat is on the mat'), comes to be correlated with the thought of the proposition which is the public meaning of those words (e.g. the proposition that the cat is on the mat). Correspondingly, as we learn to use words appropriately, the utterance of a public sentence comes to be correlated with having the thought of the proposition which is the public meaning of that sentence.

We come to have thoughts not merely through learning language; but, as animals do, through awareness of newly acquired beliefs. We shall see in Chapter 7 that there are good grounds for attributing beliefs to languageless animals, beliefs about objects and properties to which they learn to react. Beliefs are mental states, states to which the subject has privileged access. We saw earlier that there are grounds for attributing to animals sometimes an awareness of such beliefs. The brain-state which causes a belief sometimes causes initially also the awareness of that belief which is a judgement.

There is, no doubt, a natural selection explanation of how the particular links between auditory sensations and thoughts (and between the production of noises and thoughts; and the occurence of non-linguistic thoughts appropriate to their circumstances) come to be set up. A subject in whom exposure to a publicly uttered sentence causes the thought which is the public meaning of that sentence rather than some irrelevant thought, would be, for that reason, the better adapted to survive. For, given that thoughts make a difference to other thoughts and to the beliefs which an agent has (as I shall argue shortly), they will make a difference to which actions he does. And the agent who understands a public sentence about the dangers of his surroundings or the location of food in the right way, will survive for longer than one who does not. Evolution will favour mutations which lead to agents having the right thoughts when they hear public sentences, making the right public noises to express their thoughts, or being aware of their beliefs in thought (since those beliefs can then make a difference to subsequent beliefs via their trains of thought). Generally, evolution will favour the establishment of those links by which subjects come to have thoughts appropriate to their environment. (I discuss this process of how particular brain-state/ mental state links are set up more generally in Chapter 10, and I also discuss there the crucial limits to scientific explanation of such linkage.)

As a subject learns a public language, he comes, in having auditory sensations, to have thoughts of a kind expressible in that language. Certain patterns of noises set up certain patterns both of sensation and of thought. In learning the words of a language and the ways of connecting them, we acquire the ability to have the thoughts which can be expressed by those words and those ways of connecting them. Then, brain-states of a kind similar to those produced by hearing public sentences come to occur through other causes, first so as to produce auditory images of words and thereby private thoughts, and then sometimes so as to produce the thoughts without the auditory images. Public conditioning by language-learning comes to cause certain kinds of brain-state, rather than others; and so certain kinds of thought rather than others. Evolution will favour subjects whose private thoughts occur in rationally connected ways (e.g. where one thought follows deductively from another) and so leads to well-thought-out plans for attaining their goals.

Language is not of course necessarily conveyed and expressed by auditory images. Images of vision and touch may also be the vehicles of sentences. And, as we have seen, animals lacking language may still have thoughts. All the grounds for attributing thoughts to animals outlined earlier, are grounds for attributing to them thoughts of a kind about which they can have beliefs, i.e. thoughts which express the concepts involved in their beliefs. And (I shall argue in Chapter 11) the only beliefs which languageless animals can have concern states of affairs close to their daily patterns of life. It is through learning to react to objects and properties of certain kinds, as well as to react to sentences which describe those objects and properties, that subjects acquire the ability to have beliefs and so thoughts about those objects and properties. When animals have thoughts about states of affairs other than that which they are currently perceiving, picture-images of the states of affairs envisaged are perhaps, we considered earlier, the sensory accompaniments of the thoughts that those states are past, or possible, or welcome. What happens is perhaps that similar brain-states to those which produce sensory pictures of states of affairs perceived together with the belief and so the thought that things are thus, occur to produce similar sensory pictures and so thoughts in the absence of perception.

It is not logically necessary that we acquire the ability to have thoughts by being exposed to language or certain kinds of life-situation and learning to respond linguistically or non-linguistically; nor is it even naturally necessary. One day perhaps we may learn how to produce the brain-state which in turn brings about a given thought without doing so by immersing the subject in language and behaviour, as described above. But it is in practice today necessary that we acquire the ability to have thoughts in these ways. Today we can only have thoughts which are initially fairly close to our ability to express them in language or practice. But having acquired the ability to have thoughts of certain kinds, we may forget or not need all or even any images of the public words or other devices which express them. Most of us much of the time do need tags (of single words or vague images rather than full sentences) in order to have one thought distinct from some other. But for some of us, especially when the objects of our thought are very familiar ones, the tags become less and less necessary.[9]

In claiming that thoughts are unanalysable mental events, I do not wish to be thought to be denying various obvious truths. First, a thought wouldn't be a thought unless it could be expressed by some language or other. Thoughts, in the sense with which I am concerned with them, are essentially propositional in nature. Since it is plausible to suppose that every proposition must be expressible by some sentence of some language (perhaps, one as yet

[9] See Additional Note 1.

uninvented), it follows that thoughts must be expressible in language. But it does not follow that they can be expressed in a language available to the subject. Secondly, I do not wish to deny that thoughts affirm relations between things thought about (be they objects, properties, or concepts) which will be picked out by separate words in sentences which express the thoughts. In claiming that thoughts are unanalysable, I mean only that the mental events which are thoughts do not have non-cognitive parts. Nor, thirdly, do I wish to deny that we cannot have certain thoughts unless we have certain beliefs. To take Davidson's example, we cannot believe or, therefore, have the thought that the gun is loaded, unless we have beliefs such as that 'a gun is a weapon, and that it is a more or less enduring physical object'.[10] But this is because a man's thought about a gun is a thought about a weapon which is an enduring physical object and so his thought contains such thoughts, and hence his expression of it is an expression of those beliefs too. A man's thought would be wrongly described as the thought that 'the gun is loaded' unless he had those beliefs. But despite these obvious points, my claim remains that thoughts are unanalysable mental events. It is the role of public language (which we can image privately in sensory images), in developing our private thought, which makes us wrongly suppose that thought just is the utterance of noises sub-voce.[11]

It follows from all this that if (as I shall state as an assumption in Chapter 10) there is a one–many correlation between mental events and brain-events, a one–many correlation between sensations and brain-events is insufficient. (By a one–many correlation between mental events and brain-events, I mean that for any kind of mental event, there are one or more kinds of brain-event, such that whenever the former occurs, one of the latter occurs and conversely.) If the thoughts associated with qualitatively identical sensations are different, so must be the correlated brain-events.

[10] D. Davidson, 'Thought and Talk', in (ed.) S. Guttenplan, *Mind and Language*, Clarendon Press, Oxford, 1975, p. 10.

[11] This section is a defence of an account of thought attacked in Wittgenstein's *Philosophical Investigations*, §§ 316–63. It is much in agreement with the views expressed in W. J. Ginnane, 'Thoughts' *Mind*, 1960, **69**, 372–90, and in Z. Vendler, *Res Cogitans*, Cornell University Press, Ithaca, NY, 1972, ch. 3. In *Mental Acts* (Routledge and Kegan Paul, London, 1957), P. T. Geach also distinguishes between thoughts and their verbal expressions, though he is very conscious of a close connection between them. See especially § 23.

Thoughts have Effects

At the end of Chapter 2 I pointed out that there was good reason to say not merely that sensations were caused by brain-events, but that they in turn caused other brain-events. Given the Chapter 3 conclusion that sensations are indeed mental events, it follows that there is good reason to suppose that some mental events are not merely epiphenomena but are causally efficacious. One reason for supposing this, was that we could not have justified beliefs about our sensations, which to all appearances we so obviously have (does it not 'stare us in the face' that we have certain sensations?) which caused us publicly to acknowledge those sensations, unless the sensations themselves caused our beliefs. This reason operates also in the case of thoughts. My beliefs about my thoughts and my public acknowledgment of them could have no justification unless caused by the thoughts themselves. However, as we saw in Chapter 2, other reasons for believing in the causal efficacy of sensations can be given; and other different reasons for believing in the causal efficacy of thoughts can also be given.

Thoughts often set off other thoughts. Indeed much of our thought comes in chains. These may be simple chains of association of the kind studied by associationist psychology—I think of John, then I think of John's mother, then I think of John's mother's house, then I think of the railway outside John's mother's house; and so on. But they may be chains of argument. An extreme case would be where I solve a mathematical problem in my mind—say a problem of mental arithmetic, in which each thought is a stage in the argument; it follows deductively from the previous thought and provides the premisses of the next one. In these cases there are very close correlations between the content of one thought and the content of the next thought; vary the content of the first thought, and clearly you will vary the content of the second thought. It seems a soluble problem for psychology to devise, for these cases, 'laws of thought' stating for subjects with given background beliefs and a given purpose, e.g. to solve a certain mathematical problem, which thoughts will necessarily, or with high probability, follow which other thoughts. The laws will state how one thought will follow another in virtue of the content of each—e.g. the thought 'what is 35×17?' will be followed in the case of many of us by '$350 + 35 \times 7$', and that by '$5 \times 7 = 35$', '5 and carry 3' and so on, all on the assumption that the subject has the purpose of solving the problem. As I shall emphasize in more detail in Chapter 14, the subject's background beliefs are often needed to explain why he moved from this thought to that thought—e.g. his beliefs about which are good methods for solving sums and his beliefs about the answers to other simpler sums. False background beliefs will explain errors in the subject's reasoning (e.g. his false belief that $5 \times 7 = 34$ would explain how the subject reached a wrong answer to 'what is 35×17'). The operation of such 'laws of thought' is, of course, subject to the brain ticking over in the sense of keeping the subject conscious and maintaining his belief system. But the primary components of such laws of thought are mental factors—the prior thought, his background beliefs, and the agent's purpose. There is prospect of comparatively simple laws of thought of this mental kind. Simplicity, I have argued earlier, is evidence of truth. Now maybe the succession of thoughts is due to the succession of underlying processes, which are so organized that they produce the appearance of rational connection of thought (i.e. the appearance that in some way one thought is a response to the previous thought). But the greater the simplicity of connection of thought, the greater the probability that thought processes are autonomous.

There do, of course, exist computers which print out sentences corresponding to different stages in their process of calculation, where the printed sentences although having a logical connection with each other (so long as you interpret them as sentences of a certain language) in no way cause each other. But in those cases we have other evidence that the sentences do not cause each other because we know what does cause such sentences to be printed out, viz., electromechanical goings-on in the computer. Further, in such cases, there is in fact, despite initial appearances, no simplicity of connection between the sentences printed out *as such*. Simplicity only arises given a way of understanding those sentences, as having certain meanings; a way of understanding them imposed upon the sentences by the constructor and users of the computer. The computer does not itself understand its sentences as having meaning (although I could be mistaken about this). If it did, and if there were no other evidence about the causes of its printing its sentences, then it would be reasonable to suppose that those sentences were causally efficacious in producing subsequent sentences. The point stands that the greater the simplicity of connection of thought, the greater the probability that thoughts have a role in causing other thoughts. That is not to deny that brain processes of various kinds need to be operative in order that thoughts may cause other thoughts in regular ways. However, my argument is that the evidence suggests that brain processes, though they may be necessary, are not sufficient to produce the succession of thoughts.

In so far as thoughts are mediated by sensory images, then if one thought causes another it will cause the sensory images by which the latter is expressed. But normally the successions of sensations are clearly due to the successions of their physical causes. Why I have this auditory sensation followed by that one is because the blowing of the note which caused the former sensation was followed by a blowing which caused the latter sensation. With thought, I have argued, things are often otherwise. The model of brain-event/thought interaction which I advocate is thus as follows in Fig. 1. I represent thoughts by 'T's, brain-events by 'B's, and causal influence by ' → '.

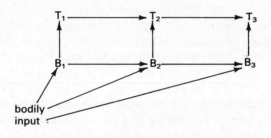

Fig. 1

5. PURPOSES

AMONG the conscious episodes to which a subject has privileged access are what I have rather clumsily called his purposings. This is a technical term, and I shall need quite a lot of this chapter to explain more carefully than I did in Chapter 1 what a purposing is, and to justify my claim that there are such conscious episodes. I do so by considering the nature of intentional action.

The Description of Intentional Action

An intentional action is something which an agent does, under some description meaning to do it (i.e. with the intention of doing it[1])—such as raising his hand, saying the word 'hand', shooting a man, or closing a door. We often do an intentional action by doing another intentional action. I kill a man by shooting him; shoot him by pulling the trigger; pull the trigger by squeezing my finger. I cheer you up by complimenting you on your work; I compliment you on your work by saying 'Well done!' When an agent does A by doing B, then normally either doing B causes some effect, the production of which is doing A; or, in the circumstances in which it is done, doing B is doing A.[2] By pulling the trigger I cause a bullet to enter the man; causing a bullet to enter the man is shooting him. Saying 'Well done!' in circumstances where these words mean that the hearer has done well (i.e. when English is spoken) is complimenting him.

In such cases we can think of the agent as simultaneously doing many different actions (pulling the trigger, shooting, killing), or as doing just one action which is described in many different ways.

---

[1] In writing about 'intention' in this chapter, I am writing about the intentions which agents have in doing what they do; not the intentions which they have now as to what they will do at some future time. My concern in this chapter is with what agents are trying to achieve as they act, not with what they have resolved to do on another occasion. I shall discuss intention for the future in Chapter 6.

[2] A. Goldman has distinguished carefully four ways in which by doing one thing, we do another, which he calls 'level generation'. See his *A Theory of Human Action*, Prentice-Hall, Englewood Cliffs, NJ, 1970, ch. 2.

Although we can think in either way, it is, I believe, more natural to think in the latter way and I shall do so. In that case the essence of the action, as it were, is the agent moving his body in a certain way, intending thereby to bring about certain further consequences.[3] If we describe the action as the bringing about of those consequences, we describe it not solely as it is in itself, but as it is (in part) in virtue of the effects which it produces. The intentional action of pulling the trigger is an action of shooting a man because it is an action of producing some bodily movement, intending thereby to cause a bullet to enter a man, in fact causing a bullet to enter a man.

Actions are events and, as I argued in Chapter 3, the same event may be described in many different ways. The event of my moving my body in a certain way has within its boundaries the movements of my body and my internal state (e.g. purposes and beliefs) yet to be analysed, which brings about those movements. A description which describes only what lies within those boundaries is an intrinsic description. A description which describes what lies within those boundaries, in whole or part in terms of its effects or what it amounts to in the circumstances of its occurrence, is an extrinsic description. If the extrinsic description of the action is one which the agent intended should apply to it, then as so described, the action is an intentional action, otherwise it is an unintentional action. If in squeezing my finger I had the intention of killing, then the resultant killing was an intentional action of mine; otherwise, it was an unintentional action.

So, of such cases which I described as cases where an agent does one action by doing another, a more correct description is that he does an action under one description by doing it under another description. He does an action of complimenting by doing that action under the description of saying 'Well done!' When an agent does an action intentionally under one description by doing an action intentionally under another description (other than the description 'trying', 'seeking', 'endeavouring', etc. to do the action under the former description), then the latter action is the same action as the former, but described by a more basic act

---

[3] 'We never do more than move our bodies: the rest is up to nature'—D. Davidson, 'Agency', in his *Essays on Actions and Events*, Clarendon Press, Oxford, 1980, p. 59. See also J. Hornsby, *Actions*, Routledge and Kegan Paul, London, 1980.

description.[4] An act is given its (most) basic act-description when it is described in such a way that the agent does not do the act under that description by doing that act under any other description, or by doing any other act.[5] When I kill the man by shooting him, etc., there is only one action and the basic act description of it is 'squeezing my finger'. I may squeeze my finger by trying to squeeze my finger, but my definition rules that out as a description of the same act. (A basic act is an act of a kind picked out by a basic act-description—e.g. any act of moving a limb or saying a word; an act of a kind which the agent just does, does not do by doing anything else.) Conversely, we may say, an action is given its ultimate (i.e. least basic) act-description when it is described in such a way that the agent does not do the act intentionally under any other description by doing the act under that description. If there is nothing else which I am doing intentionally by complimenting you (e.g. calming you down, or buttering you up), then the ultimate act-description of my act is complimenting you.

Normally for an agent to perform an action under some description is for him to bring about some event with the intention of so doing. This event is one which could have been brought about by inanimate causes (in which case the bringing of it about

[4] An agent may do an action under one description, X, by doing an action under another description, Y, in the sense that he does the act under the description Y naturally, not by following a recipe—whereas he does the action under the description X by following the recipe 'Do Y'. In such a case, the description Y is teleologically more basic than the description X. Alternatively, he may do the action under the description X by doing the action under the description Y in the sense that he does the action under the description Y intentionally in certain circumstances with that action having certain effects, and doing that action intentionally, knowing those to be the circumstances and effects, constitutes doing an action under the description X intentionally. In such a case the description of Y is causally more basic than the description of X. Normally the teleologically more basic is also causally more basic, and conversely. These seem to be the two main kinds of basic act-description among the narrower kinds distinguished by Annette Baier ('The Search for Basic Actions', *American Philosophical Quarterly*, 1971, **8**, 161–70). My concern is with causal basicness. I understand by an action described under its basic act-description, an action which the agent does not do by doing an action under any causally more basic description (except such actions as 'trying', etc.).

[5] The basic/non-basic distinction was introduced by Danto (A. C. Danto, 'Basic Actions', *American Philosophical Quarterly*, 1965, **2**, 141–48) as a distinction between different actions done simultaneously, rather than different descriptions of the same action. For a general description of different theories of when two actions are the same, see L. H. Davis, *Theory of Action*, Prentice-Hall, Englewood Cliffs, NJ, 1979, ch. 2.

would not be an intentional action). This event may be called the result of the action. My moving my hand is my bringing about the motion of my hand, which latter is the result of my action. My killing the man is my bringing about his death; his death is the result of the action. The motion of my hand and the death of the man are both events which could have been brought about by inanimate causes, and so not through intentional agency. They are, thus, the results of the two actions.

My action of saying the words 'You are a fool' (bringing it about that these words come out of my mouth) may, given the circumstances of their utterance (e.g. my looking at you), be an act of insulting you intentionally or unintentionally. The act, under this latter description, is not an act of bringing about some state of affairs which could have been brought by inanimate causes; in my sense the act under this description does not have a result. But, with one exception to which we will come shortly, its basic act-description is always a description of an action in which it consists in bringing about a result which could be brought about by inanimate causes. Inanimate causes could have caused the words 'You are a fool' to come out of my mouth. The result of an action under its basic act-description I will call its basic result. Intentional actions (described intrinsically, that is, by their basic act-description) are not always bringing about bodily movements. They may, instead, be the bringing about of some effect in or around the agent's body, as when I tie my shoelaces or say any word (e.g. 'king'). I do not intentionally move certain parts of my body in order to tie my shoe-laces or to say the word 'king'; for I would not know which parts to move to secure these ends. Rather, I intentionally bring about these effects, and certain things happen in or around my body, unintended by me, which bring about the result. Likewise, whenever I move my limbs intentionally, things have to happen in my nerves, but I do not intentionally bring about these things (even if I do know what they are)—at least, not normally. I can learn how to set up certain neural circuits or produce certain electrochemical rhythms in my brain; and then come to do these things intentionally. Mental actions, such as the bringing about intentionally of a thought or sensation, also consist in bringing about a result other than a bodily movement. As we have seen earlier—images and thoughts may either be brought about by the thinker or be caused to occur in him by other means.

There is one exception to the general thesis that intentional action (described by its basic act-description) consists in bringing about a result in my sense. Trying, endeavouring, seeking to do something, do not, as such, consist in bringing about a result, and, indeed, they may have no effect at all, but they are intentional actions all the same. I may try to bring about some bodily movement or other basic result, and simply fail. If I try to move my hand, but fail, because you are holding it down, I still perform an action—try to move my hand. Trying is something which I do intentionally. Still, I achieve nothing which I intend to achieve, apart from trying, and that is an intentional action. There is no result describable independently of the process of bringing it about. The same applies when I try to utter some word, but cannot articulate it; or try to form some mental image, but am too tired to construct the lines of my mental picture.[6]

We saw in Chapter 3 that an act described intrinsically may be described in more or less detail. The act of squeezing my finger is also the act of squeezing my finger in order to pull the trigger in order thereby to shoot my victim. All the more remote intentions of the action lie within the boundaries of the action, whereas the effects of the action (intended or not), other than its basic result, lie outside the action. We give a fuller intrinsic description of an action when we describe more fully the intention with which the agent brought about the basic result, not just as the intention to bring about that result but as the intention thereby to perform various less basic acts.

The Analysis of Intentional Action

So, then, the central notion in intentional action is that of an agent intentionally bringing about an event. Bringing about is causing. In all other cases, causation can be expressed as a relation between events. When a substance (the brick) is said to cause an event (the shattering of the window), this can be expressed as an event which

---

[6] There are a few actions which, if I try to do them, I must succeed. Trying is obviously one example; if I try to try to φ, necessarily I try to φ. Thinking that *p* in the sense of bringing about the thought that *p* (where *p* is a certain proposition) is another example. If I try to have the thought that $2 + 2 = 4$, necessarily I succeed— because the very endeavour to produce that effect involves having in mind the effect, being aware of what affect I am trying to produce. But to do that is to have that thought. However, as I claimed above, the same does not apply to images. I can try to form an image of something and fail.

is a state of that substance causing the second event—the motion of the brick caused the shattering of the window. And the wind which causes the leaves to blow about just is the motion of air. Again, when the sun causes the ice to melt, it is the sun being hot which causes the ice to melt. It is in virtue of being in this state (i.e. characterized by this property), rather than that state, that a substance causes some event, normally because it is a consequence of laws of nature that events of that kind cause events of the subsequent kind. But when an agent intentionally brings about an event, what is the state of the agent which brings it about? When I move my hand, meaning so to do, what is the state of me which brings about its motion?

There are answers of two possible kinds normally given to this question. The answers of the first kind are false; the answers of the second kind are true but misleading. Answers of the first kind consist in citing passive states of the agent which cause the events in question–desires (alias wishes or wants) plus beliefs. On such an account, when I move my hand for its own sake (not in order to achieve something thereby), what happens is that my desire to move my hand causes the movement of my hand. When I move it in order to achieve something further thereby, e.g. get a book from the shelf, what happens is that my desire to have a book from the shelf and my belief that by moving my hand I shall get it, cause the motion of my hand. We may express such an account more formally as follows. When an agent performs an intentional action, what happens is that his desire for the performance of that act under its ultimate act-description, and his belief that this will be achieved by the performance of the act under its basic act-description (via a certain series of events), cause its basic result, and thereby, via the expected series of events, achieve the performance of the act.[7] My intentionally killing the man consists in my desire that I kill him and my belief that I would kill him if I were to squeeze my finger and thus cause the gun to fire and put a bullet in him, causing my finger to be squeezed and thereby the gun to fire and a bullet to enter the man causing his death. My insulting you (or however else that act is described) consists in my desire that I insult you and my belief that I will do so by saying

---

[7] Except, that is, in the case where there is no basic result of the action but simply an unsuccessful attempt to achieve one; and in such a case there is simply the desire and the belief.

'You are a fool', causing the words 'You are a fool' to come out of my mouth, and thereby you to be insulted.

Such analyses are false in more than one way. First, they do not give sufficient conditions for action. Desires or wants (with appropriate beliefs) can cause the events desired without any intentional action taking place. A number of examples of this have been given in the literature. Here is one from Davidson:

> A climber might want to rid himself of the weight and danger of holding another man on a rope, and he might know that by loosening his hold on the rope he could rid himself of the weight and the danger. This belief and want might so unnerve him as to cause him to loosen his hold, and it might be the case that he never *chose* to loosen his hold, nor did he do it intentionally.[8]

As I shall explain more fully in the next chapter, desires, like beliefs, are passive states. They are natural inclinations to action, which an agent finds himself having. And not merely that—they are involuntary; a man cannot immediately control his desires; they come to him unsought, and sometimes unwanted. All men find themselves from time to time with desires for food, drink, rest, sex, etc.; and with more complicated desires—for power or fame, say, of this or that kind, which vary with the individual. Yet, although a man cannot help his desires, he can hold them in check, refuse to 'go along with' them and let them have sway; and so long as he so refuses, they will give rise to no intentional action of bringing about or even trying to bring about the thing desired. But the desires may still have effects which the agent does not intend or welcome—including the occurrence of the thing desired, as in Davidson's example. There is more to intentional action than desire having its effects (directly or via a route believed efficacious).

Nor is desire a necessary condition of action. An agent may perform an intentional action without in any way desiring its performance under its ultimate act-description, or any other, in the normal sense of 'desire'. I may repay my debt, not because I desire to do so nor because I have any desire (in the sense of natural inclination) to do my duty. I just do my duty because I choose to do so. (This point will be developed more fully in the next chapter.) Davidson attempts to make the general approach of intentional action as involving something like desire, plausible by

---

[8] D. Davidson, 'Freedom to Act', in his *Essays on Actions and Events*, p. 79.

talking, instead of 'desires', of 'pro-attitudes', which term covers 'desires, wantings, urges, promptings, and a great variety of moral views', etc., etc.[9] The claim, then, put in a more formal way, is that when an agent performs an intentional action, his pro-attitude towards the performance of that action under its ultimate act-description and his belief that this will be achieved by the performance of the act under its basic act-description (via a certain series of events), cause its basic result and thereby, via the expected series of events, achieve the performance of the act. Now, it is certainly true that in a very wide sense of pro-attitude, an agent must have a pro-attitude towards the performance of any action of his under its ultimate act-description, if he is to perform that action. But, now, this account, although giving a necessary condition for intentional action, on other grounds fails to give a sufficient condition. For we have pro-attitudes of some sort towards most things (it is in some way a good thing that I go upstairs, that I go downstairs, that I stay put), and those attitudes may make differences to what happens without any intentional action being performed. If Davidson's claim is to be made in any way interesting and illuminating, it must be tightened up to read not just '*a* pro-attitude' towards the performance of an action, but something like 'an attitude which holds the performance of that action to be on balance preferable to the performance of any incompatible action'. Not any pro-attitude but an overall pro-attitude; not any reason, but reasons judged overriding must cause effects if they are to be one's actions. But now the analysis will not work because of a different problem, the problem of *akrasia* or weakness of will. As Davidson himself draws to our attention in another context,[10] an agent may do the action towards which he has a lesser pro-attitude in preference to that which he believes most worth doing. A man may believe that he ought to use his money to repay his debts, that it is overall better, that he has overriding reason to repay his debts—and yet spend the money on

---

[9] D. Davidson, 'Actions, Reasons and Causes' in his *Essays on Actions and Events*, p. 4.

[10] 'How is Weakness of Will Possible' in op. cit. Davidson regards the view of this later essay ('that a reason that is causally the strongest need not be a reason deemed by the actor to provide the strongest (best) grounds for acting') as a correction to the view of the earlier essay ('that the propositional expressions of the reasons for an action are deductively related to the proposition that corresponds to the action as explained by those reasons') by denying that 'the strongest reasons are the strongest causes'. See *Essays on Actions and Events*, Introduction p. xii.

drink or gambling instead. So he does an action, towards the performance of which he has no overall pro-attitude. For these reasons I conclude that analyses of intentional actions in terms of actions (or events) brought about by passive states fail.

The question to which we are seeking an answer was—when an agent performs an intentional action, what is the state of the agent which brings about the basic result of the action? The alternative to the answer that it is some passive state or states such as desire or want (normally plus a belief) is that it is an action (normally plus a belief), only not a bodily action but an act of will. Such acts of will have often in the past been called 'volitions'. Volition theory runs somewhat as follows. When an agent does an action such as moving his arm for its own sake, what happens is that his volition to move his arm causes the motion of his arm. When he performs an action in order to achieve something further thereby, e.g. turns a handle by twisting his hand, what happens is that his volition to turn the handle and his belief that twisting his hand will cause the handle to turn causes his hand to twist and thereby the handle to turn. Intentional actions are volitions (plus beliefs) causing bodily movements, or other effects such as mental events—except in the case where the only action is trying, and then the action consists just in the volition without any effect. The volition is basically a trying, but it is only appropriate to talk of 'trying' where effort or failure is involved. When I move my hand easily and spontaneously, it seems odd to say that I tried to move my hand. However, the very same event which is called 'trying' when failure occurs is clearly involved in, and is the crucial active part of, any ordinary easily performed basic action. For suppose that I try to move my hand, yet fail, because suddenly I am paralysed. What I have contributed in the way of endeavour would clearly have been sufficient for my moving my hand intentionally to take place if I had not been paralysed. So volition theory gives to this element the technical name of 'volition'. It is an element which we usually notice only when failure or effort are involved, and then we call it 'trying'. But this thought experiment ('if I had been suddenly paralysed') reveals that it is there in every intentional action.

Volition theory seems to me basically on the right lines in the crucial respect that it does not analyse away the active element in intentional action in terms of some passive component, but acknowledges that it is there unanalysably—in the form of an act of will. However, there seem to me two highly misleading aspects of the theory as I have expounded it so far and as it is expounded by its advocates.

The first misleading aspect is that volition theory represents intentional action as a more active thing than it often is. A 'volition' is supposed to be 'an act of will', and that suggests something like a decision or a choice. This suggests that every action is a quick decision subsequently efficacious. But there are three different things wrong with that suggestion. First, intentional action is often a matter of the agent allowing certain sequences of movement to take place rather than actively bringing them about. When I fidget, tap my foot, or scratch my hand, my body is, as it were, dictating the pace, as in a reflex movement. But what makes these things intentional actions is that I allow them to happen and could at any instant, if I so chose, stop them. The volition is, in these cases, no decision: it is a giving of permission; but not the active permission of signing a permission form, but the passive permission of doing nothing to stop something. So much action is a matter of the agent not stopping his body from doing what it does naturally under its own steam. But what is allowed to happen is the performance of an action if it is something which the agent, by choosing, can readily bring about or stop occurring. Further, actions often take a long time. My walking from Madeley to Keele takes an hour, yet walking to Keele is certainly an intentional action of mine. What makes it intentional, however, is not that at the start of the walk, I decided to walk; but rather that purpose or intention guided my movements throughout the walk. The 'volition' is to be regarded as a continuing permission rather than merely an original permission. And, finally, when actions do take a long time, they are performed by performing many separate actions. I write this chapter by writing first this sentence, then that sentence, and so on. Yet there is not, as volition theory sometimes seems to suggest, a separate volition corresponding to each of the latter intentional actions. If there was, my mental life would be overcrowded with volitions. What is more plausible, surely, is that when I perform an intentional action, either there is a separate 'volition' for that action; or there is a volition to perform a longer action, one way of performing which is, I believe, by bringing about a certain series of events. In the latter case the bringing about of each event of the series constitutes an intentional action.

The volition has the general character—'to walk from Madeley to Keele'. The body selects (without any conscious choice of the agent's) a particular bodily routine to execute the volition—to put this foot here and that foot there, and so on. However, the occurrence of each part of the routine, so long as the agent believes that it forwards what he is seeking to achieve, does count as his performing an intentional action. My putting this foot there was an intentional action of mine, because, although there was nothing like a decision that the foot be there, there was a purpose of mine ('to walk to Keele') which my body was executing through a routine which involved the foot going there, and I had the belief (which, as we have already noted and as we shall see further in Chapter 7, is no conscious occurrence) that that routine (among other possible routines, perhaps) would achieve that purpose.

It is to avoid these misleading implications of volition theory, making intentional action too active a thing—implications suggested in part, I believe, by the word 'volition' itself, that I wish to replace the word 'volition' by a different word, 'purposing', and now state volition theory formally in a way which will cope with the difficulties. Purposing to bring about an event is trying to bring it about (minus any implications of effort or failure), or allowing an event to occur of a kind which the agent, by trying, can bring about, or by trying, can easily stop. When an agent performs an intentional action A, what happens is that his purposing to perform A (or a larger act of which A is, he believes, part) under its ultimate act-description and his belief that this will be achieved (in part or whole) by the performance of A under its basic act-description (via a certain series of events), cause the basic result of A, and thereby, via the expected series of events, achieve the performance of A. (The exception to this is where the intentional action does not have a basic result, viz. is simply a trying, and then it consists simply in a purposing to bring about something plus a belief as to how that is to be done.) When the basic result is a long event (e.g. the bodily movements involved in a one-hour walk), the purposing and belief last as long as, and cause, the whole event.

Note that on this theory there is not a separate purposing for the act under each description—the agent does not purpose to pull the trigger, and also purpose to shoot, also purpose to kill; simply a purposing to perform the act under its ultimate act-description.

Nor is there a separate purposing to perform each small constituent act which makes up a larger act; simply a purposing to perform the larger act which the body executes in a way which the agent believes will achieve his aim.

The Nature and Efficacy of Purposing

This purposing is clearly a mental event because the subject has privileged access to it. If my hand does not move, but you infer from my brain-states that I was trying to move it; I can have all your information. But I have further information from my own experience—I know what I was trying to do. The agent knows his purposings better than the outsider.

Among mental states, purposing is a conscious episode. It is something of which the agent is aware as guiding his movements. He does not purpose while he is asleep. I cannot really be setting myself, endeavouring, trying, meaning to do something unless I am aware of that trying. Awareness may, however, vary in degree. An agent may be giving all his attention to some action which he is performing, or he may be doing something else at the same time, with most of his attention on the latter.

Not merely must I be aware of purposings as elements of my conscious life, but I must be aware of them as the purposings they are, if they are to be my purposes. As with his thoughts, the subject's beliefs about his purposes are infallible, for purposing is pursuing a goal, and pursuing a goal involves understanding what goal it is that you are pursuing. I cannot misidentify my purpose as a purpose to go to London rather than as a purpose to go, in the opposite direction, to Edinburgh. For if I thought of myself as endeavouring to go to London, I couldn't really be endeavouring to go to Edinburgh, in the sense that this was the goal which I was pursuing. Certainly, there are purposes, such that the beliefs that he has those purposes are ones which the agent refuses to admit to himself, refuses to admit to consciouness. But he believes that he has the purposes all the same, as he may admit when psychoanalysed. And also, as with his thoughts, and for the same reason, a person may misstate his purposes when he expresses them in a public language. But he has infallible beliefs about what he is up to all the same.[11] Likewise, purposings, like thoughts, are intrinsically

---

[11] I shall consider our grounds for attributing purposes to others, in conjunction with our grounds for attributing desires and beliefs to others, in Chapter 7.

propositional. They are attitudes towards (viz. seekings to bring about) states of affairs under a description. A purposing to bring it about that p is not the same as a purposing to bring it about that q, even if p is logically equivalent to q. And purposings are the purposings they are, not in virtue of their context, but in virtue of their intrinsic content; otherwise the subject with false beliefs about the context of their occurrence could not have infallible knowledge of them.

Purposings as active, are clearly distinguished from sensations and thoughts which are passive conscious episodes. I have already distinguished between purposings and desires. Purposings are obviously distinct from beliefs; they are endeavours to change things, not simply beliefs that things are a certain way. Purposings are a separate kind of mental event. However, purposings do involve beliefs. You cannot purpose to some action without two beliefs. The first belief, which I shall articulate more fully below, is that something you know how to do will make a difference to whether or not you do that action. In other words, you cannot do some action, unless you have some idea how to set about it. I cannot even try to turn into a frog, because I wouldn't know how to begin. The second belief involved in purposing to perform some action is that the agent must believe the action to be in some way a good thing—either because it involves bringing about a good state of affairs, or because the bringing about which it involves is itself good. If you search for food, then you regard the having of food by you as a good thing; if you sing or dance, then you regard the production of the noises or movements as a good thing. And if you purpose to go to see your aged aunt instead of watching the football, that, too, can only be because you regard it as a good thing that you visit your aunt—either because being with her is good in itself, or for some further reason. You couldn't purpose to go to see your aunt if you thought that you had no duty to do so; it would give no one any pleasure, you wouldn't enjoy it, etc., etc.; if you thought that your visiting her would be in no way a good thing. I am not saying that agents always do the action which they believe to be the best available to them; indeed, I shall argue against that in the next chapter. I am simply claiming that an agent can purpose to perform an action only if he believes it to be in some way a good thing to do. These two beliefs are necessary conditions of purposing and so of intentional action, not sufficient conditions.

My first criticism of volition theory was that it made action too active a process. I have, I hope, cured this deficiency by improving the theory and, in the course of doing so, substituting a different technical term which does not carry the misleading implications of 'volition'. My second criticism of the old volition theory is in a way, I think, deeper. It is that volition theory does not make action an active enough process! This point will come out if we ask how, according to volition theory, do we discover which effects the various purposings have. We discover whether imbibing sugar or imbibing cyanide nourish or poison by noting the effects of such imbibings. If purposings are events like any other events, will we not learn what effects they have by empirical study? An agent will discover the effects of purposing to move his hand and seeing what happens—whether his hand moves or his leg moves or his tongue falls out, or whatever; and then he will have a justified belief about the effects of purposing to move his hand, which he did not have before.

That account of how we acquire beliefs about the effects of our purposings is obviously wrong. And why it is wrong is because it ignores the way in which such technical notions as purposing have been introduced. Purposing to do A is a state of the agent which, when he does A intentionally, brings about the basic result B of his intentional action A, the bringing about of which result will, the agent believes, in the circumstances of its occurrence lead to the occurrence of A. But it is not any state of the agent which brings about the basic result but that mental state which, had the basic result not occurred (e.g. because the agent was paralysed or otherwise prevented from moving his limbs), we would call 'trying'. And trying to do an action simply is initiating whatever causal chain, the agent believes, will make that action more likely to occur than it otherwise would; and since the agent believes that the occurrence of B will bring about the occurrence of A, trying to do A is simply doing whatever, the agent believes, will make B more likely to occur. We cannot describe trying, and so purposing, except in a way which already involves the agent's conception of its causal relations, that is its intrinsic nature. To try, and so to purpose, to move one's hand is not to do something which the agent might subsequently come to believe, made a difference to whether or not his hand moved; it is to act in such a way that, the agent already believes, the hand movement will be more likely to occur. (Of course other things, such as bodily malfunctioning, may, on occasion, cause the agent's purposings to have unintended effects, or to have no effects at all, and the agent may suspect in advance that this will happen. All that he needs to believe if he is to purpose is that his purposing is more likely to produce the result sought than his failing to do so.) A purposing to move my hand is not to be confused with thinking about moving my hand or saying to myself 'I will move my hand'; with respect to these there are independent intrinsic descriptions of what is going on which make no reference to their causal influence on hand-moving. But there is no other intrinsic description of trying and so of purposing (or volition) except in these causal terms.

It is only if an agent believes that he can make a difference to whether something happens, that he can purpose to do so. For if he does not believe that he can make any difference, he cannot do what, he believes, will make a difference; there is nothing for him to do. It is for this reason that I cannot try (i.e. purpose) to turn into a frog. For having no belief that anything I do will make my turning into a frog more likely to occur, I have no idea how to try. The only way to achieve any result is to try to bring it about. Someone might suppose otherwise—that there are better ways of getting things done than trying to get them done—as in the saying 'The way to sink a putt is not to try.' But that saying is misleading. What it really means is that the way to sink a putt is not to concentrate on the putting alone; it is to hit the ball towards the hole, while thinking and talking of other things at the same time. The ball landing in the hole is a result best achieved by doing other things. The saying is telling us that there is a recipe for sinking a putt; if trying is to be successful, it will have to be conjoined with a belief that getting the ball into the hole is best achieved by doing certain acts described under other basic act-descriptions (e.g. 'thinking and talking of other things'); the putter will have to abandon the belief that 'sinking a putt' is for him a basic act description—it isn't; he can't sink a putt just like that, he can only do it by doing something else as well. It remains the case that there is no other way to sink a putt or to do anything else except to try— but in the case of many actions, you need the right beliefs about which basic actions will achieve your goal; you need the right recipe. But basic actions are those for which there is no recipe. An agent who tries to move his arm (without using other limbs) does not have any beliefs about how to do it. The only description of his action which he sees as applying to it is as 'trying to move his arm', i.e. 'doing what, he believes, will make his arm more likely to move'. That is the intrinsic nature of the action. Note that purposings may vary in degree. Less technically, one may try, and then try harder, and then try harder still. The agent must regard trying harder as exerting more causal influence.

Now although an agent must believe that his purposings make a difference, an observer need not. I may believe that when you try to move your arm, that makes no difference to whether your arm is going to move; but I cannot believe that of myself. On any given occasion, or perhaps on all occasions, the agent may be mistaken about whether he is making the action causally more likely to occur. He may even think that he is intentionally making his hand move when he is doing no such thing. Bodily processes which do not involve his purposing may bring about the hand motion; but his purposing makes no difference to what happens. In such a case the purposing remains, as I have described, doing whatever the agent believes will make the result causally more likely to occur. The intrinsic description of the purposing involves reference to its 'causal efficacy', but only its believed causal efficacy.

But, as we have seen, an agent has to think of his purposing as more than that, as, in fact, his making causally more likely the result of his basic action; and if the agent is correct in his beliefs, that is what it is. When my purposing is successful, the act of purposing to move my arm (intrinsic description) is, in virtue of its causal efficacy, the act of intentionally causing my hand to move (extrinsic description). Since it must seem (epistemically) to the agent that he makes certain things causally more likely to occur, if he is to act at all, he ought, by the principle of credulity described in Chapter 1, to believe that he does, in the absence of counter-evidence. And knowing that others are like himself in their mental life and modes of behaviour, he will realize that he can only think of himself as making a difference to his bodily movements, if he thinks of others as doing so also.[12]

---

[12] That causation is part of the content of the experience of acting has been very well argued in J. R. Searle, *Intentionality*, Cambridge University Press, 1973, chs. 3 and 4. He argued that in acting we experience ourselves as causing, and in perception we experience ourselves as being caused. (We cannot regard ourselves as seeing something unless we regard our visual experience as being caused by the object seen.) He shows how our knowledge of events causing events in the

Other arguments in favour of our purposes affecting our brains, and so our bodily movements (and so not being mere epiphenomena), are as follows. First there is an argument similar to that used in Chapters 2 and 4—we couldn't have justified beliefs about our purposes unless our purposes had effects; and we couldn't state our purposes publicly with justification, unless they had brain, and so bodily, effects. Secondly, between purposings that there occur bodily movements of certain kinds and the occurrence of the movements purposed there are very regular correlations—for normal people in normal circumstances invariable correlations—of a very simple kind (a purposing that X occur is followed by the occurrence of X). There is an obvious and natural hypothesis to explain this—viz. that (for a normal person in normal circumstances) purposings that bodily movements X occur cause the occurrence of X. To avoid this by postulating a common cause would be to put forward a very much more complicated hypothesis; and so, by the principle of simplicity, one much less likely to be true. For it would involve postulating that a brain-event which has, as it were, no description of a bodily movement, say the movement of my hand, built into it, can cause both the purposing to move my hand and the movement of the hand. That is indeed logically possible. But the issue is whether in the absence of evidence that the situation is like that, it is reasonable to suppose that it is— when there is such an evident plausible rival hypothesis. We saw earlier that this second reason (of regular correlation) cannot be an agent's sole ground for believing in the efficacy of his own purposes, but it is, nevertheless, a substantial reason for belief in the efficacy of purposes.

Sometimes of course parts of our body get out of control, or even the whole body may temporarily get out of control—as in an epileptic fit—and the agent's purposes are inefficacious. But the regularity under normal conditions is good evidence that under those conditions purposes are efficacious. And that evidence is reinforced by the fact that when conditions become abnormal, you can often make your purposes effective if you try a bit harder. The fact that if you have Parkinson's disease, then ordinary purposing to raise your arm in a straight line is not efficacious but an intense

inanimate world derives from our knowledge of experienced causation, and not the other way round—as is commonly supposed in accounts of causation deriving from Hume.

degree of purposing (i.e. trying very hard) has the intended effect, suggests that that sort of thing is what makes the difference, including when conditions are normal.

I have argued against epiphenomenalism and in favour of the causal efficacy of conscious episodes on bodily events and on other mental events, with respect to sensations, thoughts, and now purposes. A final argument for the causal efficacy of conscious episodes is this. If conscious episodes were not causally efficacious, there would be no evolutionary advantages in an organism developing them. Whereas, if sensation is needed for the acquisition and understanding of beliefs of many kinds, and thought is needed for reaching certain kinds of rational conclusions, which result in action, and if purposing is needed for certain kinds of long-term co-ordinated goal-seeking movements, then there is a good Darwinian explanation of why creatures with sensation, thought, and purpose develop. Otherwise, sensations, thoughts, and purposings would have to be a mere by-product of brain-states which convey no evolutionary advantage. That could be so, but—other things being equal—we ought to suppose that striking features of animals do have some evolutionary function.

6. DESIRES

The Nature of Desire

THE words 'desire' or 'want' are, like 'thought', used in a number of different ways in ordinary language, and it is important to distinguish these if 'desire' is to be used as a useful technical term. A 'desire' or 'want' as I shall understand these terms (and as I also believe to be their normal sense) is a natural inclination to do some action with which an agent finds himself. We cannot (immediately) help our natural inclinations but what we can do is choose whether to yield to them, or resist them and do what we are not naturally inclined to do. When we resist our natural inclinations, we do so because we have reasons for action quite other than ones naturally described as the satisfaction of desire—e.g. we do the action because we believe that we ought to, or we believe it to be in our long-term interest.

The natural inclinations of agents are to perform certain actions, seen as separate from some of their properties and consequences, or to bring about certain states of affairs, seen as separate from the process of bringing them about. An action or state of affairs is seen as having certain properties and consequences which belong to it, and other properties and consequences which are separate from it. The former we may term its central properties and consequences, the latter its peripheral properties and consequences. Whether John is rightly to be said to desire to go to a party of Alan's depends on what is seen as involved therein. The party is a party with Alan and his family, but Jane will be there. He likes Jane but he does not like Alan. We can say of him either that he does not want to go to the party, but he wants to meet Jane—and so perhaps goes; or, redescribing the same facts, we can say of him that he does want to go to the party because Jane will be there. If we say the former, we think of the party as a party with Alan (Jane being there being something separate from the party in itself—i.e. a peripheral property of the party); if we say the latter, we think of the party as a party at which Jane is present (this being a central property of the party).

When an agent desires a state of affairs—say his owning a large and sumptuous house—then he has a natural inclination to bring about such a state of affairs, when the bringing about is thought of as separate from its normal properties and consequences—e.g. the trouble and embarrassment involved in the process of acquisition.

The object of desire is normally thought of as separate from its evaluative properties, its properties of being good or bad in some respect or overall, including its moral properties, such as being obligatory to do or not to do. A man is said to desire or not to desire some state of affairs or to do some action in view of an attitude towards it which abstracts from his beliefs about its moral, or other, worth. Whatever other of its properties are thought of as central to the action of going to the party, that it is a party which it is John's duty to attend or (alternatively) his duty not to attend, is thought of as something peripheral. If John believes that he ought not to go to the party, that in no way normally affects whether he can be rightly said to desire to go to the party.

There are different ways of carving up actions, and according to what is seen as central to the action, so the agent is said to desire or not to desire to do the action. But obviously the most useful way to describe an agent's desires is to treat as separate, features of actions towards which he has very different inclinations, rather than lump them together and consider a total inclination.

Note that this central/peripheral distinction is a different distinction from the intrinsic/extrinsic distinction of Chapters 3 and 5. The latter distinction was a distinction between different ways of describing events, and so actions. An action described intrinsically was one described simply as the bringing about of a certain bodily movement with certain purposes and beliefs. An action described extrinsically was one described, at least in part, in terms of its surroundings or consequences—e.g. as the successful achievement of some goal. But an agent, considering whether to do some action, or a spectator, may think of it primarily in extrinsic terms— e.g. as the achievement of that goal; and so may regard as central to that action, in determining his atttitude towards it, some extrinsic feature of it, such as its having a certain consequence. John's going to a party is an extrinsic description of an action; it is a description of his moving his body in a certain way with a certain purpose, in terms of the fulfilment of that purpose. Yet, central to his action, as he views it, would be succeeding in being at the party, and maybe being at a party with Jane.

And what is a 'natural inclination'? It is a readiness (of which the agent can become aware in consciousness) spontaneously to do the action when, in the agent's belief, the opportunity arises—but for any belief he may have about the peripheral consequences and properties of the action, and but for any desire to do a rival action which the agent believes cannot be done at the same time. I desire to smoke a cigarette (considered as an action separate from any consequences to my health or the health and inconvenience of others) if involuntarily I am all organized to smoke a cigarette when I have the opportunity (e.g. I am offered one) and have no desire to do something which I believe incompatible (e.g. chew gum), and when I have no beliefs about it having bad peripheral consequences. Humans (and animals) have sets of responses all ready to make spontaneously in different circumstances—they are all ready to respond in various ways to bells and lights, commands and smells, and they are aware of themselves as so prepared.

But some of these readinesses to act are voluntarily formed intentions so to act, intentions which we could easily abandon at will if we saw reason for doing so. Desires, on the other hand, are readinesses which we find in ourselves and are not alterable at will. It is this passive and involuntary character of desire which I was seeking to capture by the word 'inclination'.

We can see the difference by comparing a desire with a conditional intention otherwise similar but formed at will, and able to be abandoned at will. Suppose that I know that I shall be offered by my host a choice between playing a game of tennis and making a visit to a stately home, and that it will be a good thing to choose quickly and sound enthusiastic about one of these. I have no prior desire to do one rather than the other. Having no beliefs that one or other of these will have subsequent consequences for my life which the other will lack, or moral worth which the other lacks, I form a conditional intention (as a result of tossing a coin, perhaps) that, when offered the choice but given no further information about consequences or moral worth, I will choose to play tennis. I resolve so to respond. But I do not thereby create in myself a desire to play tennis which I did not have before, since the intention is alterable at will. By contrast, I am aware of myself as organized spontaneously to respond in a certain way if offered a choice between rice pudding and chocolate éclair in a situation where I have no beliefs that choosing one or other of these will have subsequent consequences for my life which the other will lack or moral worth which the other lacks. I am already organized to choose the éclair.

The account so far is circular in that a 'desire' is defined in terms of how a man is inclined to act but for any rival 'desire'. This circularity can however easily be removed by a regressive definition. A man has a desire to do X if he is inclined to do the action but for beliefs about its peripheral consequences and properties. He then also has a desire to do Y if he is inclined to do Y but for the stated beliefs and but for a belief that he had the opportunity to do X. He then has a desire to do Z if he is inclined to do Z but for the stated beliefs and but for beliefs that he had the opportunity to do X or Y. A man desires to do some action if such a conditional is true of him that he is inclined to do the action but for beliefs about its peripheral consequences and properties and but for beliefs about rival actions open to him. The scheme of definition then yields a natural comparative measure of strength of desire. A desire to do Y is stronger than a desire to do Z if the agent is inclined to do Y rather than Z in circumstances when he believes both to be available to him but for beliefs about their peripheral consequences and properties. Two desires are equal in strength if the agent has no inclination to do one action rather than the other in those circumstances.

Desire is, as I have so far defined it, the inclination to spontaneous action in the absence of beliefs about peripheral consequences and properties, including worth, and in the absence of rival opportunities. And if agents are to have desires, they must have inclinations to act under such narrow circumstances. But it is the fate of humans that their desires which give rise to action under such narrow circumstances, also influence action when the agent believes the action to be overall bad. The agent still finds himself ready-geared to do the action, even when he believes it immoral. But in those circumstances it is up to the agent whether to restrain or indulge the desire, as I shall bring out more fully shortly.

Enjoyment or pleasure consists in the satisfaction of desire; not in the mere satisfaction of an intention subject to voluntary control, but in the yielding to involuntary inclination. I enjoy playing golf if I yield to natural inclination in playing golf; and I get pleasure out of sunbathing if my natural inclination is to let the sun continue to warm my body. I enjoy doing something, or having something happen to me, if I do it or it happens when I want to do it or want it to happen. I am not saying that my enjoyment consists in yielding to an inclination which I had before I yielded; for when I yield, I may find that that to which I yield gives no pleasure.[1] I mean, rather, that this enjoyment consists in yielding to an inclination to yield which I possess while I am yielding. To enjoy eating consists in eating while I am naturally inclined to eat.

There certainly could be creatures who formed or readily changed all their intentions as to which actions they would to in all circumstances including in the absence of beliefs about their peripheral consequences and properties, without finding a prior inclination already present in themselves which was in any way difficult to alter. But they would not have desires, merely conditional intentions, and enjoyment and pleasure could not be theirs. It is because pleasure consists in the satisfaction of desire that in all known systems of morality the satisfaction of desire (of the agent or of other people close to the agent or of all people) forms a central element of the good life, indeed for many systems of morality the whole of the good life. A system of morality very different from any known system of human morality would be needed to prescribe conduct in a community of agents who lacked desire. But although it is necessary for pleasure there should sometimes be an inclination to act, but for beliefs about peripheral consequences and properties, what is not necessary is that the inclination should still be present when the agent has a belief that the action has overall bad peripheral consequences and properties, and, above all, has the belief that these are such as to make the act overall a bad one to do. It is, as we have seen, the fate of humans that the inclinations to act needed for enjoyment still move towards action (make the actions easier, more natural to do) when the agent believes the action overall bad. That desire so operates in humans is a contingent feature of desire.

---

[1] In his book *Reason and Value* (Cambridge University Press, 1983), E. J. Bond frequently makes the point that satisfaction of desire does not in itself necessarily give pleasure. (See e.g. p. 61.) But by this he means that the satisfaction of pre-existing desire does not do this.

That we have such inclinations to spontaneous action in various ways under various circumstances is a fact about our conscious life which is captured by saying that we have desires. Facts about an agent's desires are facts about the inclinations towards intentional action in himself, not facts about how he has behaved in the past, or what he says that he wants, or even about what he would do if he did in fact believe that the opportunity to act had arrived and he had no evaluative beliefs which stood in his way. It is always possible that an agent's desire to eat chocolate might suddenly vanish when he ceased to believe that eating chocolate did him harm. Since an agent can know everything which everyone else knows about his behaviour, and yet can feel (in a way which others cannot) the inclinations to which he is subject, desires are mental events.

Our awareness of a desire is an awareness of an inclination which we find in ourselves, and which we suppose continues to exist while we are unaware of it or anything else. We thus think of desires as continuing mental states to which we have access from time to time. We think in this way for two reasons—first, because the process of asking ourselves what we want and providing an answer comes to us as a process by which we become aware in ourselves of a readiness to act, which does not seem created by the enquiry, but to be there ready to manifest itself in appropriate circumstances. That is, desire comes to us phenomenologically as something uncovered and not created by enquiry. Secondly, it is normally the case with the desires of which agents are aware at a given time, that they are aware of the same desire at any time over a continuing period when they have occasion to wonder whether they have the desire, or are presented with an opportunity for doing the act desired. We know that from their reports. Also, those same desires often influence any actions they may perform over the same continuing period. The continuing period is a fairly short one with respect to desires such as those for food, drink, and sleep. The period is often a much longer one with respect to desires which have causes partly of a social and cultural kind, such as the desire for success in an examination, a marriage, or a career. But in all these cases, when the agent reflects, he is aware of the same inclination to act over a continuing period, and that inclination influences, often decisively influences, his behaviour during that period.

None of this applies generally to sensations, thoughts, and purposes. We do not think of ourselves when investigating these, as bringing to consciousness states of affairs which existed for long periods while we were unaware of them, and it would not facilitate the explanation of behaviour to suppose that these were such states—with one exception. We see certain thoughts, viz. those which are judgements, as awarenesses of an underlying state, belief; I will discuss this exception in the next chapter. Desires, however, are naturally and usefully thought of as continuing mental states to which we have access from time to time.

There remain, however, two possible ways of understanding this talk—the dispositional or the categorical. On the dispositional understanding, to say that an agent has some desire of which he is currently unaware is just to say that, if asked, he would become aware of it, or, if the opportunity arose to do the action desired, doing it would come easily to him. There is some state of the agent—and in order to reduce alternatives to manageable proportions I shall assume with most advocates of such a view that it is a brain-state, which remains the same and causes the agent's thought and action to be influenced in the same way from time to time. On this understanding, the mental nature of desire consists in the subject's privileged access, whenever he chooses, to a feelable inclination to action. But the only 'real' categorical state which exists while the agent is unaware of his inclination is a brain-state ready to influence thought and action. The manifestation of the desire in consciousness is *intrinsically* propositional; it is the manifestation of the desire it is, quite independently of its surroundings, causes and effects; a desire to bring about a state of affairs under a description, e.g., to eat this meal rather than to eat corn (even if this meal is corn). Whereas when the subject is unaware of his desire and all that exists is the brain-state, what makes it true that the subject has this desire rather than that desire is the effects to which the brain-state would give rise in appropriate circumstances; there is no continuing intrinsically propositional state.

On the categorical understanding of desire, what continues when an agent is unaware of some desire is an attitude towards a state of affairs, which is just the same as the attitude of which he is aware when he is aware of his desire, except for the fact that he is unaware of it. To say that an agent has a desire of which he is currently unaware is to say that he has such an attitude. Desires are intrinsically propositional, even when not being manifested. I shall consider in Chapter 14 which of these understandings of desire is the correct one.

Are desires causally efficacious? On the dispositional view there is nothing more to a desire than its manifestations. These manifestations of the desire are not caused by anything other than a brain-state. There is not a continuing intrinsically propositional state, to which awareness in consciousness gives intermittent access, and which in any way causes that awareness or anything else. The awareness in consciousness of a desire can, like thought, no doubt have effects; but that is the only new specimen of psychophysical causality which comes in with desire. For the existence of a desire is simply the existence of a disposition, and dispositions are mere 'would-be's', they are not events which can have effects. On the categorical view, however, desires are more than their manifestations, and the question arises as to whether these intrinsically propositional states can have effects—either in causing the manifestations of desires (making subjects aware of their desires, and act as they do), or in some other way. We shall consider this issue also in Chapter 14.

Knowledge of Desires

Is our access to our desires infallible? Do we know infallibly what we desire? An agent will know infallibly what he desires, when in his belief he has the opportunity to manifest his desires in action, and no belief about peripheral consequences and properties of the action and no belief about other incompatible actions, desired or thought good, which is relevant to his acting. For in those circumstances he will manifest his desire in purposive action if he has it; and not manifest it if he does not. The circumstances being ones in which he has certain beliefs and, as I shall argue in Chapter 7, our knowledge of our beliefs is infallible; and since, as I argued in Chapter 5, our knowledge of our purposes is infallible, we have infallible knowledge of our desires in these circumstances. If I am offered chocolate and have no beliefs that it will do harm for me to eat it, and still I do not eat it (nor do I do instead some action believed incompatible with eating chocolate—e.g. chew gum), that shows that I do not desire to eat it. And if I am offered chocolate and have no beliefs that it will do me good or that it is my duty to eat it, and still I eat it, that shows that I desire to eat it. But what about when there is no chocolate available? An agent may first report (honestly) that he has an inclination to eat it under the stated circumstances (when he believes the opportunity to be available, when he has no rival desires and no belief that eating it has bad peripheral properties or consequences); and then after considering the matter more fully, without being aware of any change in his inclinations, report that he has no such inclination. This shows that desire is a thing about which we can come to form too quick a belief (as about the details of sensations, of all of which we need not be aware, while they exist—see p. 31). Although the inclination is 'naked' to our eye, through inadequate attention, we may acquire a false belief about it.

I shall consider our grounds for ascribing desires to other men in the next chapter, along with our grounds for ascribing purposes and beliefs to them.

Desires Distinct from Other Mental Events

It is important to contrast desire in the crucial sense which I have now delineated with the agent's belief about what he will enjoy doing or having.[2] As we have seen, enjoyment consists in the satisfaction of desire, in the yielding to inclination. To enjoy playing golf is to be playing golf and in doing so to be yielding to inclination. To enjoy being in Spain is to be in Spain when you want to be in Spain (i.e. when you would be naturally inclined to put yourself in Spain if you were not there already). But it is one thing to have a present desire to do some action or be in some situation; and a different thing to have a present belief that when you are doing it you will be satisfying a desire existing at that time.

It follows that an agent may desire now to do some action or bring about some state of affairs which he believes he will not enjoy, when he has succeeded. This is obvious as regards states of affairs. A man may desire his own death or a certain disposition of his property after death. You cannot enjoy what you do not know about; and you cannot believe that you will enjoy that of which,

[2] 'An object, such as fame, knowledge, or the welfare of a friend, is desired, not because we foresee that when obtained it will give us pleasure; but vice versa; obtaining it gives us pleasure because we previously desired it or had an affection carrying us to it and resting in it'—Richard Price, *A Review of the Principal Questions in Morals* (third edition, 1787), ed. D. D. Raphael (Clarendon Press, Oxford, 1974), p. 75. The final clause suggests that 'previously' is to be interpreted as 'immediately previously'.

you believe, you will have no knowledge. But there are examples, too, which concern actions, which necessarily the agent will know that he is performing when he performs them. There is the man with the desire to run a Marathon, which he believes he will in no way enjoy doing when he is doing it.

Can a man believe that he will enjoy doing something and yet not desire to do it? I shall argue shortly that necessarily an agent has some desire for what he believes to be good. Since, I suspect, no agent can have a conception of the good unless he regarded the satisfaction of desire as in some respect a good thing (even if on balance not a good thing), all agents must have some minimal desire for future enjoyment by themselves and by others. But it is evident that a desire to perform a future action or bring about a future state of affairs which an agent believes that he will enjoy, may be fairly weak compared with such desires as to avoid the trouble and embarrassment of bringing these things about. A man's desire to go to a party which he believes that he will enjoy when he gets to it may be fairly weak.

However, it is a notable feature of humans that their desires are in general largely and sometimes exclusively for actions and states of affairs which they believe they will enjoy when they get them. The examples which I gave where desire diverges from belief about future enjoyment are unusual ones. Men could have been so made that they desired the future happiness of their fellows as much as their own future happiness. But they are not so made, or, at least, not in general. They do sometimes have desires for the well-being of others, but the desires are for the well-being of those very close to them and often are not nearly as strong as desires for their own well-being. A belief that one will enjoy doing a certain action often goes with occurrent thoughts of viewing with pleasure the prospect of doing the action (i.e. the yielding to having such thoughts being the yielding to inclination), and occurrent thoughts of regret at its present absence (which force themselves upon us, despite inclination). Since belief in future enjoyment normally goes with desire, such a pattern of thoughts is a good indication of desire. But it is not to be equated with it; since a desire may exist in the absence of a belief that one will enjoy the thing desired and *a fortiori* in the absence of thoughts about that thing. When social scientists measure strength of desire, they may be measuring any of three different things, or some weighted average thereof. They may be measuring strength of desire in my sense, i.e. comparative strength of spontaneous inclination to action in the absence of beliefs about consequences or worth. They may be measuring what agents believe that they will enjoy most. Or they may simply be measuring what agents do. Clearly, often these will diverge. A man may be faced with a choice of slouching before the TV, going to the theatre, or going to church. He may be most inclined naturally to slouch in front of the TV; that is his desire (in my preferred sense). But he may believe that he would enjoy going to the theatre most—if only he made the effort to get there. Yet he may go to church all the same, believing that to be the most worthwhile thing to do.

Desires are distinct from mental events of the other kinds which I have claimed to be the elementary constituents of the mental life. I have already distinguished desires from beliefs and thoughts about future enjoyment, and there are no more plausible beliefs and thoughts with which to equate desire. The natural inclination which is desire is different from any belief or thought about it or its consequences. Desires are also distinct from sensations—my desire for fame need have nothing sensory about it. There are, however, desires which are accompanied by sensations, e.g. hunger, the desire for food which is accompanied by 'pangs' of hunger, i.e. by sensations which, we believe, the satisfaction of the desire will remove and which we desire to remove. But the desire for food is not the same as, and need not at all involve, the occurrence of unpleasant sensations. And finally, desires are distinct from purposings. Desires are inclinations to act in the absence of various beliefs, but, faced with beliefs about the worth and consequences of the act, an agent must choose whether to yield to desire, or purpose to act contrary to it.

Acting on Desire versus Acting on Believed Worth

Men often purpose to do what they desire to do most. But there are reasons why often they do not purpose to do so. To start with, they may not realize that they have the opportunity to do so. A man may desire food; there may be food in the cupboard. But he will not go to the cupboard to get the food unless he believes that it is there. Then, a man may have a conflicting desire, i.e. a desire to do an action or bring about a state of affairs, the doing or bringing about of which he believes to be incompatible with a given action. I may believe, rightly indeed, that a desire to meet Linda in London on Monday evening and a desire to meet Elspeth in Edinburgh on Monday evening cannot be co-satisfied. So, if I seek to achieve the former I cannot seek to achieve the latter. One case of conflicting desire is where an agent desires to do some action, considered as separate from certain of its properties and consequences but also desires not to do an action with those properties or consequences. An agent may desire to acquire a certain book, but also desire not to pay out the money involved in acquiring the book. These actions cannot be co-satisfied, and so the agent may not purpose to do what he desires to do, viz. acquire the book.

An action is normally considered apart from its moral nature or, more generally, its worth (which is seen as a peripheral property) in order to assess an agent's desire to do it. And agents often do not do what they desire to do because they believe it to be overall a bad action, and for that reason they choose not to do it. And conversely, they often do what they do not much desire to do because of a belief that it is overall better to do so.

We saw in the last chapter that purposing to do an intentional action involves believing the action to be in some way a good thing; and when an agent is faced with conflicting possible actions among which he has to choose, all of them, even to be candidates for action, must be regarded by the agent as in some way a good thing. Hence, an agent can desire only that which he believes to be in some way a good thing. But he will regard some actions as better than others, and one perhaps as overall the best. Men rank actions as better than others on various grounds; because they bring benefit in the immediate short run, or because they produce greater benefit in the long run; because they bring pleasure to the agent (i.e. satisfy his desires) or because they bring pleasure to many people; or because they are more worth while for reasons which have nothing to do with the pleasure they confer—a man may think listening to Beethoven more worth while than listening to Top of the Pops. Different men give different weights to different grounds, so that they reach different beliefs about the overall worth of actions. For some agents its promotion of their own long-term interest is what makes an action overall the best. But crucial among the grounds which most men have for ranking one action as better than another is that it constitutes the satisfaction of a (moral) obligation, a duty owed to some fellow being.

To see an action as in some way a good thing to do is to have a reason for doing it. To say that someone believes that he has a good reason for doing something involves holding that if there are no equally good reasons for not doing that being and if no factors other than reasons influence him, he will do that thing.[3] Likewise, to say that someone believes that one action is overall better than another, that he recognizes overriding reasons for doing the action, is to say that he will do the former rather than the latter if he has to choose, unless factors other than reason (in the form of beliefs about relative goodness) influence his choice. If you said that you recognized that overall it would be better for you to go home rather than to go to the cinema, and then you went to the cinema, we should have to suppose either that you were lying or had changed your mind, or that factors other than reasons influenced what you did. An explanation of your behaviour is needed, not only in terms of what you believed about the relative merits of the actions, in terms that is of reasons; but also in terms of other factors which led you to do what you did not recognize adequate reason for doing. These other factors will be natural inclinations to do the actions, causes which incline a man to do an action which he may not regard as overall the best action, viz. desires. An agent's having a desire to do some action is always a reason for his doing it. But he may often believe that, although that is a reason for doing it, there are other and better reasons for not doing the action. Desire, in that case, inclines a man to act contrary to his beliefs about worth, including his moral beliefs. Hence the phenomenon of weakness of will.[4] In this situation the

---

[3] This point, that reason alone, without 'desires' or 'purposes' or 'pro-attitudes', suffices to explain behaviour, barring the operation of irrational factors, is made at length in D. Locke, 'Beliefs, Desires, and Reasons for Actions', *American Philosophical Quarterly*, 1982, **19**, 241–49. Bond (op. cit., e.g. p. 14) claims that unless an agent has in some wide sense a 'desire' to do an action, there will be nothing to motivate his doing it. But there is no clear content to this thesis, since the only understanding which Bond can provide of his wide sense of 'desire', is that it is whatever is necessary to motivate action. Bond seems to be trying to save a false thesis—'people do only what they desire to do'—by saying that the crucial word 'desire' must be understood in whatever way is necessary to make the thesis true.

[4] Weakness of will is an agent not doing what he believes to be most worth doing (e.g. what he believes to be morally obligatory). It is important to distinguish genuine cases of weakness of will from the cases where a man does not do what some moral code lays it down that he ought to do. He may fail to care for his aged parents, and comment 'I know that I ought to but I'm not going to'. But it may be in such a case that all that he means by 'I ought to' is 'people think that I ought to' or

agent sits, as it were, in the middle of a circle of alternative possible actions, some very easy to perform (those which he desires to perform), and others which he judges to be much more worth performing. He must choose whether to conform to reason or yield to his desire. It needs effort, struggle, and self-persuasion to resist desire, and if the agent does nothing the strongest desire will win.

Since agents desire only that which they believe to be in some way good, and in the absence of other desires, they will do that which they believe to be overall the best, we may say that all agents have a desire for the good as such, in proportion to its goodness. The trouble is that they also have desires for things believed to be good not in proportion to their goodness. But is it not possible that some agents may have desires for the good as such, in proportion to its goodness, which far outweigh other desires? For them the discovery that some action was overall the best open to them would lead automatically to their moving to do it, spontaneously and eagerly rushing into it. Such agents, on my definition, would have a strong desire for the good; and so (although we normally regard the evaluative properties of an action as peripheral to it), such agents would have a strong desire to do a particular action seen as involving its evaluative properties. I suspect, however, that a strong desire for the good, as such, is a very rare desire. The good is too abstract a category to incline humans strongly to action. Do not misunderstand me. There are, of course, many people who are strongly inclined to do many of

'Society's moral code prescibes that I ought to'. He may not, in fact, consider himself to be under a binding obligation to help his parents. In that case he is using the word 'ought' in what Hare called the 'inverted comma' sense (see R. M. Hare, *The Language of Morals*, Clarendon Press, Oxford, 1952, pp. 124 ff.); he is merely reporting Society's moral views, in no way endorsing them.

There is a tradition in Western philosophy that if an agent does not do what he believes to be most worth doing, this can only be because he is compelled to act contrary to his belief. One recent writer who has argued strongly for this thesis is R. M. Hare. (See his *Freedom and Reason*, Clarendon Press, Oxford, 1963, ch. 5.) For discussion of the views of Hare and Davidson ('How is Weakness of Will Possible', op. cit.) on this issue, and powerful advocacy of the position taken in this book, that an agent can fail to do what he believes most worth doing without being compelled not to, see D. Pears, *Motivated Irrationality*, Clarendon Press, Oxford, 1984, chs. 9 and 10.

On Weakness of Will explaining a man's failure to act on reasons of prudence, see T. Nagel, *The Possibility of Altruism*, Clarendon Press, Oxford, 1970, especially ch. 8.

the actions, which they also believe to be good actions. There are many naturally altruistic people who are strongly inclined to seek the happiness of others, many to whom promising and truth-telling is 'second nature', many who love to do the will of God as they see it. But their strong inclination is not towards the good as such, but towards the things which they also believe to be good. The test, that that is so, is—suppose that they come to believe that some action of one of the above kinds is not on occasion, or ever, good at all, do they automatically cease to have a strong inclination to do it? I suggest that normally they do not cease to have that inclination; and that confirms my suggestion that a strong inclination towards the good is a rare thing. Most of us have no strong in-built spontaneous inclination to pursue the good, as such, despite desires to do other things. If we are lucky, or have so conditioned ourselves, we may have desires to do actions and bring about states of affairs which we also believe to be good. But, otherwise, we need to resist our in-built inclinations to spontaneous action if we are ever to do what we believe to be overall best.

In the absence of beliefs about worth in conflict with desire, agents will act on their strongest desire; and where their strongest desires are strong, there is a considerable probability that they will do so anyway, despite any belief about worth in conflict with their strongest desire. Bodily desires, for food, drink, etc. occur fairly predictably in response to bodily stimulation; and culturally induced desires (such as the desire for success in school examinations) last for long periods. It is in consequence of these facts that much human action is predictable. Knowing of a man that he does not believe it wrong to eat when he desires to eat, and knowing when he will desire to eat, we can predict when he will eat.

But in a situation where desires and evaluative belief are in conflict, mere knowledge of an agent's evaluative beliefs and the relative strengths of his desires will not allow us to predict with certainty what he will do. For, evidently, in similar situations of choice agents with the same evaluative beliefs and the same relative strengths of desire have done different actions. Thank goodness, there have always been men who have resisted the worst torture which torturers could devise for them, while others with similar beliefs and desires have yielded to it. And, similarly, for situations of less agonizing choice. And, more generally, mere knowledge of mental properties (i.e. properties to which the agent has privileged access in consciousness) is often insufficient to allow us to predict what the agent will do. (One might say that knowledge of the numerical strength of an agent's desires, measured by some quantitative scale, rather than mere knowledge of their relative strengths would make possible prediction of his actions. But I suggest that we could only calculate a numerical strength for desire which would enable us to make such predictions, by taking into account factors other than mental ones.) For this reason psychological determinism, in the sense of all actions being necessitated by mental factors alone, seems false. That does, however, leave open the question of whether men are predetermined by brain-states in respect of whether they yield to the strongest desire, or whether they do the action which they believe to be most worth while (or whether they do some intermediate action which they believe to be of some value and which they have a fairly strong desire to do). I shall come to that question in a later chapter.

The Modification of Desire

Desires have various causes—some, such as the desire to eat, are often caused by physiological causes alone; others are largely the product of culture. In a later chapter I will be examining in more detail the processes by which desires are formed and changed. All that I wish to note here is that there are various techniques open to an agent himself to modify his own desires. Desires being by their nature involuntary inclinations, they cannot be changed just like that. It requires effort over some time to change one's desires, and such effort may not always be successful. The methods by which an agent can seek to change his desires are many and various. He can increase or decrease his desire for food or nicotine or sex, by taking drugs. He can prevent a desire from increasing by avoiding the occasions which stimulate it. The drunkard should keep clear of the pub; the gambling addict should keep clear of the casino. And desires to do some action may be weakened or stimulated by the agent thinking through the nature and consequences of that action.

A major reason which agents have for modifying their desires is thereby to affect the pattern of their future actions. I seek to abolish my desire to smoke in order that I may cease to smoke. That, however, is not the only reason which agents have for modifying their desires. They often think (rightly) that it makes for a good or bad character to have certain desires and not others, whether or not you ever have occasion to indulge them. It matters not merely that you do certain actions, but that you are naturally inclined to do them. It matters not merely that you take an interest in your children but that you want to take an interest in your children.[5] Also a man may seek to have a desire, in order to know what that desire feels like. There is Frankfurt's[6] example of the doctor who desires to experience the desire for heroin not in order to take heroin, but in order to know what an addict feels like. An older example is Odysseus who sought to hear the Sirens' song and have the desire which it produces without doing the action normally resulting from that desire.

The possibility of modifying our desires allows for the possibility that we may desire to do so; and hence the phenomenon of second-order desire to which Frankfurt drew our attention. We sometimes have natural inclinations to develop certain desires and suppress others—either for their own sake, as in the heroin example, or for the sake of their consequences (i.e. we have a desire to develop or suppress the desire considered as including its consequences). A man ordered to parachute from an aeroplane may want (i.e. desire) to desire to jump, fearing that he will not otherwise do so. And (some) cigarette smokers desire not to desire to smoke cigarettes.

Intention for the Future

The modification of desire, that hard-to-change *involuntary* readiness to act which we find within ourselves, is not the only, or even the most frequent, way by which agents influence their future actions. There is also the method of forming a *voluntary* intention, i.e. making a decision, and it is important to contrast the two methods. By the method of forming a voluntary intention I mean forming an intention today to do something tomorrow, or the next day, or for the rest of my life—to go to London tomorrow, to apply for the job, or to marry Jane. Such an act is a decision, a choice. Today's decision affects tomorrow's movements not

---

[5] I take it that it is this kind of point which St Paul is making by saying: 'Though I bestow all my gifts to feed the poor . . . and have not charity, it profiteth me nothing'. (1 Cor. 13: 3.)

[6] H. G. Frankfurt, 'Freedom of the Will and the Concept of a Person', *Journal of Philosophy*, 1970, **68**, 5–20.

blindly but only in so far as it is recalled. It affects them by giving me a very good reason for doing the appropriate action when the appropriate time arrives. If I decide today to go to London tomorrow, I give myself a reason which I will recognize tomorrow (barring exceptional circumstances) as an overriding reason for going to London, whatever other reasons I mave have now or then for going or not going. It provides such a reason because I believe that (barring exceptional circumstances) I ought to do what I have decided to do. I hold this view because I think that on important matters I ought to do what the balance of reasons indicates that I should do. Before reaching a decision, I consider that balance carefully and reach a view as to whether I should go or not. Tomorrow I shall have no time to reach a balanced view; but I shall know that I did so today and that I incorporated it in my decision. Hence I shall know that the way to act on a balanced view is to act on my decision. Also, I know the value of having a fixed course of action, not broken off by continual changes of mind. For these two reasons I regard the fact of a decision having been made as a reason for carrying it out. True, between now and tomorrow something quite unexpected may happen—e.g. my wife may get ill—which will give me even stronger reason for not going to London. In that case I will recognize that I ought not to act on my decision. But in general I will recognize that I ought so to act. The believed worth of an act is, we saw earlier, something which will lead an agent to perform that act—in the absence of contrary desire. My decision to do it gives me a new reason for doing the act in question. As well as thinking it right to act on my decisions, I may also have a desire, a natural inclination, to do so. In that case, too, the decision does not act by modifying my desires; they remain as before. It acts by using an existing desire—to carry out my decisions, which I believe in general to be a good thing—and adding to it belief that the way to satisfy that desire is to do so-and-so, e.g. to go to London. Forming an intention is thus doing an intentional act which is performative—rather like making myself a promise. It provides me with a reason for action which did not exist before and it may also provide me with a way of satisfying a pre-existing desire.

Some decisions are a matter of the agent saying to himself 'I will do so-and-so'; other decisions are simply a matter of an agent beginning a course of action (e.g. a journey to London, or writing a chapter of a book) when he regards having started the action as constituting a reason for finishing it. Only those who make decisions, at least of this latter kind, are likely to get very far in attaining any long-term goal. For, notoriously, reasons in the form of tiredness and other things to do will crop up before the goal is achieved. In those circumstances the fact of the past decision gives an additional reason for continuing to pursue the goal, and may also bring into play another desire (to do what I have decided), additional to the desire (which may now be weakening) to achieve the goal for other reasons.

Among the decisions or intentions which people form are conditional intentions—to do so-and-so if and when such-and-such circumstances arise. My earlier example of deciding to choose to play tennis when asked was an example of the formation of a conditional intention. Of course, some people don't make decisions; some people don't have any strong moral view about the keeping of decisions, or any desire to keep them. And even if they do believe that on balance they ought to fulfil their decisions, they may not do so—weakness of will again may operate. But decision remains for many people an efficacious means of affecting future conduct.

Decision is for many people the means by which they continue to pursue long-term goals, such as writing a thesis, building a house, or walking across Antarctica. The decision to do so gives them a reason for continuing the project when the desire to pursue the project has grown weak.

7. BELIEFS

The Nature of Belief

THE final component of a man's mental life are his beliefs. At any time a man has hundreds of thousands of beliefs—some true, some false, some well justified, some ill justified, some which he is ever repeating to himself and investigating, and some which he seldom puts into words. A man's beliefs include particular beliefs that today is Monday, or that I have two children; general beliefs—that all men are mortal; conditional beliefs—that if I jump out of an upstairs window I will hurt myself; and so on. We think of beliefs, like desires, as existing while the subject is giving them no thought, and indeed while he is asleep.

An agent's beliefs are his map or view of the world, what he holds to be true about it. He is aware of himself as having this, that, and the other belief from time to time (e.g. when he asks himself what he believes about some subject), and such awareness is the thought that this is his belief which I called judgement in Chapter 4. A man is aware of himself as believing that today is Monday by the judgement occurring to him 'today is Monday' rather than, say, 'today is Tuesday', or 'today is Wednesday', if and when he had thoughts about what the day is.

Among an agent's beliefs are what I shall call his means–ends beliefs, i.e. beliefs about which actions will attain which goals; and these determine how a man will execute his purposes. If, purposing to get butter, I go to the cupboard, that can only be if I believe that I shall get butter by going to the cupboard. If I go to the Senate Room in executing my purpose to attend a committee, that can only be if I believe that I shall get to the committee by going to the Senate Room. Men normally hold means–ends beliefs because these follow from more theoretical beliefs, but executing a given purpose by a given course of action may be manifesting any of very many different theoretical beliefs. Thus, purposing to go to London, I get on a train. That shows that I hold the belief that if I get on the train, I will get to London. I may hold this means–end belief because I hold the more theoretical belief that the train will shortly travel along the railway to London. Or I may hold the means–end belief because I hold the more theoretical belief that those on the train are going to be given free air tickets to London. Or I may hold the means–end belief because I believe that London is situated at the end of a short tunnel accessible from the train. And so on. An agent can, by asking himself, make himself aware of which more theoretical belief lies behind his means–end belief.

The means–end belief which determines how an agent will execute his purposes will inevitably be one which in judgement be acknowledges himself as having. For if an agent found himself bringing about X when he was purposing to bring about Y, while it did not seem to him by introspection that bringing about X would bring about Y, he could not regard himself as bringing about X in order to bring about Y. 'In order to' implies a view that the one leads to the other. The criterion of belief that an agent's beliefs are shown in the way he seeks to execute his purposes is but a special case of the criterion that an agent's beliefs are how things seem to the agent in thought.[1]

Beliefs are mental events in that whatever means others can use to learn about them (e.g. by observing which public actions an agent performs), the subject can also use; yet he has the additional means not available to others of his own awareness of his view of the world. Further, since belief just is the way an agent looks at the world, the way he sees it as being, he cannot be in error about

---

[1] Traditionally, however, these two criteria have been the foundation of two apparently very different theories of belief—the Humean Theory and the Dispositional Theory. According to Hume, to believe something is to have a 'lively' (as opposed to a faint) idea of it. See D. Hume, *A Treatise of Human Nature* (first published 1739, ed. L. A. Selby-Bigge, second edition, Clarendon Press, Oxford, 1978), 1. 3. 7. Since a man's beliefs continue while a man is giving them no thought, we must amend Hume so as to claim that to believe something is to have a 'lively' idea of it when you have an idea of it at all. If we understand 'lively idea' as 'judgement', we then have the judgement-criterion as stated in the text. A dispositional theory claims that a man's beliefs are a matter of how he behaves; but we must qualify it, as in the text, by saying that it is a matter of how he behaves so as to fulfil some given purpose. Dispositional theories tend to ignore this qualification and suppose erroneously that belief can be read off public behaviour. There is a well-known classical exposition of a qualified version of the Dispositional Theory by R. B. Braithwaite in 'The Nature of Believing', *Proceedings of the Aristotelian Society*, 1932–3, **33**, 129–46 (reprinted in (ed.) A. Phillips Griffiths *Knowledge and Belief*, Oxford University Press, London, 1967); and many more modern theories of belief such as the account given by Lewis (see n. 5), are, I think, dispositional in essence.

this.[2] Whatever he believes to be his view of the world is his view of the world. An agent may, however, refuse to admit to himself some belief, refuse to spell it out in judgement, and thus repress it from consciousness. Also, as I noted with respect to thought in Chapter 4, and the same goes for purposes and desires, an agent, knowing well what his beliefs are, may misstate them to himself in thought, and though seeking to be honest may misstate them in public language—for the various reasons which I gave with respect to thought in that chapter.[3]

Ambiguity of Ordinary Talk about Belief

What is meant by saying in ordinary language that someone s believes some proposition p is not always clear. But what is normally meant (and what I have understood by 'belief' so far) is, I suggest, that in s's view the world is more probably one in which p is true than one in which any alternative is true, i.e. s believes p to be more probable than any alternative. I suggest that the primary concept of belief is believing this proposition as against this alternative. My grounds for this suggestion is that sometimes agents are unclear about what is meant by saying that they believe some proposition, until belief is spelled out in this way; and, as we shall see, this relative belief is the concept of belief which is

---

[2] Sometimes a person will say that he does 'not know what he believes' about some matter. That assertion is, I suggest, to be taken as an assertion that he is not aware of himself as having a belief about some matter that things are this way rather than that way; and so, it follows, he does not believe one proposition about the matter rather than its negation.

[3] Two recent writers have given similar accounts, very different from the one above, of the relation between an agent's beliefs and his judgement as to what are his beliefs. According to John Vickers ('Judgement and Belief' in (ed.) K. Lambert, *The Logical Way of Doing Things*, Yale University Press, New Haven, 1969) and D. H. Mellor ('Consciousness and Degrees of Belief' in (ed.) D. H. Mellor, *Prospects for Pragmatism*, Cambridge University Press, 1980) belief is something manifest in public behaviour, while the agent's 'judgements' or 'assents' are his views expressed to himself or publicly about that pattern of public behaviour. We have seen, however, that mere public behaviour will not show an agent's beliefs. We would use an agent's judgements as further evidence of his beliefs to the pattern of his public behaviour. Another difficulty with their view is that while any discrepancy between what an agent says about his own beliefs and the belief manifest in behaviour seems strong evidence of deceit or self-deceit, there is no reason on this account why it should do. It is simply misobservation or misinterpretation of public behaviour—which, like any other misobservation or misinterpretation of the public, may be quite lacking in any such self-deceit.

manifested in action—which is why agents have a clearer grasp upon it.

The normal alternative with which a belief is contrasted is its negation. The negation of a proposition p is the proposition not-p or 'it is not the case that p'. The negation of 'today is Monday' is 'it is not the case that today is Monday' or 'today is not Monday'. Normally to believe that p is to believe that p is more probable than not-p. To believe that Labour will win the next general election is normally to believe that it is more probable that Labour will win than that they will not win. In other words, normally, I suggest, to believe that p is to believe that p is probable (i.e. has a probability of greater than $\frac{1}{2}$; and so not-p has a probability of less than $\frac{1}{2}$). (I understand p being certain as an extreme case of p being probable; it is p having a probability of 1 or close thereto.) What can be said in favour of this claim? To start with, if I do not believe that p is probable, I cannot believe that p is true. If I believe that it is more probable that not-p than that p, I cannot believe that p. Examples bear this out. If I believe that it is not probable that Liverpool will win the cup then (barring considerations to be discussed below, arising, from the existence of a number of alternatives) I cannot believe that they will win. But what about the other way round? Suppose that I do believe that p is probable. Must I believe that p? Clearly, if either I am to believe that p or I am to believe that not-p, I must believe the former. But might I not believe that p is probable without believing that p or believing not-p? If I believe that p is very, very probable, surely I believe that p. Cases where we would say the former are always cases where we would say the latter. If I believe that it is very, very probable that Liverpool will win the FA Cup, then I believe that Liverpool will win. The only difficulty arises when I believe that p is marginally more probable than not. Here we might be hesitant about whether to say that I believe that p. The hesitation arises not from ignorance about any unobserved matters, but because the rules for the application of the concept of belief are not sufficiently precise. Maybe some men do use 'believe' so that s has to believe that p is significantly more probable than not if s is to believe that p. But certainly others are prepared to allow that s believes that p if s believes merely that p is marginally more probable than not. It seems tidier to follow this latter usage. For, if we do not follow this usage, there would have to be some value of probability θ between

½ and 1, such that only if a man believed that *p* had a probability greater than θ would he believe that *p*. But any value chosen for θ would be extremely arbitrary. I conclude that although our ordinary rules for the use of words *may* not be sufficiently precise for my suggestion to be clearly analytic (i.e. to bring out our current understanding of the concept of belief), there is a case, if we are to have a clear concept of 'believe', for tightening up usage so that the words of my suggestion do now express a logically necessary truth.

Although normally the sole alternative to a belief that *p* is its negation, sometimes there will be other alternatives. This will be the case where *p* is one of a number of alternatives being considered in a certain context. In that case to believe that *p* will be to believe that *p* is more probable than any one of these alternatives (but not necessarily more probable than the disjunction of the alternatives). Sometimes, if in answer to a question 'Who do you believe will win the election?' I reply 'Labour' I may mean simply that I believe that it is more probable that Labour will win than that the Conservatives will win; and that it is more probable that Labour will win than that the SDP–Liberal Alliance will win, and more probable that Labour will win than that no party will win. I may believe these things without believing that it is more probable that Labour will win than that they will not win (and so that election will have some other, I know not what, result). Again, the belief that Liverpool will win the Cup may be the normal strong belief that it is more probable that Liverpool will win the Cup than that they will not, but it may be simply the weak belief that it is more probable that Liverpool will win than that Leeds will win, and more probable that Liverpool will win than that Aston Villa will win. And so on. But certainly normally to believe that *p* is to believe that *p* is more probable than not–*p*.

Belief, Passive and Involuntary

Belief is a passive state; believing is a state in which you are, it is not a matter of you doing something. And it is an involuntary state, a state in which you find yourself and which you cannot change at will. I believe that today is Tuesday, that I am now in Keele, that Aquinas died in *AD* 1274, etc., etc. I cannot suddenly decide to believe that today is Monday, that I am now in Italy, or that Aquinas lived in the eighteenth century. That belief is involuntary was a claim of Hume's. 'Belief consists', he wrote, 'merely in a certain feeling or sentiment; in something that depends not on the will, but must arise from certain determinate causes and principles of which we are not masters.'[4] But what Hume does not bring out is that this is a logical matter, not a contingent feature of our psychology. For suppose that I could choose my beliefs, i.e. bring them about by purposing, I would know that I was doing this. For, as we have seen, purposing is a conscious episode, about which the subject has infallible knowledge. But if I knew that what I called 'my beliefs' were the result of my choice, I would know that they were not forced upon me by outside forces, that they were not formed by the evidence. So I would know that what I 'believed' was in no way influenced by what was the case in the outside world; what I 'believed' was simply what I chose to believe. But then I would know that I had no reason for believing 'my beliefs' either to be true or to be false. But if I knew with respect to some opinion that I had no reason for believing either it or its negation to be true, I would know that the evidence supported it and its negation equally well—that it was not more probable than not, and so I would believe that it and its negation were equally likely to be true. So I would not believe it (as against its negation). We believe our beliefs to be true because we know that we do not choose them, but we believe that they are forced upon us by evidence from the outside world.

It is true that while I cannot change my beliefs at an instant, I can set about trying to change them over a period and I may have some success in this. I can set myself to look for more evidence, knowing that may lead to a change in my beliefs. Or I can deliberately set about cultivating a belief—e.g. by looking selectively for favourable evidence, and then trying to forget the selective character of my investigation. Or I can try to get myself to adopt new standards for assessing the old evidence. But any such process of self-conditioning inevitably takes time and is difficult to achieve. If forgetting was achievable at will, I would know that it was, and so I would know that my new collection of evidence might well be a very biased one, and that would lead me to distrust the resulting belief. And any new standards which I might adopt for assessing evidence will not seem plausible unless I can be got to view them as implicit in or continuous with standards which I had

---

[4] D. Hume, *Treatise of Human Nature*, Appendix, p. 624.

previously regarded as correct; and so there must be some continuity in my changing standards, and that involves their changing slowly. However, beliefs are not normally changed as a result of a long process of self-conditioning conducted by the subject. They normally change (in a way unplanned by the subject) as a result of all his perceptions of the world, his thoughts about them, and the arguments which others give to him. A man's beliefs change in the light of the evidence to which he is exposed and his standards for assessing that evidence (which may or may not be rational ones).

Belief and Action

An agent's beliefs, we have noted, affect the way in which he executes his purposes. Let us now attempt a more precise account of how belief is manifested in behaviour. Suppose to start with that a man has just one purpose—to achieve x, and a number of beliefs p, q, r from which there follow a number of means–end beliefs about the relative probability of different actions attaining the goal x. Thus it may follow that it is more probable that A_1 will attain x than that A_2 will, and more probable that A_2 will than that A_3 will, and so on. Then if A_1, A_2 and A_3 are incompatible actions (i.e. the agent can do at most one of them), it follows that the agent will do the action which, it follows from his beliefs, will most probably attain his goal.

Thus suppose that I am walking along and come to a junction. My one purpose in life is to get home. I believe that it is more probable that the left-hand road leads home than that the right-hand one does. It follows that it is more probable that I will get home if I walk along the left-hand road than if I walk along the right-hand one. Given that, I must take the left-hand road. If I do not, it cannot be both that I have the one purpose in life to get home and that I have the cited beliefs. In real life my situation is unlikely to be as simple as this. First, I shall have other beliefs which will complicate things. I may believe that a bus leaves the junction for home soon. I hold this belief with a certain degree of probability and also believe that there is a certain probability that the bus will be full up. Given the theoretical beliefs, different means–ends beliefs follow about the relative probabilities of success of different methods of getting home. But the general result remains—that an agent will do that action (among incompatible actions) which, it follows from his beliefs, will achieve its purpose more probably than will any other action.

Secondly, of course, I shall have other purposes which I am seeking to achieve. I shall not normally just be seeking to get home, but to get there without travelling for a long time, without getting wet or dirty, and so on. Which action an agent will perform in a situation where he has many purposes depends on just how keen he is on the fulfilment of the various purposes x_1, x_2, x_3 and so on; and just how probable he believes that it is that the various actions A_1, A_2, A_3 etc. will lead to the fulfilment or non-fulfilment of each of them. Thus suppose my purposes are x_1 (getting home), x_2 (not spending more than an hour on the journey), x_3 (remaining clean and dry). The alternative actions are A_1 (taking the left-hand turn), A_2 (taking the right-hand turn), A_3 (waiting for a bus). I have various beliefs which I hold with different degrees of probability—p (that the right-hand road leads home) being much more probable than q (that the left-hand road leads home); r (that the right-hand road is muddy) being much more probable than s (that the left-hand road is muddy); and so on. What determines what I will do is which purposes I am most keen to achieve (e.g. whether or not I mind very much about getting muddy), and just how much more probable it is that one action will achieve the purposes on which I am most keen than that others will. I will do that action which (it follows from my theoretical beliefs) will most probably achieve my purposes best (as many of them as possible, but especially those which I seek most). That the belief which affects behaviour is a belief that a certain action will more probably achieve a given goal than will another one (rather than, say, a belief that a certain action will almost certainly achieve a given goal) confirms my earlier claim that the primary concept of belief is a belief that one thing is more probable than another.

My discussion so far of how beliefs affect actions has made the crucial assumption that agents draw the correct conclusions from their theoretical beliefs, in the sense that they also believe their consequences for actions. They may not. A man may have a theoretical belief which entails that if he does a certain action, he will certainly achieve his goal; and yet he may not do the action through failing to draw the correct conclusion, i.e to believe what follows from his theoretical belief. My conclusions about the consequences for action of the means–end beliefs which follow from an agent's more theoretical beliefs, only follow in respect of those consequences which he understands as involved in his more theoretical beliefs.

Most people do believe most of the fairly immediate consequences of their beliefs; and everyone must believe some of the consequences of any belief which he has. You could not be said to understand some proposition unless you understood something of what was involved in it, nor therefore to believe a proposition unless you understood it as involving some of its more immediate consequences. However, we see the more remote consequences of some of our beliefs, especially those beliefs which we regard as important and whose consequences for action we regard as important, and we do not see the more remote consequences of other of our beliefs.

So in these, albeit complicated, ways, an agent's beliefs determine the actions by which he will seek to achieve his purposes. With respect to many of his more theoretical beliefs, even if he sees their more remote consequences, an agent may lack any purposes which are such that they affect his actions. But so long as he has the purpose of telling the truth, any belief of his however theoretical will make a difference to what a man says when asked what his beliefs are. My belief that time has no beginning will have little effect on most of my actions, but if I am asked 'Do you believe that time has a beginning?' and I have true beliefs about the meaning of the sentence 'Do you believe that time has a beginning?' and the meaning of the words 'Yes' and 'No', and I have the purpose of telling the truth in answer to such a question, I will say 'No' rather than 'Yes'.

Our Knowledge of the Beliefs, Purposes, and Desires of Others

My own beliefs and purposes are known to me infallibly; those of others are not, I have to infer them from public behaviour. Yet only with knowledge of his purposes can I infer infallibly from his public behaviour to an agent's beliefs; and only with knowledge of his beliefs can I infer infallibly from an agent's public behaviour to his purposes. An agent walks along a certain cliff path. If we know that he has the sole purpose of getting to the next town, we can infer that he believes that the path is safe. If we know that he believes that the path is so dangerous that he is certain to fall off, we can infer a purpose of committing suicide. But the mere fact that he walks along the path by itself allows no deductive influence either to his beliefs or to his purposes.

Nor, as we have seen, does what an agent says show infallibly what he believes. It does so only given that he has a purpose of truth-telling and certain further beliefs about the meanings of words, and these again are not things evident on the surface of his behaviour. Indeed, any given stretch of an agent's public behaviour is compatible with his having various beliefs and purposes. If you are prepared to attribute any strange purpose you like to him, you can attribute any belief you like to him. I fire a gun at someone. This is compatible with any belief you like to take about guns or anything else—e.g. the belief that firing a gun at someone gives him long blond hair—as long as you are prepared also to attribute to a man strange purposes in his actions—e.g. to make someone have long blond hair. However, although compatible with any given belief or purpose, a man's conduct rules out very many combinations of beliefs and purposes. If S fires a gun at T, it cannot be both that S has the purpose of keeping T alive and that S believes that firing guns at them kills people.

Although a man's public behaviour may be formally compatible with his having all sorts of extraordinary beliefs and purposes we infer from their public behaviour to the beliefs and purposes of others, and we do so using the principles of simplicity and charity; that is, in the same way as, we saw earlier, we infer to the sensations and thoughts of others. We use the principle of simplicity in attributing to men relatively stable purposes and beliefs. We assume, other things being equal, that the beliefs and purposes manifested in a man's actions today and yesterday are similar; that different men have similar purposes in similar situations; and that men acquire similar beliefs when presented with similar stimuli. We use the principle of charity in assuming that, other things being equal, other people have purposes of a kind which we also have ourselves and come to acquire beliefs in ways similar to that in which we do. These assumptions are then qualified in so far as is necessary to construct a theory of purpose and belief compatible with observed public behaviour, but qualified so as to complicate as little as possible. Application of these principles allows us to reach reasonably justified conclusions about what a man believes. If we show to a man S other men being killed by being shot in the heart, we reasonably suppose that S will come to believe that shooting kills (since we ourselves would come to hold that belief when shown what S was shown), and so if we then see S intentionally shooting someone else T, we infer that he believes that he will kill T, and so has the purpose of killing T. We assume that purposes do not come and go completely randomly, and so if failing to hit T with his shot, S then tries to strangle him, we infer that S believes that strangling kills (because S's purpose of killing T has remained). And so on.[5]

Our inference to a man's desires from his public behaviour is also of this kind, utilizing the principles of simplicity and charity. Other things being equal, we assume that what a man purposes he also desires. But from a study of his education and (by the principle of testimony) from what he says publicly, we infer his beliefs about what reasons there are for doing various actions other than that he desires to do them. Where, we infer, an agent has a belief that it is good to do some action for a reason other than he desires to do it, we cannot automatically infer from his doing it that he desires to do it. In such a case the agent's own testimony is good evidence on whether he had a desire to do the action. We infer also by the principles of simplicity and charity that, other things being equal, men have the same desires as ourselves and as each other. In this way we can build up a justified picture of a man's desires, as we can of the other elements of his mental life.

Use of the principles of simplicity and charity also allows us to infer to the purposes, desires, and beliefs of the higher animals (although with less confidence than similar inferences to the mental lives of other men), in virtue of the similarity of many of their patterns of behaviour to some of our own. But use of the principle of charity can only give highly tentative results in the case of animals with very different brains from ourselves. It becomes a more and more shaky inference that others have desires like our desires, the more different their brain-structure is from ours. And any use of the principle of simplicity to infer the mental life of animals different from ourselves must involve postulating simple principles about the formation and expression of beliefs, purposes, etc. which are specific to closely related animals; or which state how the way in which they are formed and expressed varies with the brain-structure of the animal.

[5] I have given here the kind of description of the inductive principles at work, given (e.g.) in D. Lewis, 'Radical Interpretation', *Synthese*, 1974, **27**, 331–44.

Purposes, desires, and beliefs are, like thoughts, intrinsically propositional events; that is, they consist in an attitude to a state of affairs under a certain description, i.e. as described by a certain proposition. Purposes are purposes that some proposition be made true; beliefs are beliefs that some proposition is true. We have to describe the intrinsically propositional states of others in our own language, and that may be ill suited for describing the states of animals very different from ourselves. The sentence of our language which gets closest to describing some animal belief may carry implications that the animal has some other belief which he does not in fact have. We saw this in Chapter 4 with respect to thought.

Although we infer to a man's beliefs from his behaviour by means of the principles of simplicity and charity, we assume that the conclusion yielded by such principles is only probable, not necessarily true.[6] *S* may ask *R* for an aspirin, *R* may take a pill out of his aspirin bottle and give it to *S*, *R* may in general have behaved benevolently towards *S* so far; yet the pill turns out to be a cyanide pill which kills *S*. We infer from his generally benevolent behaviour that *R* did not have the purpose of killing *S*, and hence that he did not believe that the pill would kill *S*. But we could be wrong, and *R* could know that we were wrong. A man's beliefs are not necessarily what an inference from his observable behaviour would, by the principles of simplicity and charity, lead us to infer that they are. And the same goes for his purposes, and for his desires. When public evidence supports equally well two different theories of an agent's beliefs, an agent having this privileged access could know which belief was his. And, more than that, an agent may know better than the outsider even when the public evidence supports (and perhaps even supports fairly strongly) one of two rival theories of an agent's beliefs.

---

[6] Thus, in the article referred to above, Lewis claims that if we knew all the actual and hypothetical behaviour of a person (i.e. not merely . . . what he does, but what he would do in unrealized circumstances), all described in physical terms, and drew conclusions therefrom about his beliefs and purposes, we would know everything about his beliefs and purposes. If the data gave equal support to more than one theory about the man's beliefs and purposes, there would be no factual difference between such theories. My argument above suggests that this is false. If, for example, there was more than one such theory, what a man admitted to himself, although not publicly, about his beliefs and purposes would seem to select one such theory as true and another as false.

Belief a Continuing Mental State

His beliefs are accessible to an agent in the form of judgements that so-and-so is the case. Why should we think of their being anything more than the judgements; why not suppose that there are mental events of four kinds only? Why should we think of a judgement as tapping an independently existing continuing mental state rather than simply expressing a view which lasts only as long as the judgement itself?

We do, however, think of beliefs as continuing for periods during which we are unaware of them, and for the same reasons as we think of desires as continuing mental states. First, there is the phenomenological reason. The process of asking ourselves what we believe and providing an answer comes to us as a process by which we find in ourselves a view of the world, which does not in general seem created by the enquiry but to be there ready to manifest itself in appropriate circumstances. Belief, like desire, comes to us phenomenologically as something uncovered and not created by enquiry. Secondly, it is normally the case with the beliefs of which agents are aware at a given time, that they are often aware of the same beliefs at certain moments of the near past or future; and where relevant, those beliefs have influenced the agent's conduct at nearby points of time. All of this gives reason for believing that if the agent asked himself about his beliefs on the subject in question at any moment of a period of time including the present, he would have got the same answer; and the same belief, if relevant, would have influenced his conduct cover that period.

If I am aware in thought at 2.00 p.m. of a belief that there is butter in the cupboard, and I am aware in thought at 3.00 p.m. of a belief that there is butter in the cupboard, then in general if at 2.30 p.m. I were to ask myself about this matter, I would also be aware of such a belief (and would express to myself the judgement that there is butter in the cupboard); and also if I were to have the sole purpose of getting butter, I would go to the cupboard.

The above applies generally to many beliefs. There are beliefs which the agent is aware of himself as coming to have at a given time, sometimes as a result of enquiry. The agent is aware of his present perceptual beliefs (what he is now seeing, and hearing) as acquired at this moment and not pre-existing. And he is also aware of himself as acquiring new beliefs by reasoning. It is important not to confuse the process of asking oneself what one already believes, with the process of asking oneself what ought one to believe (e.g. given one's previous beliefs). Asked whether my house is more than 2.23 miles from the University, I may consider the matter and reply 'Yes'. But here I am drawing a conclusion from what I already believe—that my house is 3 to 4 miles from the University—initiating a process which allows a belief which follows from pre-existing beliefs rationally to be created, rather than reporting a pre-existing belief. Why describe things thus? Because the belief that my house is more than 2.23 miles from the University comes to me phenomenologically thus, I previously made no judgements about it, nor was my previous conduct affected by it as opposed to being affected by other beliefs which do seem to me to have been believed by me before (e.g. that my house is 3 to 4 miles from the University).

The general continuity of beliefs which influence action and of which agents are aware over a period of time, and the phenomenological fact that agents seem to be discovering pre-existing beliefs makes it natural and useful to think of beliefs as mental states continuing while the agent is unaware of them. But as with desires, there are two possible ways of understanding this talk—the dispositional and the categorical. On the dispositional understanding to say that an agent has some belief of which he is currently unaware is just to say that if the agent made a judgement about the matter in question, it would be the one which expressed that belief; and if the belief had as a consequence which actions of the agent would achieve some purpose and he sought to achieve that purpose, he would do those actions. The continuing existence of a belief is the continuing of a disposition to thought and action; and the appropriate thoughts and actions are caused by some state of the agent, and in order to reduce alternatives to manageable proportions, I shall assume that state to be a brain-state. Belief is propositional, for it is belief that so-and-so is the case. Its manifestation in thought is intrinsically propositional, for, as we saw earlier, thoughts are intrinsically propositional. Its manifestation in action would not be intrinsically propositional, for what makes a belief so manifested the belief that it is, is which action A is performing and which more ultimate purpose G he is purposing to achieve thereby. It is the occurrence of A and G which constitute the belief that A will lead to G, or a belief of which that is a consequence. And when a belief is not being manifested it is not intrinsically propositional, for what makes it the belief it is the hypothetical context—what would happen if the subject had a thought on a certain subject or had to perform an action of a certain kind.

On the categorical understanding of belief, what continues when an agent is unaware of some belief is an attitude towards a state of affairs which is just the same as the attitude of which he is aware when he is aware of his belief except that he is not aware of it. Beliefs are intrinsically propositional even when not being manifested. I shall be considering in Chapter 14 which of these understandings of belief is the correct one.

Are beliefs causally efficacious? On the dispositional view there is nothing more to a belief than its manifestations. These manifestations of the belief are not caused by anything other than a brain-state. There is not a continuing intrinsically propositional state, to which awareness in consciousness gives intermittent access, and which in any way causes that awareness or anything else. The awareness of belief in consciousness, being a judgement and so a thought, may have effects, as I have already argued. On the dispositional view the existence of a belief is simply the existence of a disposition, and dispositions are mere 'would-be's'; they are not events which can have effects. On the categorial view, however, beliefs are more than their manifestations, and the issue arises as to whether these intrinsically propositional states can have effects—either in causing the manifestations of beliefs (making subjects express judgements to themselves, and act as they do), or in some other way. We shall consider this issue also in Chapter 14.

The Five Elements

I have suggested that there are three kinds of conscious episode, three elements which make up the stream of consciousness— sensations, thoughts (often mediated via sensations), and purposings. The agent is aware from time to time of his desires and beliefs; and it is useful to think of this awareness as an awareness of continuing mental states (even if we adopt a dispositional account of what this continuing consists in). Beliefs and desires form a background within which an agent has his sensations, thinks his thoughts, and forms his purposes.

I now suggest that all other mental events can be analysed in terms of these five elements. There is no space to demonstrate this in detail, but in this section I shall give and provide some justification for this claim by providing the analysis of mental events of a few other kinds.[7]

I begin by taking again from Chapter 2 the example of *perception*. The central case of perception is where one perceives an object of a certain kind or a particular object, believing that one does perceive an object of that kind or that particular object. There are cases where one perceives something without believing that one does—one may see the Prime Minister without believing that it is the Prime Minister. Such cases are to be analysed as perceiving an object which is ϕ, believing that one does; where that ϕ object is in fact ψ (although the subject does not believe this). To see the Prime Minister (without believing that one does), is to see a person who has certain characteristics, e.g. of visual appearance, believing that one does, where that person is in fact the Prime Minister (although one does not believe that). The central case of perceiving an object which is ϕ, believing that one does, is to be analysed as the object which is ϕ (a public thing) causing the subject to have certain sensations and the belief that the sensations are caused by a ϕ—object. Seeing involves visual sensations, hearing auditory sensations, and so on. The sensations are characteristic of the object, the mode of perception, and the angle and distance of the object; and are related to the belief in the way analysed in Chapter 2.

Although philosophers dispute much about the correct analysis of *knowledge*, almost all agree that knowledge is belief of a certain kind in certain circumstances. The traditional analysis of '*S* knows that *p*' is that *S* believes that *p*, *p* is true, and *S* is justified in believing that *p*. The second component, '*p* is true', is not a mental component, and if the third component is analysed as involving mental elements, it is always other beliefs of *S* (e.g. a belief that the evidence supports *p*).

[7] In *Intentionality*, pp. 30–6, J. R. Searle provides analyses of various intentional attitudes (i.e. attitudes towards some proposition, such as regretting, fearing, expecting) in terms of desire and belief. Thus, being disappointed that *p* is analysed as believing that *p*, when previously the subject believed that *p* would not happen, and desiring that *p* not happen. His work brings out that desire and belief are the simple mental attitudes towards states of affairs, in terms of which other attitudes are to be analysed.

Memory may be the name either of a continuing mental state or of a conscious episode. In the former case memory is a kind of knowledge, the mental element of which is belief; it is knowledge of a certain sort caused in a certain way. People are said to remember things while they are giving them no thought (e.g. while they are asleep), and in such a case 'remember' is being used to describe a continuing mental state. Factual memory is memory that certain things are so, that the Battle of Hastings was fought in 1066, or that Edinburgh is to the north of London. Factual memory is present knowledge caused in part by past knowledge, and believed by the subject to be so caused. To remember that the Battle of Hastings was fought in 1066 is to know that this is so in part because one knew it previously, and to believe that that is the source of one's knowledge. Personal memory is a species of a factual memory. It is knowledge that things are so when this knowledge is knowledge that the agent did certain things or had certain experiences, and where the present knowledge was caused in part by his past knowledge at a certain time that he was doing or experiencing those things at that time, and is believed by the agent to be so caused. I now remember having gone to London if I know that I went to London partly as a result of my having known at the time that I was going there, and I believe that past knowledge to be the source of my present knowledge.

More usually 'memory' is the name of a conscious episode, that is for the judgement that certain things are so, where the belief which that judgement expresses amounts to knowledge, the belief being caused in part by previous knowledge and the agent believing it to be so caused. Remembering is then recalling. Where the knowledge recalled is knowledge at a time that the agent did or experienced certain things at that time, the memory is personal memory. Otherwise it is mere factual memory. My remembering seeing him fall down consists in me now having the judgement that I did see him fall down being caused in part by the knowledge at the time that I was seeing him fall down, when I believe that it was so caused. The judgement may be mediated by sensation; I may have a vague visual image, which I believe to correspond very roughly in shape and pattern to the sensations involved in the past perception of him falling down. So memory involves (as well as public elements) thought, sensation, and belief (the mental element in knowledge). As with perception, to the extent that the memory is erroneous, the public element will be absent. An apparent memory is it seeming (epistemically) to the subject that he remembers. An apparent factual memory is an inclination to believe that things are so in a certain respect together with an inclination to believe that the former inclination was caused in part by previous knowledge that things are so. An inclination to believe, it will be recalled, is a state which would be belief but for any other evidence. Alternatively, it is a conscious episode—a thought that probably things are thus, together with a thought that the former thought probably was caused in part by previous knowledge (probably, but for any other, less direct, evidence there might be). An apparent personal memory is it seeming to the subject that he did or experienced this or that, and it seeming to him that it so seems in part because at the time he knowingly did or experienced this or that.

There is a further qualification, however, to be put on the above account. The causal chain whereby the past event causes the present belief (or thought) must be of a special kind, and the subject must believe it to be of this kind if the belief is to amount to memory. If the belief is to be a personal memory, a causal chain of this kind must run between the agent's knowledge at the time that he was doing or experiencing this or that and the agent's present belief that he was, and the agent must believe that it does so run. If I had some experience in the past, told Jones about it and then forgot about it; he tells me about the experience years later, my present knowledge of it (although caused indirectly by my past experience) is not a memory of it. If the causal chain goes through an informant, that rules out the resulting belief from being a memory. The same applies if it goes through a diary. If my knowledge of what I did is due to my reading what I wrote in my diary it is not memory. What is necessary is that the causal chain goes through my body or some other part of me (I shall argue in the next chapter that there is another part of me), and not through anything outside me, if my belief is to amount to memory; and I must believe that it does. If a belief (or thought) of mine is to be an apparent memory, then I must be inclined to believe it to be caused by a causal chain of this kind.[8]

---

[8] The above account is a fairly rough one. One difficulty concerns the exact limits to a body. Suppose I carry with me a box which is plugged into my brain and which tapes my experiences; only when I am plugged into the box again, do I

Emotions normally involve sensations, beliefs, thoughts, and desires. There are occurrent emotional sensations—I may have a twinge of fear at 2.00 p.m.; and continuing emotional states—I may fear lions all the week, including periods while I am asleep without a conscious life. To have a twinge of fear is to have a sensation, perhaps a sinking feeling in the stomach, caused by a thought that a certain thing may be going to happen (e.g. that the lion will catch me), and a desire that that thing do not happen. The continuing state of fear consists of a continuing belief (that something may be going to happen) and a continuing desire that it should not, which under appropriate circumstances or from time to time, manifests itself in occurrent thought that the thing will happen, causing sensations.

Emotional states differ from each other according to the different thoughts, beliefs and desires which enter into them. If my belief is that the thing will certainly happen, not just possibly or probably happen, and I desire that it shall not, my emotion is rather regret, sadness, or dread (according to the strength of my desire). If I believe that something bad has certainly already happened, and my desire is that it should not have happened, the emotion is sadness. If the thing believed to have happened is the loss of a loved one, the emotion is grief. Emotional sensations involve occurrent thoughts rather than mere beliefs. The same sensation is then the sensation of a different emotion according to the different desires and thoughts which cause it. Thus a stab of anger is a stabbing sensation caused by a thought (viz. a judgement) that something bad has happened brought about by some person or thing X, and a desire to cause immediate hurt to X. If the desire is to hurt X over a longer period in less violent ways—e.g. by speaking ill of him and refusing favours to him—we would call the stab one of resentment.[9]

acquire the belief that they occurred. Is this memory? My inclination is to say that it is. Another difficulty is that, it is logically possible there may be no causal chain. The past event might cause the present belief without doing so via any intermediate states. This would be 'causation at a temporal distance', a kind of causation to which Russell gave the name 'mnemic causation' (B. Russell, *The Analysis of Mind*, Lecture 4). In such a case also, I suggest, we have memory. There is only not memory where the causal chain from past event to present belief runs outside the person. For the original discussion of the kind of causal chain which is necessary for memory, see C. B. Martin and M. Deutscher, 'Remembering', *Philosophical Review*, 1966, **75**, 161–96.

[9] Jenefer Robinson has argued that it is characteristic of the role of desire in emotion that the desire causes the thought (viz. the judgement). If I am afraid of a

To take *pleasure* in doing something, or to get enjoyment out of doing it, is, as I argued in Chapter 6, simply to do it, to want (i.e. desire) to be doing it, and to want the circumstances to be as they are, and not to want much to be doing anything else instead or to be instead in any other circumstances. Pleasure is not a sensation which people get as a consequence of doing something. There is no sensation which a man enjoying writing philosophy gets in the process; but his enjoyment consists in the satisfaction of desire. *Pain*, by contrast, as I argued in Chapter 2, is a sensation accompanied by a desire that the sensation do not occur. The sensation must be of a certain kind, which can be illustrated by examples, but which can occur at very low intensity. Only if a sensation of that kind occurs at sufficiently great intensity does the subject desire not to have it and only then does it count as pain.

bear, I don't just judge that the bear is dangerous, and then desire to escape. Rather, my desire for life determines how I view the bear. See J. Robinson, 'Emotion, Judgment, and Desire', *Journal of Philosophy*, 1983, **80**, 731–41.

PART II

THE SOUL

8. BODY AND SOUL

So far in this book I have been analysing the structure of man's mental life. I have been arguing that there are mental events of various kinds—sensations, thoughts, purposings, desires, and beliefs—and that these interact with brain-events, which are physical events. I now come to the crucial question of the nature of that substance, the man (or human being) of which the mental events are states. Is a man just his body, an organized system of molecules, or does a man consist of two parts—body and soul?

This second part of the book is a defence of substance dualism. As stated in Chapter 1, I understand by substance dualism the view that those persons which are human beings (or men) living on Earth, have two parts linked together, body and soul. A man's body is that to which his physical properties belong. If a man weighs ten stone then his body weighs ten stone. A man's soul is that to which the (pure) mental properties of a man belong. If a man imagines a cat, then, the dualist will say, his soul imagines a cat. Talk of a man's body and its properties is of course perfectly natural ordinary-language talk; talk of a man's soul less so. The dualist would, however, claim that souls do feel and believe, even if we do not naturally talk in that way. (In ordinary talk perhaps minds, rather than souls, are, however, often given mental predicates—to be said to imagine things or feel weary, for instance.) On the dualist account the whole man has the properties he does because his constituent parts have the properties they do. I weigh ten stone because my body does; I imagine a cat because my soul does. Mixed mental properties, as I defined them in Chapter 1 are those mental properties which can be analysed in terms partly of a physical component. Writing a letter is a mixed property because it involves purposing to write a letter (mental property) being followed by the hand so moving that a letter is written (physical property). The instantiation of the mental property is followed by (and, I argued in Chapter 5, causes) the instantiation of the physical property. On the dualist view the mixed property belongs to the man, because its pure mental-property component belongs to his soul, and its physical-property component belongs to his body. I write a letter because my body makes certain movements and my soul purposed that it should.

A person has a body if there is a chunk of matter through which he makes a difference to the material world, and through which he acquires true beliefs about that world. Those persons who are men have bodies because stimuli landing on their eyes or ears give them true beliefs about the world, which they would not otherwise have; and they make differences to the world by moving arms and legs, lips and fingers. Our bodies are the vehicles of our knowledge and operation. The 'linking' of body and soul consists in there being a body which is related to the soul in this way.

Some dualists, such as Descartes, seem sometimes to be saying that the soul is the person; any living body temporarily linked to the soul is no part of the person. That, however, seems just false. Given that what we are trying to do is to analyse the nature of those entities, such as men, which we normally call 'persons', we must say that arms and legs and all other parts of the living body of a man are parts of the person. My arms and my legs are parts of me. The crucial point that Descartes[1] and others were presumably trying to make is not that (in the case of men) the living body is not part of the person, but that it is not essentially, only contingently, part of the person. The body is separable from the person and the person can continue even if the body is destroyed. Just as I continue to exist wholly and completely if you cut off my hair, so, the dualist holds, it is possible that I continue to exist if you destroy my body. The soul, by contrast, is the necessary core which must continue if I am to continue; it is the part of the person which is necessary for his continuing existence. The person is the soul together with whatever, if any, body is linked temporarily to it.

By saying that the person '*can*' continue if the body is destroyed I mean only that this is *logically* possible, that there is no contradiction in supposing the soul to continue to exist without its present body or indeed any body at all (although such a soul would not then, on the understanding which I have given to 'man'—see

[1] There are passages in Descartes which can be interpreted as saying that the body is no part of the person and other passages which can be interpreted as saying that the body is a part, but not an essential part, of the person. For examples and commentary, see pp. 63–6 of B. Smart, 'How can Persons be ascribed M-Predicates', *Mind*, 1977, **86**, 49–66.

pp. 4 f.—be a man or part of a man, although it would have been part of a man). Whether this normally happens, is another question; and one to which I shall come later. My concern in this chapter is to show that a man has a part, his soul, as well as his body—whether or not in the natural course of things that part continues to exist without the body.

So much for what dualism is. Now for its general defence. My initial argument in its support has two stages. I argue first that knowledge of what happens to bodies and their parts, and knowledge of the mental events which occur in connection with them will not suffice to give you knowledge of what happens to those persons who are (currently) men. Talk about persons is not analysable in terms of talk about bodies and their connected mental life. And more generally, it is logically possible that persons continue to exist when their bodies are destroyed. Secondly, I argue that the most natural way of making sense of this fact is talking of persons as consisting of two parts, body and soul—the soul being the essential part, whose continuing alone makes for the continuing of the person.

So then for the first stage of the argument. It is, I suggest, a factual matter whether a person survives an operation or not. There is a truth here that some later person is or is not the same as some pre-operation person, but it is, I shall suggest, a truth of which we can be ignorant however much we know about human bodies and the fate of their organs.

How much of my body must remain if I am to survive an operation? Plausibly, with respect to all parts of my body other than the brain, if you remove them I survive. Cut off my arm or leg, replace my heart or liver, and I continue to exist; there is the same person before as after the operation. Remove my brain, on the other hand, and put it in the skull of another body, and replace it by a different brain, and intuitively the rest of the body that was mine is no longer. I go where my brain goes. We treat the brain as the core of the body which determines whose body it is. That is because with the brain goes the characteristic pattern of mental life which is expressed in behaviour. The brain gives rise to a man's mental states—his beliefs, including his apparent memories, and his desires, their expression in public behaviour, and his character-istic pattern of unintended response to circumstance. The brain gives rise to memory and character which we see as more intimately connected with personal identity than the digestive processes. But what if only some of my brain is removed? Do I survive or not?

The brain, as is well known, has two very similar hemispheres—a left and a right hemisphere. The left hemisphere plays a major role in the control of limbs and of processing sensory information from the right side of the body (and from the right sides of the two eyes); and the right hemisphere plays a major role in the control of limbs of and processing of sensory information from the left side of the body (and from the left sides of the two eyes). The left hemisphere normally plays the major role in the control of speech. Although the hemispheres have different roles in adults, they interact with each other; and if parts of a hemisphere are removed, at any rate early in life, the roles of those parts are often taken over by parts of the other hemisphere.[2] Brain operations are not infrequent, which remove substantial parts of the brain. It might be possible one day to remove a whole hemisphere, without killing the person, and to transplant it into the skull of a living body from which the brain has just been removed, so that the transplant takes. There would then appear to be two separate living persons. Since both are controlled by hemispheres originating from the original person *p*, and since apparent memory and character and their manifestation in behaviour are dependent on factors present in both hemispheres, we would expect each publicly to affirm such apparent memories and to behave as if he had *p*'s character. It is possible that appearances might be misleading here—that one of the apparent persons was simply a robot, with no life of conscious experience at all, but caused to behave as if it had. But, if we suppose that appearances are not misleading here, the transplant will have created two persons, both with *p*'s apparent memories and character. But they cannot both be *p*. For if they were, they would both be the same person as each other, and clearly they are not—they have now distinct mental lives. The operation would therefore create at least one new person—we may have our views about which (if either) resultant person *p* is, but we could be wrong. And that is my basic point—however much we knew in such a situation about what happens to the parts of a person's

[2] For a simple readable account of the current state of psychological research of the different roles of the two hemispheres, see S. P. Springer and G. Deutsch, *Left Brain, Right Brain*, W. H. Freeman, San Francisco, 1981.

body, we would not know for certain what happens to the person.

I can bring the uncertainty out strongly by adapting Bernard Williams's famous mad surgeon story.[3] Suppose that a mad surgeon captures you and announces that he is going to transplant your left cerebral hemisphere into one body, and your right one into another. He is going to torture one of the resulting persons and free the other with a gift of a million pounds. You can choose which person is to be tortured and which to be rewarded, and the surgeon promises to do as you choose. You believe his promise. But how are you to choose? You wish to choose that you are rewarded, but you do not know which resultant person will be you. You may have studied neurophysiology deeply and think that you have detected some all-important difference between the hemispheres which indicates which is the vehicle of personal identity; but, all too obviously, you could be mistaken. Whichever way you choose, the choice would, in Williams's telling word about his similar story, be a 'risk'—which shows that there is something other to the continuity of the person, than any continuity of parts of brain or body.

It is a fashionable criticism of an argument of this kind that it assumes that personal identity is indivisible. We do not make this kind of assumption with respect to inanimate things, such as cars and countries. These survive in part. If half the bits of my old car are used together with bits of another old car in the construction of a new car, my car has survived in part. And if the other bits of my old car are used in construction of another new car, then my old car has survived in part as one car and in part as another car. If we succeed in dividing humans, why should not human survival be like that? If half my brain is put into one body, and half into another body, do I not survive partly as one person and partly as another?

However, persons such as men are very different from inanimate beings such as cars. They have hopes, fears, and memories which make it very difficult to give sense to the idea of their partial survival. Consider again the victim in the mad surgeon story. If he survives to the extent to which his brain survives, his choice of who is to suffer will make no difference; however he chooses one person who is partly he will suffer, and one person who is partly he

---

[3] For the original, see B. Williams, 'The Self and the Future', *Philosophical Review*, 1970, **79**, 161–80.

will be rewarded. In that case he has reason both for joyous expectation and for terrified anticipation. But how can such an attitude of part joyous expectation and part terrified anticipation be justified, since no future person is going to suffer a mixed fate? It is hard to give any sense to the notion of there being a half-way between one having certain future experiences which some person has, and one not having them, and so to the notion of a person being divisible.

But even if this notion of partial survival does make sense, it will in no way remove the difficulty, which remains this. Although it *may* be the case that if my two brain hemispheres are transplanted into different bodies, I survive partly as the person whose body is controlled by one and partly as the person whose body is controlled by the other, it may not be like that at all. Maybe I go just where the left hemisphere goes. As we have seen, the fate of some parts of my body, such as my arms and legs, is quite irrelevant to the fate of me. And plausibly the fate of some parts of my brain is irrelevant—can I not survive completely a minor brain operation which removes a very small tumour? But then maybe it is the same with some larger parts of the brain too. We just don't know. If the mad surgeon's victim took the attitude that it didn't matter which way he chose, we would, I suggest, regard him as taking an unjustifiably dogmatic attitude. For the fact that a resultant person has qualitatively the same memory and character is certainly no guarantee that he is me—in whole or in part. For while I continue to exist quite untouched by any change of brain or character or memory, some other person *p* with my character could, through a long process of hypnosis, be given 'my' apparent memories in the sense of being led to believe that he had the same past experiences as I did. But that would not make me any less than fully me; and if I remain fully me, there is no room for *p* to be me, even in small part.

My argument has been that knowledge of what has happened to a person's body and its parts will not necessarily give you knowledge of what has happened to the person, and so, that persons are not the same as their bodies. I have illustrated my argument by considerations which, alas, are far from being mere thought-experiments. Brain transplants may well happen in a few decades time, and we need to be armed with the philosophical apparatus to cope with them. But it suffices to make my point to point out that the mere logical possibility of a person surviving with only half his brain (the mere fact that this is not a self-contradictory supposition) is enough to show that talk about persons is not analysable as talk about bodies and their parts.

My arguments so far, however, show only that some brain continuity (or other bodily continuity) is not sufficient for personal identity; which is something over and above that. They do not rule out the possibility that some bodily matter needs to continue *as well*, if personal identity is to continue. Thought-experiments of more extravagant kinds rule out this latter possibility. Consider life after death. It seems logically possible that any present person who is currently a man, having the mental properties which we know men to have and which I have described in previous chapters, could continue to be with loss of his present body. We understand what is being claimed in fairy stories or in serious religious affirmations which affirm life after death. It seems self-consistent to affirm with respect to any person who is the subject of mental properties that he continue to have them, while his body is annihilated. This shows that the very notions of sensation, purposing, etc. involve the concepts of a subject of sensation and purposing of whom it makes sense to suppose that he continues while his body does not.

This suggestion of a man acquiring a new body may be made more plausible, to someone who has difficulty in grasping it, by supposing the event to occur gradually. Suppose that one morning a man wakes up to find himself unable to control the right side of his body, including his right arm and leg. When he tries to move the right-side parts of his body, he finds that the corresponding left-side parts of his body move; and when he tries to move the left-side parts, the corresponding parts of his wife's body move. His knowledge of the world comes to depend on stimuli to his left side and to his wife's right side (e.g. light rays stimulating his left eye and his wife's right eye). The bodies fuse to some extent physiologically as with Siamese twins, while the man's wife loses control of her left side. The focus of the man's control of and knowledge of the world is shifting. One may suppose the process completed as the man's control is shifted to the wife's body, while his wife loses control of it. At that stage he becomes able to move parts of what was his wife's body as a basic action, not merely by doing some other action.

Equally coherent, I suggest, is the supposition that a person who is a man might become disembodied. A person has a body if there is one particular chunk of matter through which he has to operate on and learn about the world. But suppose that a person who has been a man now finds himself no longer able to operate on the world, nor to acquire true beliefs about it; yet still to have a full mental life, some of it subject to his voluntary control. He would be disembodied. Or suppose, alternatively, that he finds himself able to operate on and learn about the world within some small finite region, without having to use one particular chunk of matter for this purpose. He might find himself with knowledge of the position of objects in a room (perhaps by having visual sensations, perhaps not), and able to move such objects just like that, in the ways in which we know about the positions of our limbs and can move them. But the room would not be, as it were, the person's body; for we may suppose that simply by choosing to do so he can gradually shift the focus of his knowledge and control, e.g. to the next room. The person would be in no way limited to operating and learning through one particular chunk of matter. Hence he would have no body. The supposition that a person who is currently a man might become disembodied in one or other of these ways seems coherent.

Not merely is it not logically necessary that a person have a body or brain made of certain matter, if he is to be the person which he is; it is not even necessitated by laws of nature.[4] For let us assume what I shall later call into question, the most that is claimed for natural laws, that they dictate the course of evolution, the emergence of consciousness, and the behaviour and mental life of men in a totally deterministic way. In 4000m BC the Earth was a cooling globe of inanimate atoms. Natural laws then, we assume, dictated how this globe would evolve, and so which arrangements of matter would be the bodies of conscious men, and so, also, just how those men would behave and what mental life they would have. My point now is that what natural laws still in no way determine is which animate body is yours and which is mine. Just the same arrangement of matter and just the same laws could have given to me the body (and so the behaviour and mental life) which are now yours, and to you the body (and so the behaviour and

[4] I owe this argument to an article by John Knox, Jr, 'Can the Self Survive the Death of its Mind?', *Religious Studies*, 1969, **5**, 85–97.

mental life) which are now mine. It needs either God or chance to allocate bodies to persons; the most that natural laws could determine is that bodies of a certain construction are the bodies of some person or other who in consequence of this construction behave in certain ways and have a certain mental life. Since the body which is presently yours could have been mine (logic and even natural laws allow), that shows that none of the matter of which my body is presently made is essential to my being the person that I am.

And so I come to the second stage of my argument. How are we to bring out within an integrated system of thought, this fact which the first stage of my argument has, I hope, shown conclusively—that continuing matter is not (logically) essential for the continuing existence of persons. For persons are substances, and for substances of all other kinds continuing matter *is* necessary for the continuing existence of the substance. If a substance S_2 at a time t_2 is to be the same substance as a substance S_1 at an earlier time t_1 it must (of logical necessity) be made of the same matter as S_1, or at least of matter obtained from S_1 by gradual replacement. If my desk today is to be the same desk as my desk last year it must be made largely of the same wood; a drawer or two may have been replaced. But the desk would not be the same desk if all the wood had been replaced. In the case of living organisms such as plants, we do allow for total replacement of matter—so long as it is gradual. The full-grown oak tree possesses few if any of the molecules which formed the sapling, but so long as molecules were replaced only gradually over a period while most other molecules continued to form part of the organized tree, the tree continues to exist. That continuing matter was necessary for the continued existence of a substance, was a central element in Aristotle's account of substances. But now we have seen that persons can survive (it is logically possible) without their bodily matter continuing to be part of them. In this situation we have a choice. Either we can say simply that persons are different—in their case continuing matter is not necessary for the continued existence of the substance. Or we can try to make sense of this fact by liberalizing Aristotle's account a little. We can say that the continuing existence of some of the stuff of which a substance is made is necessary for the continued existence of the substance. Normally the stuff of which substances are made is merely matter, but some substances (viz.

persons) are made in part of immaterial stuff, soul-stuff. Given, as I suggested earlier, that persons are indivisible, it follows that soul-stuff comes in indivisible chunks, which we may call souls.

This liberalized Aristotelian assumption I will call the quasi-Aristotelian assumption: that a substance S_2 at t_2 is the same substance as an earlier substance S_1 at t_1 only if S_2 is made of some of the same stuff as S_1 (or stuff obtained therefrom by gradual replacement).

Given the quasi-Aristotelian assumption, and given, that for any present person who is currently conscious, there is no logical impossibility, whatever else may be true now of that person, that that person continue to exist without his body, it follows that that person must now actually have a part other than a bodily part which can continue, and which we may call his soul—and so that his possession of it is entailed by his being a conscious being. For there is not even a logical possibility that if I now consist of nothing but matter and the matter is destroyed, that I should nevertheless continue to exist. From the mere logical possibility of my continued existence there follows the actual fact that there is now more to me than my body; and that more is the essential part of myself. A person's being conscious is thus to be analysed as an immaterial core of himself, his soul being conscious.[5]

If we are prepared to say that substances can be the same, even though none of the stuff (in a wide sense) of which they are made is the same, the conclusion does not follow. The quasi-Aristotelian assumption provides rather a partial definition of 'stuff' than a factual truth. To say that a person has an immaterial soul is not to say that if you examine him closely enough under an acute enough microscope you will find some very rarified constituent which has eluded the power of ordinary microscopes. It is just a way of expressing the point within a traditional framework of thought that persons can—it is logically possible—continue, when their bodies do not. It does, however, seem a very natural way of expressing the point—especially once we allow that persons can become disembodied. Unless we adopt the more liberal quasi-Aristotelian assumption, we shall have to say that there can be substances which are not made of anything, and which are the same substances as other substances which are made of matter.

There is therefore abundant reason for saying that a man

---
[5] See Additional Note 2.

consists of body plus soul. A man's physical properties (e.g. having such-and-such a shape and mass) clearly belong to his body and to the person in virtue of belonging to his body. If the man dies and ceases to exist (i.e. his soul ceases to exist), there need (logically) be no change in the way those properties characterize his body. A man's pure mental properties, however, belong to his soul and to the man in virtue of belonging to his soul; for it is logically possible that those properties continue to characterize the person who is that man, when his body is destroyed. Hence mixed properties belong to the person in virtue of their physical-component properties belonging to his body and their pure mental-component properties belonging to his soul.

Note that on the dualist view which I am expounding, although the identity of persons at different times is constituted by the identity of their souls (and these are not publicly observable things), it remains the case that all claims about personal identity are verifiable, in the sense that there can be evidence of observation for or against them. For although continuity of brain and of apparent memory (i.e. a man's apparent memory of who he was and what he did) do not constitute personal identity, they are evidence of it, and so evidence of sameness of soul. Why they are evidence of personal identity is an issue to which I shall come in the next chapter.

And not merely are all claims about personal identity verifiable via observations of other things, but over a short period personal identity is itself experienceable by the subject, as directly as anything can be experienced, in the continuity of his perceptions and other mental events. Human perception is perception of change. The perceptual beliefs to which our senses give rise are not just beliefs that at one time things were arranged thus, and at another time in a different way, and at a third in yet a third way. For as a result of perception we come to know not merely what happened, but in what order things happened—that first things were arranged like this, and subsequently like that, and yet subsequently like that. Sometimes, of course, we infer from our perceptions and our general knowledge of how things happen in the world, the order in which those perceptions and so the events perceived[6] must have occurred. Knowing that, in general, babies

---

[6] We learn through perceptions of the effects which we ourselves bring about that, in general, spatially near events are perceived at approximately the instant of their occurrence. See my *Space and Time*, Macmillan, London, second edition, 1981, p. 145.

get bigger and not smaller, I may infer that my seeing the small baby John occurred before my seeing the medium-sized baby John, which occurred before my seeing the large baby John. But not all knowledge of the order of our perceptions can derive from inference. For first, we have much knowledge of the actual order of perceptions, when as far as our general knowledge of the world goes, the events perceived could as easily occur in one order as in the other—such as a ball moving on a particular occasion from left to right rather than from right to left. And secondly, in order to infer the order of our perceptions, we need that general knowledge of the order in which events of the kind perceived occur. Yet our beliefs about the latter (e.g. our knowledge that in general babies get bigger) would be without justification (and so would not amount to the knowledge which we surely rightly believe them to be) unless they were grounded in many perceptions made by ourselves or others of actual such successions.

So the perceptual beliefs to which our senses give rise include (and must include if we are to have knowledge, grounded in experience) beliefs about the order in which things happen. That is, we perceive things happening in a certain order. The most primitive things which an observer sees include not just the train being here, but also the train moving from here to there, from there to the third place. When a train moves along a railway line, the observer S on the bank has the following successive perceptions: S sees (train T at place p followed by T at place q); S sees $(T$ at q followed by T at $r)$; S sees $(T$ at r followed by T at $u)$, and so on. He acquires the belief that things were as perceived. But then that is not quite a full description of the beliefs which he acquires through perception. For if those were all his data, he would have no grounds for believing that the second event which I have described succeeded the first event (rather than being one which occurred on an entirely different occasion). Why he does have such grounds is because he also acquires, through having the succession of perceptions, the further perceptual beliefs that the first perception is succeeded by the second perception, and that the second perception is succeeded by the third perception. He acquires, through experience, knowledge of temporal succession. And, more particularly, the further perceptual beliefs which he acquires are that *his* first perception is succeeded by his second perception, and so on. The content of his further perceptual beliefs is that there has been a succession of perceptions had by a common subject, viz. himself. Using the word 'experience' for a brief moment in a wide sense, we may say that the succession of perceptions is itself a datum of experience; *S* experiences his experiences as overlapping in a stream of awareness. As John Foster, to whom I owe this argument, puts it, 'It is this double overlap which provides the sensible continuity of sense experience and unifies presentations [i.e. perceptions] into a stream of awareness . . . It is in the unity of a stream that we primarily discern the identity of a subject'.[7] That is, one of a subject's basic data is of the continuity of experience, which means the continuity of the mental events of a common subject, the person.

In a famous passage Hume wrote: 'When I enter most intimately into what I call *myself*, I always stumble on some particular perception or other, of heat or cold, light or shade, love or hatred, pain or pleasure. I never catch *myself* at any time without a perception'.[8] It may well be that Hume never catches himself without a 'perception' (i.e. a conscious episode) but his bare datum is not just 'perceptions', but successions of overlapping 'perceptions' experienced by a common subject. If it were not so, we would have no grounded knowledge of succession. Hume says that he fails to find the common subject. One wonders what he supposed that the common subject would look like, and what he considered would count as its discovery. Was he looking for a common element in all his visual fields, or a background noise which never ceased? Is that the sort of thing he failed to find?[9] Yet the self which he ought to have found in all his mental events is supposed to be the subject, not the object of perception. And finding it consists in being aware of different mental events as had by the same subject.

Further, among the data of experience are not merely that certain mental events are the successive mental events of a

---

[7] J. Foster, 'In *Self*-Defence' in (ed.) G. F. MacDonald, *Perception and Identity*, Essays presented to A. J. Ayer, Macmillan, London, 1979, p. 176.
[8] *A Treatise of Human Nature*, 1. 4. 6.
[9] Because our awareness of ourselves is different in kind from our awareness of objects of experience, Berkeley chose to say that we have a 'notion' of the former but an 'idea' of the latter. 'To expect that by any multiplication or enlargement of our faculties we may be enabled to know a spirit as we do a triangle, seems as absurd as if we should hope to see a sound'—G. Berkeley, *Principles of Human Knowledge*, 1710, § 142.

common subject, but also that certain simultaneous mental events are states of a common subject. At a single moment of time you feel cramp in your leg, hear the noise of my voice, and see the movement of my arms. It is among the data of your experience (i.e. among basic data, not inferable from anything closer to experience) that these are all *your* mental events.

Yet that mental events are states of the same subject is something that knowledge of brains and their states and knowledge of which mental events were occurring would be insufficient to tell you. As I noted earlier, some sensory nervous impulses (including those from the right-side limbs and right sides of the two eyes) go in the first instance to the left brain hemisphere, and some (including those from the left-side limbs and the left sides of the two eyes) go to the right brain hemisphere; and the two hemispheres control different parts of the body (the left hemisphere controlling speech, as well as the right arm and leg). However, in the normal brain the signals to one hemisphere are immediately transmitted to the other, and the 'instructions' given by one are correlated with events in the other. But if the brain operation of cerebral commissurotomy (cutting the main tract between the two hemispheres) is performed, the hemispheres act in a much more independent way, and it is a crucial issue whether by the operation we have created two persons. Experimenters seek to discover by the responses in speech, writing or other means whether one subject is co-experiencing the different visual, auditory, olfactory, etc. sensations caused through the sense organs or whether there are two subjects which have different sensations. The subject (or subjects) is aware of one or more kinds of sensation and the experimenter seeks to elicit information about his (or their) sensations from him (or them). That is not quite as easy as it sounds. If the mouth confesses to seeing a green object but not to hearing a loud noise; while the left hand denies seeing a green object, but claims instead to hear a loud noise; that is not enough in itself to show that no subject co-experienced a loud noise and saw a green object. For, first, mouth and hand may sometimes, as may any limb, give a reflex response to a question rather than a considered judgement (the reflex may be out of a subject's control without being in the control of some other subject), and the reflexes available to different limbs may relate to information of different kinds (the left hand may be able by pointing to give the answers to questions about objects presented to the left side of the visual field only without the subject being aware of the objects presented and/or the responses of the hand); and secondly, there may be kinds of belief (about his mental events) which the split-brain subject can convey only by one means rather than another. The effect of cerebral commissurotomy is not immediately evident, and various complex experiments are needed before any one hypothesis about what has happened can gain significant support.

That hypothesis about how many subjects of experience and action, i.e. persons, there are, will be best supported the better it can be filled out as a detailed claim about which beliefs, desires, and other mental events the one or more different subjects have, which explains in a simple way many observed data. For example a hypothesis that there are two persons becomes more plausible if we can in certain circumstances attribute to each not merely distinct sensations and beliefs about them, but distinct beliefs and desires of a general character, i.e. different views about what is good and bad in the world, and different inclinations to bring about long-term states of affairs, and these different beliefs and desires are continuing beliefs which explain whole patterns of limb movements—e.g. the left hand and the mouth express different complex moral claims. For then the patterns of response of the different sets of limbs would be more analogous to the conscious responses of men by which they manifest beliefs of which they are conscious, than to patterns of mere unconscious reflex. And it would be simpler to suppose that similar patterns of response (of all limbs in normal persons, and of one set of limbs in split-brain persons) have similar explanations (viz, in distinct sets of beliefs and desires) than to suppose that the unity of response in the latter case does not arise from the unity of a person with a continuing mental life.[10]

What is clear in these cases is that what the investigator is trying to discover is something other than and beyond the pattern of the subject's responses, as it is also something other than and beyond

[10] On the results and interpretation of such experiments, see Springer and Deutsch, op. cit., chs. 2 and 10, articles referred to therein (especially J. E. LeDoux, D. H. Wilson, and M. S. Gazzaniga, 'A Divided Mind: Observations on the Conscious Properties of the Separated Hemispheres', *Annals of Neurology*, 1977, **2**, 417–21), and, most recently, D. M. and Valerie Mackay, 'Explicit Dialogue Between Left and Right Half-Systems of Split Brains', *Nature*, 1982, **295**, 690–1.

the extent of the connections between the two hemispheres. That something is whether there are one or two subjects of experience and action, i.e. persons. Whether one person is having both sensations is something of which he will be immediately aware, but which others have to infer (fallibly) from the complex public data. In considering simultaneous experience as in considering experience over time, we see that which persons are the same as other persons are facts additional to publicly observable facts. Dualism can make sense of why there is sometimes (i.e. in cases of cerebral commissurotomy) a difficult problem of discovering how many persons there are. Dualism, in claiming that a person is body plus soul, explains the problem as the problem of discovering the number of souls connected to a given brain. Since the outsider can only discover this by fallible inference from bodily behaviour and brain-states, discovering the answer can be difficult and we can always go wrong. However, co-experience is no artifical construct; it is as primitive a datum of experience for the subject as anything could be. The subject's awareness is an awareness of himself as the common subject of various sensations (and other mental events).

My conclusion—that truths about persons are other than truths about their bodies and parts thereof—is, I suggest, forced upon anyone who reflects seriously on the fact of the unity of consciousness over time and at a time. A framework of thought which makes sense of this fact is provided if we think of a person as body plus soul, such that the continuing of the soul alone guarantees the continuing of the person.

9. THE EVIDENCE OF PERSONAL IDENTITY

WHAT are the criteria that some person P_2 at time t_2 is the same person as a person P_1 at an earlier time t_1—e.g. that the person lecturing to you one week is the same person as lectured to you the previous week; or more extravagantly, that some ghost who appears to you one week is the same ghost as appeared to you in a previous week. Personal identity being constituted by sameness of soul, my question boils down to—what are the criteria which show that the souls are the same? By the criteria, I mean the discoverable evidence which renders some claim of identity probable; fallible evidence, not certain evidence which conclusively proves personal identity.

The two main criteria which philosophers discuss are the criterion of brain continuity and the criterion of apparent (personal) memory. As we saw in the last chapter, the brain-continuity criterion derives from a bodily criterion. The brain is taken as the core of the body which determines personal identity because it is that bodily organ whose continuing normally guarantees the continuing of apparent memory and character. The brain-continuity criterion is satisfied to the extent to which P_2 at t_2 has the same brain as P_1 at t_1; in so far as some of that brain has been removed and replaced by other brain material, and in so far as such removal has been sudden and not gradual, to that extent the criterion is not satisfied.

Personal memory, as I defined it in Chapter 7, is memory of a man's own deeds and experiences. It is to be distinguished from remembering how (e.g. to swim or to ride a bicycle) and from mere factual memory, which is simply the continuing availability of knowledge previously known (e.g. that $2 + 2 = 4$, or that the Battle of Hastings was fought in 1066), because it was previously known and has remained with the subject. Personal memory is revived knowledge of one's own deeds and experiences, which one has because it has remained in one during the intervening period and is not caused by external causes such as being told about one's experiences by some witness or reading of them in one's diary.

Apparent personal memory is whatever seems to the subject to be personal memory, although he may misremember. The criterion of apparent memory is satisfied to the extent to which P_2 seems to remember doing and experiencing whatever P_1 did and experienced, and to the extent to which they share apparent (personal) memories of the past earlier than t_1; or to the extent to which P_2 and P_1 are connected by a chain of continuous apparent (personal) memory—viz. there are intermediate persons P', P'' such that P_2 seems to remember doing and experiencing whatever P' did and experienced; P' seems to remember doing and experiencing whatever P'' did and experienced; P'' seems to remember doing and experiencing whatever P_1 did and experienced; and there are similar links of shared apparent memories of the past. To the extent to which I apparently remember or am linked by a chain of apparent memory to someone who was called 'Richard Swinburne' and looked like me last year, to that extent the criterion of apparent memory for me being him is satisfied. If it is satisfied because there is much brain continuity between the two persons (as there normally will be), then to that extent the criterion of brain continuity will also be satisfied. But the criterion of apparent memory could be satisfied when there is no brain continuity. And the criterion of brain continuity could be satisfied when there is no apparent memory; because although normally brain continuity produces continuity of apparent memory, it need not do so always (as with the amnesiac who is entirely ignorant of the past of the person with his body and brain).

What a person apparently remembers is something known infallibly to himself (because it is a belief, and a subject knows his beliefs infallibly), but known to others only in so far as he chooses to tell them; and he may lie or be silent about his apparent memories. However, by the principle of testimony, we ought to believe what anyone claims that he has experienced, in the absence of counter-evidence. To the criterion of apparent memory is normally added a lesser criterion, that of continuity of character. There is continuity of character between P_2 and P_1 to the extent to which P_2 has the same central beliefs about the world (including moral beliefs) and the same general desires, leading to the same natural reactions to circumstances; or they are connected by a chain of persons with similar characters to those adjacent to them in the chain. The criterion is less central, because obviously sometimes people do change their characters quite rapidly; and anyway many people have very similar characters. For the sake of simplicity of exposition, I shall largely ignore this addition to the criterion of apparent memory.

When the two criteria of brain continuity and apparent memory are well satisfied—when P_2 has the same brain (without any splitting) as P_1 at t_1, and apparently remembers deeds and experiences which were in fact done and had by P_1, then P_2 is beyond reasonable doubt the same person as P_1. And when the two criteria are clearly not satisfied—when P_2 has none of P_1's brain and apparently remembers none of his deeds and experiences—then beyond reasonable doubt P_2 is a different person from P_1. Most questions of personal identity can be settled with as much certainty as most matters of factual dispute; although, as with most such matters, there is no infallible knowledge to be had. Whether your claim is about recent political history, or atoms and molecules, or life on Mars, you can never verify them in such a way as to put them beyond all possible future controversy. The same applies to claims about personal identity. Serious dispute only arises when the two cited criteria give uncertain or conflicting answers; and we shall be able to shed a little light on how evidence is to be weighed in such cases later in the chapter.

Although the two tests of brain continuity and apparent memory (and character) are those most discussed by philosophers, clearly in practice we use other tests too; and it is important to see the relation of these subsidiary tests to the primary tests. The most frequent test to be used is the test of similarity of visual appearance. You judge some man to be the man who was lecturing to you last week because he looks like him. To similarity of visual appearance, we must add similarity of appearance to the other senses—e.g. sound of voice (and, no doubt, for people with poor vision and hearing, smell or feel). Similarity of a person's appearance covers not only instantaneous appearance, but appearance over time in the ways in which he manifests his presence—e.g. the way he walks, and the gestures he makes. More technical tests used today are sameness of fingerprints and blood groups.

Evidently the latter tests are used because they are evidence that other of the tests, more difficult to apply, would be satisfied if we could use them. We use fingerprints as evidence of personal identity because of an empirical discovery (suspected many centuries ago, but established fairly well scientifically in the nineteenth century) that when two persons are by other criteria pretty conclusively the same, they have the same fingerprints, and when two persons are by other criteria pretty conclusively distinct, they have distinct fingerprints. That suggests that when we have evidence of sameness of fingerprints but no other evidence one way or the other about some more central test of personal identity such as bodily continuity, nevertheless bodily continuity holds. Fingerprints are thus indirect evidence of personal identity, in the sense that they are evidence of what would be shown by other and more central criteria of personal identity. The same evidently goes for blood groups and other physiological tests.

What of similarity of appearance? It, too, I would suggest, is an indirect test in the stated sense. We take similarity of appearance at different times as evidence of personal identity because we believe it to be evidence of bodily identity and this (via brain identity) to be evidence of personal identity. (Likewise we take dissimilarity of appearance to be evidence against personal identity, because we believe it to be evidence against bodily identity). We can see the test to be an indirect one for the reason that if two persons P_2 at t_2 and P_1 at an earlier time t_1 looked the same but were shown to have totally different bodies, the similarity of their appearance would in no way be regarded as grounds for supposing them to be the same person. We do, however, take similarity of appearance as evidence of sameness of body, and thereby of personal identity, because we believe that in general each body has a distinctive appearance—two bodies observed at different times which are to all appearances qualitatively indistinguishable are very probably the same body; and two bodies observed at different times which are qualitatively distinct in appearance are very probably different bodies. Our grounds for this belief is that, when we keep bodies under observation for limited periods, any great change of appearance is very rare indeed, and bodies of totally similar appearance are also very rare indeed. It is simpler to suppose that this constancy and distinctness of appearance holds when bodies are not under observation, as well as when they are; rather than to suppose that things change suddenly when we are not observing them.

We find by experience the limits to the application of the criterion of similarity of appearance, and the ways in which it should be applied. Thus we find that appearance changes gradually with time; faces become lined, hair becomes grey. We know this because we observe that often a body which we judge to be the same as a body observed on the previous day on the basis of its similarity of appearance, and to be the same as a body on the day before that, on the basis of similarity of that to the body on the middle day, and so on until you reach a body years earlier, looks different if you compare its appearance directly with its appearance years earlier. Having discovered empirically the ways in which appearances change, we can then allow for these (i.e. discount differences in appearance of bodies observed at intervals of a number of years in respect of face-lining and hair colour) in judging similarity of appearance.

Again, we learn empirically (from those who have kept bodies under continuous observation and judged them to be the same body on the basis of similarity of appearance of most of their parts) that sometimes some parts of bodies (e.g. faces as a result of plastic surgery) change their appearance very quickly. But because such events are rare, we take radical difference of appearance to show distinctness of body, in the absence of evidence of the occurrence of such an event as plastic surgery. Also, we learn empirically, by seeing them side by side, that sometimes two different bodies are indistinguishable in appearance. (There are identical twins.) And in those cases we hesitate to take similarity of appearance as evidence of sameness of body.

So then similarity of appearance at different times is an indirect criterion of personal identity, because it is evidence of bodily identity which in turn is evidence of personal identity. But we have already seen in Chapter 8 that bodily identity is only used as evidence of personal identity, given that the body retains the same brain. In other words, because brain transplants (very probably) do not yet occur, bodily identity is now wellnigh conclusive evidence of brain identity. So it too is indirect evidence of personal identity. And why is brain identity so important? As we have seen, we choose the brain as the organ whose continuity is vital for personal identity because it is that organ, the continuity of which normally guarantees continuity of apparent memory and character. If P_2 and an earlier P_1 have the same brains, P_2 will in general apparently remember the deeds and experiences of P_1 and behave in somewhat similar ways to P_1. And if (as neurophysiology leads us reasonably to suppose) brains are split, both hemispheres or smaller parts of the brain would bring about some continuity of apparent memory and character in the persons into whose skull they were transplanted. Our selection of brain continuity as evidence of personal identity, because that is that part of the body which is correlated with continuity of apparent memory and character, suggests that but for a correlation with apparent memory and character we would not use any part of the body as evidence of personal identity.

We can see that that is so by asking ourselves what we would say if the following occurred. Suppose that a person in body B_1 on even days apparently remembered (almost) everything done and experienced by the person in another body B_2 on odd days, but nothing done and experienced by the person in B_1 on odd days nor anything done and experienced by the person in B_2 on even days. Conversely the person in B_1 on odd days and the person in B_2 on even days have the same apparent memories, which concern the deeds and experiences only of the person in B_1 on odd days and the person in B_2 on even days. These apparent memories of deeds and experiences are true beliefs about what was done and experienced by a person with the body in question. Suppose too that character goes with apparent memory (e.g. that the persons in B_1 on odd days and B_2 on even days have the same character), and that there are no transplants of any parts of the body.

If this kind of apparent body-swap was a normal, regular, exceptionless feature of life, it seems patently obvious that we would not claim that bodily continuity (or continuity of any part thereof) ensured personal identity. What might be more open to question is whether we would then claim that a person was who he apparently remembered that he was. Might we not suppose instead that persons lasted for only one day? It seems to me unlikely that we would suppose this in view of the enormous continuity of memory, and the general beliefs and attitudes towards the world which are involved in character, which I suppose to hold between people in different bodies on different days. I suggest that in these circumstances not merely would we suppose that personal identity went with apparent memory, but that we would be right to suppose this. That we would be right follows directly from the principle of credulity itself.

Recall that by apparent memory we mean apparent personal

memory, and that this is simply what it seems to the subject that he did or experienced where that seeming seems to be caused by his own past deeds and experiences. Apparent memories may be shown in various ways not to be genuine memories—e.g. by showing that no one did the things which the subject purports to remember, or by showing that the source of his information was a diary. But although apparent memories may be shown not to be genuine memories, they are, I suggest, to be taken at their face value as evidence of that of which they are apparent memories, in the absence of counter-evidence. For by the principle of credulity, a subject ought to believe that things are as (epistemically) they seem to him—in the absence of counter-evidence. If it seems to me that there is in front of me a brown table, or a Greek vase, then probably there is; and I ought so to believe, unless counter-evidence turns up. Reliance on apparent memory is just a special application of the principle of credulity. For apparent memory is it seeming to the subject that he did and experienced certain things, and that this seeming has its source in past knowledge. Apparent personal memory is a special kind of apparent memory. Reliance on it is therefore justified, unless it conflicts with other evidence— the testimony of other men about what happened or some general theory of how the world works which it seems to us to be true (no doubt because we remember having read that it was well supported by experimental test).

An objector might say that one is justified in believing one's apparent memory only if it coincides with the apparent memory of someone else. But a man often believes his memory of what he alone has seen, and intuitively it seems right so to do. Anyway, after someone else has borne testimony to his apparent memory which coincides with yours, your subsequent reliance on the joint memory depends on your own apparent memory of the coincidence between what you did and what he claimed to remember.

For knowledge of the past it needs to be the case that there are people to whom it seems that so-and-so happened. Then in the absence of counter-evidence, we ought to believe that so-and-so did happen; and that gives us a start in constructing our picture of the past. But in practice it is not going to seem to us that so-and-so happened, unless such seeming comes to us in the form of an apparent personal memory that we saw so-and-so happen, or made so-and-so happen. There may be the odd person who is absolutely convinced that his father was born in 1900, although he denies any source for his knowledge in the way of being told this or having read it in a book or whatever. But in general all claims to knowledge of the past depend directly or indirectly on apparent personal memory, and the knowledge so obtained suggests that other claims are unreliable. I may make a discovery about the past by looking at my diary or someone's record of his experiments. But the diary or record only records what it seemed to the subject that he apparently personally remembered. If I rely on some geological or chemical method for inferring from present traces to their past causes, I or someone else who tells me, need apparently to remember seeing that certain experiments had certain results which makes its probable that those methods are reliable, and so on. Knowledge of what happens to brains and their parts is also ultimately dependent on the apparent personal memory of observers who kept them under observation.

Even if there were other sources of knowledge of the past which did not depend on apparent personal memory, it certainly still follows from the principle of credulity that it is right to rely on apparent personal memory, among any such sources, in the absence of counter-evidence. This general argument confirms that in the apparent body-swap thought experiment, we would be right to judge that a person did and experienced the things he apparently remembered having done and experienced, and so was who he apparently remembered that he was.[1]

The division between what we perceive and what we remember having perceived is a fairly arbitrary one. Do I remember what I first came to know through perception two seconds ago, or is it part of what I am still perceiving? The boundaries of the 'specious present' are unclear. My memory of what I perceived merges into my present perception. So my memory of who I was merges into my awareness of myself as a common subject of different perceptions at very close moments of time, which I discussed in the last chapter.

---

[1] Joseph Butler (in his essay 'Of Personal Identity') gives an argument of this kind for relying on apparent memory as evidence of personal identity, concluding that 'it is ridiculous to attempt to prove the truth of those perceptions, whose truth we cannot otherwise prove, than by other perceptions of exactly the same kind with them, and which there is just the same ground to suspect; or to attempt to prove the truth of our faculties, which cannot otherwise be proved, by the use of means of those very suspected faculties themselves.'

So brain continuity provides only indirect evidence of personal identity; our justification for using it is that in general when, and only when, two persons P_2 at t_2 and P_1 at t_1 are connected by continuity of apparent memory (viz. P_2 apparently remembers the deeds and experiences of P_1 or is connected with P_1 by a chain of such persons) they also have the same brain; and that is reason to suppose that where parts of brains are transplanted, persons connected at any rate by some continuity of brain matter are also connected by continuity of apparent memory. This evidence of what almost invariably happens makes brain continuity in some particular case strong evidence of personal identity—in the absence of counter-evidence—when we do not have any evidence from apparent memory.

But what about where a person P_2 has no apparent memory of the deeds and experiences of P_1, even though he tries to recall such deeds and experiences (and they are not connected by any chain of apparent memories)? And what about where the two criteria are in conflict? Suppose that P_2 at t_2 has the same brain as P_1 but apparent memory of the deeds and experiences of some person P_1^* at t_1, with whom no other person at t_2 has continuity of brain or apparent memory? Shall we say that P_2 is P_1 or that he is P_1^*?

Here a different factor enters in. One would expect apparent memory to be sometimes in error. Just as I sometimes misobserve things in front of me now and misremember facts about the positions and properties of material bodies, so one would expect me sometimes to misremember what I did and experienced. I noted earlier two ways in which apparent memories can be shown to be in error. We saw in Chapter 1 that the fundamental principle for correcting any claims accepted via the principle of credulity, is to adopt the simplest theory compatible with a vast number of claims accepted via the principle of credulity, and to reject any remaining claims incompatible with the resulting theory. We correct apparent perceptions (i.e. what it seems to the subject that he is perceiving) and apparent memories of the positions and properties of material bodies, by selecting as the most probable hypothesis the simplest hypothesis about what is perceived or remembered which has the consequence that the overwhelming majority of our apparent perceptions and memories are correct. Application of this fundamental principle of simplicity leads us to adopt more detailed principles with respect to various kinds of bodies—e.g. that metal bodies do not normally change their shape. We then use these principles to reach particular beliefs, e.g. in the way illustrated in Chapter 1 with respect to the round-looking metal object. The detailed principles are themselves corrigible and may need to be corrected or to have exceptions made to them, in order that we may continue to hold correct the overwhelming majority of our apparent perceptions and memories.

It follows from the principles of credulity and simplicity that we ought to deal with apparent memories of who one was in the same kind of way. We find, as we have seen, that in general apparent memory reveals that personal identity goes with brain continuity. It is a simple supposition which has the consequence that the vast majority of our apparent memories are correct, to suppose that brain continuity is in practice a necessary condition of personal identity and hence that apparent memories are in error when they are apparently of the deeds of a person who has none of the subject's brain. That will not tell us what is the right answer when brains are split; nor does it cast any doubt on the fact that the ultimate foundation for the belief that personal identity is carried by brain continuity is apparent memory, and that any general failure of the correlation between continuity of apparent memory and continuity of brain must lead us to take brain continuity no longer as evidence of personal identity.

So then our general reliance on apparent memory is justified a priori, and it shows us—in the absence of counter-evidence—what was done; and, as Reid put it, 'My memory testifies not only that it was done, but that it was done by me who now remembers it.'[2] Some recent writers have wished to restrict reliance on memory to what was done (and experienced), and to deny that we are justified in relying on it (without further empirical evidence) to show who did and experienced what was done and experienced. Parfit[3] claims that the only datum provided by memory is an awareness of psychological continuity, an awareness, that is, of an overlapping series of quasi-memories (memories 'from the inside' that so-and-

   [2] T. Reid, *Essays on the Intellectual Powers of Man*, III, 4.

   [3] D. Parfit, *Reasons and Persons*, Clarendon Press, Oxford, 1984, Part III, 'Personal Identity'. Thus (p. 224): 'As Locke and Kant argued . . . such awareness [of our past experiences] cannot in fact be distinguished from our awareness of mere psychological continuity.' Psychological continuity is defined by Parfit (p. 222) in terms of overlapping quasi-memories.

so was done and experienced, which do not have as part of their content that the doer was the same as the rememberer). But that is just false. It is as much part of what seems to the subject to be the case that he did or experienced so-and-so as that so-and-so was done or experienced. It needs a positive argument to show that memory cannot provide the information which it claims to provide—for otherwise, because of the principle of credulity, its witness must be taken. There are indeed circumstances under which the subject should cease to assume that his apparent memories do concern his own past deeds and experiences. For example, my apparent memories might include apparent memories of the experiences of two different past people, both of whom cannot have been me. Then, for those experiences I should cease to make the assumption that my apparent memories must be about my own experiences. And if that kind of experience was very common indeed, I would cease to rely on apparent memory as evidence of what I experienced and merely rely on it as evidence of what was experienced.

But the same argument applies to any facet of memory. If my apparent memories prove mistaken—as shown by other of my apparent memories and by the evidence of others, ultimately dependent on their apparent memories—in some respect, I cease to rely on them in that respect. If it proves that my apparent memories of faces are unreliable in that I fail by means of them correctly to identify people, I rely on their voices instead. If it proves that I cannot remember what I did more than twenty years ago, I rely in this respect on the memories of others instead. But in the absence of such positive counter-evidence, I have every justification for relying on my apparent memory. If I do not, then, as we saw, I can have no knowledge of the world.

There is a well-known argument[4] which could be deployed to back up Parfit's position, although it is not one which he uses himself. Claims about publicly observable past events involved in claims of apparent memory can be checked. If I claim (because it seems to me that I saw it) that there was a hole in the road yesterday, my claim can be checked, by finding others who apparently remember observing the same thing. But my claim that I myself did or experienced something (e.g. saw the hole) is

---

[4] See S. Shoemaker, *Self-Knowledge and Self-Identity*, Cornell University Press, Ithaca, NY, 1963, especially pp. 199–202.

uncheckable unless my body is evidence of my presence. If I claim to have been in London, my claim is checkable only if the presence of my body in London is evidence of the presence of me in London and its absence is evidence of my absence. So without some sort of physical evidence of a person's presence—and the obvious evidence is that provided by the bodily criterion of personal identity (as amended to a brain criterion)—a person's claims to the effect that he was the person who did and experienced certain things would be uncheckable. So, the argument could go, apparent memory is to be believed where it can be checked—e.g. about physical matters—but not where it cannot be checked; and it can only be checked in its claims about a person's past deeds and experiences if we rely on the bodily criterion of personal identity. Hence the primacy of the bodily criterion (and, through it, of the brain criterion) over the memory criterion.

This argument is not to be accepted. To start with it assumes that if there is no possibility of cross-checking some claim, either that claim has no truth-value or at any rate no one is justified in believing it. These are very dubious assumptions, but even if we grant them, it remains the case that apparent memory can itself be checked by apparent memory. If P_3 at t_3 apparently remembers the deeds and experiences of P_2 at an earlier time t_2 and of P_1 at a yet earlier time t_1, the reliability of this can be checked by investigating whether P_2 apparently remembered the deeds and experiences of P_1. The claim of P_3 to be identical with both P_2 and P_1 is backed up by the evidence of apparent memory that P_2 and P_1 are identical with each other. This evidence may be obtained by others if at t_2 P_2 made public memory claims and P_3 did likewise at t_3. In order to make public memory claims, P_2 and P_3 must manifest their presence publicly. They may do this by being embodied and speaking through mouths—and this can happen and be seen to happen without our needing to take for granted that they are embodied in the same bodies. The cross-checkable memory claims would then be evidence that the two persons were the same, without any bodily criterion needing to be employed.

It may be urged by an opponent that there must be at least a short period of embodiment in a continuous body (and so satisfaction of the criterion of sameness of body) for memory claims to be identified as the claims of a single claimant at all—five minutes, say, while through the same mouth a man makes his memory claims. But even that is unnecessary. A voice might speak from mid air, and be reasonably judged to be the voice of the same speaker over a period of time by the sameness of its accent and the grammatical and logical coherence of its message; in those circumstances the principle of simplicity shows us that it is more probable that the noises derive from one speaker than from many.

It follows that the criterion of apparent memory can be used and its deliverances can be checked privately and publicly without any reliance on any bodily criterion. The previous argument to show the primacy of the criterion of apparent memory as a criterion of personal identity stands.[5] A person ought to be judged to be (i.e. to have the same soul as) whom he remembers himself to have been. This criterion has to be weighed against other criteria—e.g. bodily continuity. And in a particular case, other criteria may indeed outweigh the memory criterion. But what this chapter sought to show is that this could not happen in general. In general people must be judged to be whom they claim to have been. This verdict must be reached because other criteria derive their ultimate authority from the memory criterion itself. So it can only be outweighed on a particular occasion because in general the memory criterion authenticates some other criterion which outweighs on that occasion the memory criterion. But any general break between the deliverances of the memory criterion and other criteria would destroy the authority of the other criteria.

---

[5] In applying this criterion, we do also bring in, as I noted earlier, sameness of character. Clearly one reason why we use this criterion is that it is found by experience that very often two persons who are the same by any of the other criteria which we have discussed have similar characters, at least if the times involved are not far apart from each other. This criterion is thus to some extent an indirect criterion. This reason is not, however, the only reason. There are a priori considerations why sameness of character may be expected to go with sameness of apparent memory; see my contribution to S. Shoemaker and R. Swinburne, *Personal Identity*, Blackwells, Oxford, 1984, pp. 62–5.

10. THE ORIGIN AND LIFE OF THE SOUL

THE arguments of Chapter 8 showed that a man's having a mental life must be understood as a non-bodily part of the man, his soul, having a mental life. In this chapter I come to the questions of when the soul begins to exist in the individual human (e.g. at conception or at birth), and when it began to exist in evolution (i.e. which non-human animals, if any, have souls). Although the answers to these questions depend in part on the answers to detailed questions of physiology which I shall not attempt to provide, I hope to show what kind of physiological information is relevant to answering my main questions. A crucial philosophical issue which we shall need to consider is what is it for a man to have a soul when he is not having any conscious episodes (e.g. during some periods of deep sleep). The answers to these questions lead me on to two further questions—how far could the science of the future explain the evolution of souls; and are organisms which do not belong to the family of Earth-born animals (e.g. organisms on some distant planet, of a totally different construction from any animal on Earth), or organisms constructed by men by means other than normal sexual reproduction, likely to have souls?

The Existence of Consciousness

The soul may be said to function when it has conscious episodes, (viz. sensations, thoughts, or purposings). The evidence of neurophysiology and psychology suggests most powerfully that the functioning of the soul depends on the operation of the brain.

As we saw in Chapters 2, 4 and 5, any person who has thoughts or purposings, will be aware of them; and although he may have a sensation of which he is not aware, this will only be because he is aware of some other conscious episode. A man who is conscious, will be aware of the fact. (This is not to say that he can put the claim that he is conscious into words; only that if he had the vocabulary, and sought to tell the truth about the matter, he would claim to be conscious.) The evidence available to others that some man is currently conscious will, we saw in earlier chapters, be his testimony and certain patterns of bodily behaviour which manifest his conscious life (e.g. screaming when in pain). At later times a man will have his own apparent memory of his conscious episodes, others will have his testimony to this and their apparent memory of his previous testimony and the patterns of his bodily behaviour. We may call evidence of the above kinds direct evidence of consciousness. (By a person being conscious I understand not his being conscious of his surroundings, but his having conscious experiences. Thus a man knocked out and so rendered unconscious in the former sense may still be having sensations and so be conscious in my sense; the dreamer too is conscious in my sense.) This direct evidence of consciousness is found to be correlated with physiological phenomena. When direct evidence shows that he is conscious, the electrical rhythm of a man's brain, his EEG, is found to have a certain pattern. The EEG varies with the kind of consciousness—there is one kind of EEG rhythm for intense thought, another kind when a man is mentally inactive but awake, another kind when he is dreaming (as evidenced by his own testimony if woken up shortly afterwards); and there are different rhythms for sleep of different kinds, when the man has no recollection of dreaming (if woken up shortly afterwards). EEG rhythms are thus indirect evidence of consciousness. Yet evidence of the connection of EEG rhythm with consciousness, means that (since a man's own apparent memory of whether he was at some time conscious or not can err, like all memory) it can be used to correct apparent memory—e.g. if a man woken up from what by EEG rhythm evidence is deep dreamless sleep claims that he was woken from a long dream, the EEG evidence acts at least to cast doubt on his claim to have been conscious. Thus EEG evidence of consciousness, just like brain evidence of personal identity, though only taken as evidence because of the general correlation of its results with those of apparent memory, acquires independent status and can be used (on particular occasions, though not in general) to correct the deliverances of apparent memory. The same goes for the evidence of rapid eye movements during sleep (REMs) showing that a man is dreaming.

By all this evidence there are periods of deep sleep in which a man is not conscious at all. There are periods during which a man's body shows no pattern of movement evidential (by the criteria of Chapters 2, 4 and 7) of conscious episodes (e.g. he does not speak); subsequently he can recall no conscious episodes. During those periods there are no REMs, and the electrical rhythm of the brain is that characteristic of unconsciousness. So often the evidence is quite unanimous that there are such periods. The absence of consciousness for those periods is clearly dependent on the state of the brain, and not vice versa. A man can be made unconscious—by drugs, being knocked out, etc.—or woken up. The functioning of the soul depends on the correct functioning of the brain.

Given that, what physiology indicates further of course is that there is no conscious life before some point between conception and birth. No one can recall conscious episodes immediately after conception, there are no bodily movements evidential of sensations, thoughts, or purposings, and there is no brain to evince the electrical patterns characteristic of consciousness. The evidence suggests that consciousness originates when the foetus has a brain with the kind of electrical rhythms characteristic of consciousness, viz. about twenty weeks after conception (the time of quickening, the first muscle movements, which are probably connected with the first brain activity).

The Existence of the Soul

What I have argued so far is that without a functioning brain, the soul will not function (i.e. have conscious episodes)—not that it will not exist. But what does it mean to suppose that the soul exists at some time without functioning? The distinction between existence and functioning is clear enough in the case of a material substance, which has some sort of life (e.g. a plant) or some sort of working (e.g. a machine). The substance continues to exist so long as the matter of which it is made continues to exist in roughly the same shape (with the possibility perhaps of gradual replacement of parts). But it functions only so long as normal life-processes or machine-use continue. The clock exists, when it no longer tells the time, so long as the parts remain joined in roughly the normal way; and a dead tree is still a tree, although it no longer takes in water through its roots and sunlight through its leaves.

The distinction is not, however, at all clear in the case of the soul, an immaterial substance. The soul functions while it is the subject of conscious episodes—while it has sensations or thoughts or purposes. But is it still there when the man is asleep, having no conscious episodes? This calls for a decision of what (if anything) we are to mean by saying of some soul that it exists but is not functioning.

We suppose that persons continue to exist while asleep, having no conscious life. In saying that some such person still exists, we mean, I suggest, that the sleeping body will again by normal processes give rise to a conscious life, or can be caused to give rise to a conscious life (e.g. by shaking it), a conscious life which by the criteria of Chapter 9 will be the life of the person existing before sleep. Now, we could describe this latter fact by saying that, although persons only exist while they are conscious, the bodies which they previously owned continue to exist during the periods of unconsciousness and become thereafter the bodies of persons again (indeed the same persons who previously owned those bodies). However, that would be a very unnatural way to talk, largely because it has the consequence that certain substances (persons) are continually popping in and out of existence. Although there seems to me nothing contradictory in allowing to a substance many beginnings of existence, it seems a less cumbersome way to describe the cited fact to say that persons exist while not conscious, and mean by this that normal bodily processes or available artificial techniques can make those persons conscious. This will have the consequence that persons normally have only one beginning of existence during their life on Earth.

Our grounds for saying that persons exist while not conscious are similar to the grounds which I gave in Chapters 6 and 7 for saying that persons have desires and beliefs when they are not aware of them, i.e. that they can easily be made aware of them and that those desires and beliefs will influence their actions when they are put in appropriate circumstances.

Conscious persons consist of body and soul. We could say that souls exist only while conscious; while a person is asleep, his soul ceases to exist but it is made to exist again when he is woken up. But this would be a cumbersome way of talking. It is better to understand by a soul existing when not functioning that normal bodily processes on their own will, or available artificial techniques can, make that soul function. In saying this I am laying down rules for the use of a technical term, 'soul'. With this usage, a soul exists while its owner exists; and a soul will normally have only one beginning of existence during a man's life on Earth.

But the boundaries of this usage are not as clear as they look. It all depends on what we understand by 'normal' bodily processes and 'available' artificial techniques. If a drowned body of a person can be revived by artificial respiration, that person certainly exists before the respiration is given. And the same perhaps goes for the man rendered unconscious through injury who will not become conscious again except by use of the latest techniques available to the best doctors. But what about the man in a coma for reviving whom there are no techniques available to doctors at that place and time, though there will be such techniques usable a few years later? Are there, then, 'available' techniques? If the man's body is kept alive, it is unlikely that he will recover spontaneously, but it is possible. If he recovers, have 'normal processes' made his soul function again? Shall we say that a normal bodily process 'can' make a man's soul function, revive that soul, only if it leads to revival almost invariably, or is it enough that occasionally it shall lead to revival?

Any spelling out of what constitutes 'normal' bodily processes, or 'available' techniques will bring out how arbitrary a matter it often is whether we say that some person exists, although unconscious; or whether we say that he does not exist although perhaps may be caused again to exist. However, if we are to bring precision and consistency into our talk of this matter, we must, I think, develop the account which I have given so far by giving fairly arbitrary stipulative definitions of 'normal' bodily processes and 'available' techniques. If our talk of persons existing is not to depart too wildly from ordinary usage, we must deny that it is sufficient for the existence of a man merely that it is logically possible that he be brought to life again; for in that case all dead men would continue to exist (as a mere logical consequence of once having existed). And if we are to keep our talk about souls in line with our talk about men, we must not say this of souls either. I suggest that we understand in this context by a bodily process being 'normal', that it will yield its outcome with a high degree of predictability given normal nutrition, respiration, etc., without sophisticated medical intervention; and by a technique being 'available', that it is available to doctors during that period of history within a region of the size of the average county. Alternative definitions are possible of what it is for a person and so his soul to exist, when not conscious, but I do not think that they will prove any less arbitrary than the suggested one. (Any definition in terms of it being *naturally* or *physically* possible, for some agent at some time or place, to revive the person runs into the difficulty that there may not be any general laws connecting the physical and the mental—as I shall argue later in the chapter, and so one cannot know what is physically possible in general, only what is practically possible under certain familiar circumstances.) My preferred definition does allow that it sometimes happens that a person (and so his soul) ceases to exist and then by an unexpected accident comes to exist again. It thus allows a substance to cease to exist and then to come into existence a second time; but I cannot see any good reason for not talking in that way. What this discussion will, I hope, have brought out is that little turns on whether some soul exists unfunctioning (e.g. after death). The real issue is just how easy it is to get it to function again.

So, given that the soul functions first about twenty weeks after conception, when does it come into existence? There exist normal bodily processes by which the fertilized egg develops into a foetus with a brain after twenty weeks which gives rise to a functioning soul. If the soul exists just because normal bodily processes will bring it one day to function, it surely therefore exists, once the egg is fertilized, at conception.[1] On the other hand one might say that normal processes need to be fairly speedy ones if the soul is to exist during their operation; and so that the soul begins to exist, only shortly before it first begins to function. Once again it seems an arbitrary matter when we say that the soul begins to exist, requiring a further stipulation as to how 'normal bodily processes' are to be understood. It seems to me somewhat more natural to describe things in the second way. What is important, however, is to keep clear the factual and conventional elements involved in claiming that the soul comes into existence at a certain time.[2]

[1] But not before conception, since the union of the two cells at fertilization constitutes a sharp break, and is hardly a normal process analogous to growth.

[2] That the human soul (the rational or intellectual soul as the medievals called it) comes into being (connected to the body) sometime between conception and birth is the traditional Catholic doctrine. The human soul is present when there is specifically human functioning. In the last century or two it has been normal for Catholic writers and pronouncements to assume that that soul comes into being at conception. St Thomas Aquinas on the other hand held that the fertilized egg began to grow first as an animal (or, alternatively, first as a living non-conscious thing and then as an animal), and only later as a human; that is, it was animated first

Animal Souls

We have seen in earlier chapters how the grounds for attributing a mental life of sensation, thought, purpose, desire, and belief to other men are provided by the pattern of their public behaviour, including above all what they say. There are, as we noted there, similar grounds for attributing a mental life characterized by these elements to the higher animals, especially mammals. They have many reactions to stimuli which cause in them sensations similar to our own. Most mammals cry out when cut or bruised. Complex patterns of animal movement are explicable by combinations of purposes somewhat similar to ones which we have and beliefs acquired in ways similar to those in which we acquire beliefs. Some cat's body might show complex patterns of limb movement which, in the absence of obstacles, might lead to his being in the kitchen; if there is an obstacle a different pattern of movement is initiated which has the same final state, the cat being in the kitchen. (He may go through the window as opposed to the door.) We may explain these movements in a simple way by supposing that he has somewhat similar capacities to ourselves (e.g. his leg movements are intentional actions), the purpose of getting food, the beliefs that there is food in the kitchen, and that going through the door or the window will get him to the kitchen. We can explain his purpose as arising from a desire for food which arises in him with the kind of frequency in which such a desire arises in ourselves. We can explain his beliefs as originating from past stimuli (optical and kinaesthetic) in the same way as such beliefs would be caused in ourselves. Many animal purposes are for goals to achieve which men also have desires, and for reasons which I will give in the next chapter, they will not have purposes to perform actions which they do not desire to perform. Hence their purposes show their desires.

by a sensitive soul (or first by a vegetative soul and then by a sensitive soul) and only later by an intellectual soul (see *Summa Theologiae*, Ia, 76. 3, ad 3 and IIa, IIae, 64. 1). Aquinas owed this view to Aristotle. It was listed as an error by Pope Leo XIII in 1887 (H. Denzinger, *Enchiridion Symbolorum*, 1910). Aquinas would not have denied that abortion was wrong, even when (because done soon after conception) it was not the killing of a human being and so murder. He would have said that it was still wrong in virtue of being the destruction of a potential human being, or the frustration of a natural process. Aquinas's view that the foetus is animated by a human soul only at some time much later than conception, seems to have been a general view in the Western Church until the nineteenth century—see G. R. Dunstan, 'The Moral Status of the Human Embryo: A Tradition Recalled', *Journal of Medical Ethics*, 1984, **1**, 38–44.

In the circumstances in which in humans acquisitions of belief give rise to thought, animals sometimes show the facial signs which humans show when struck by thought; and so the principles of simplicity and charity provide grounds for attributing thoughts to such animals.

The similarity of brain structure and material to that of humans, of the higher animals and especially the mammals, provide further grounds for attributing to them a mental life similar to ours. Many of them have brain parts, similarly constructed out of similar material, the operation of which in humans is found to be necessary for them to have sensations of certain kinds and memories of certain kinds.

But of course the most obvious difference between the higher animals and ourselves is that they do not have a structured language; and this, I shall argue in the next chapter, has the consequence that there are beliefs and thoughts, purposes and desires which we have and they cannot have. It also means that we do not have the kind of evidence about their mental life, which is available to us with respect to the mental lives of other humans; and this means that any conclusions we reach about their mental lives must be much more tentative than any conclusions we may reach about the mental lives of other men.

As we move down the evolutionary scale, and come first to birds, reptiles, and amphibians, and then to the invertebrates such as crabs, spiders, and ants, their patterns of behaviour become much less similar to ours. Their behaviour is very stereotyped. Their behaviour is far less naturally explicable in terms of purposes similar to ours and beliefs acquired in similar ways to ours. They lack any organ very similar to our brain. And so there become less and less grounds for attributing to them a mental life.

At some stage in evolutionary history for the first time some animal became conscious. An organism can have sensations without having mental events of other kinds; and my suspicion is that the conscious life of the first conscious animals was purely sensory, consisting perhaps of smells, pain-sensations, heat-sensations, and touch-sensations. Before that time animals merely withdrew limbs in a reflex way when pricked by a spike or burnt by fire, but felt no pain on being thus stimulated. Now pain and other sensations began to intervene between stimulus and response. Next, I suspect, there evolved creatures who did not merely have limbs moving in some direction, but purposed to move those limbs in order to achieve some goal. Since, as I shall argue, creatures without language cannot have moral concepts, desire alone must move such creatures to action. So desires will have arrived on the evolutionary scene at the same time as purposes.[3] Since the executing of a purpose involves a belief that certain movements will attain the purposed goal (more probably than other movements), beliefs must have been present in all purposing animals. Sooner or later animals must have formulated their beliefs to themselves in thought. Such is my hesitant sketch of the evolution of the facets of consciousness present in our nearest relations, the apes. The exact stages by which the facets evolved may be uncertain. But it seems overwhelmingly certain that seas and rocks do not have such a mental life, and humans do; and so, suddenly or gradually, the mental life must have evolved in the course of evolutionary history. A fairly gradual evolution seems the hypothesis best consonant with the observable data of geology, animal behaviour, and animal physiology.

Evolution has given to animals, and then humans, gradually changing capacities to perform intentional actions and gradually changing powers to acquire by means of the senses true beliefs about the environment. Our animal relatives can through purposing move different limbs and move limbs in different ways from humans; and they have different senses which provide different kinds of information about the world from ours. What embodiment amounts to varies with the agent embodied.

Now the claim which I made in Chapter 8 about the need to describe humans as composed of body and soul applies to conscious animals as well. The moment some animal is conscious, there is a truth about whether he has reason to fear or hope to have the sensations of some later animal; and this truth is one not necessarily revealed by knowledge of what happens to the parts of the animal's body. If you divide my cat's brain and transplant the two halves into empty cat skulls and the transplants take, there is a truth about which subsequent cat is my cat which is not necessarily

---

[3] 'The behaviour of animals that lack reason is prompted by physical appetites and by emotions . . . It would be quite implausible to suppose that the advent of intentional action had to wait until reason began to exercise control'—(Pears, op. cit., p. 213).

revealed by knowledge of what has happened to the parts of my cat's body.

Animals do indeed in my sense have souls. Talk about animal souls as well as human souls was normal in Greek philosophy and Christian medieval thought. The idea of a very sharp division between animals who had no souls, and men who had souls, arrived in the seventeenth century with Descartes and his strange view that animals were unconscious automata. Our experience is against that strange view. The difference between animals and men, as the medievals well recognised, was not that men had a mental life and so souls, and animals did not; but that man had a special kind of mental life (mental capacities which went beyond those of animals) and so a special kind of soul. The medievals called this soul the rational or intellectual soul, as opposed to the animal or sensitive soul.[4]

Scientific Explanation of Animal Evolution

I shall concern myself in Part III with the processes of evolution of the specifically human soul. In this section, I shall ask how far science can explain the process of evolution up to the level of the apes, in other words the evolution of animal souls, which have in common with human souls the mental life of sensation, thought, purposes, desire, and belief. How far can science explain the evolution of these forms of consciousness?

Most writers who discuss the relation of mind and body and consider the possibility of scientific explanation in this field normally make an assumption of one–many simultaneous mind–brain correlation. That is, for each kind of mental event there are one or more kinds of brain-event, such that whenever one of the latter occurs, the former occurs simultaneously and conversely. Thus, given a specific kind of sensation, a round red image of a certain hue and size against a black background, there will be one or more kinds of brain-events such that whenever one of the latter occurs, the image occurs; but the image never occurs without one of the latter occurring. The evidence for this commonly made

---

[4] They also believed that plants had a special kind of soul, a vegetative or nutritive soul. But if the soul is to be thought of, as it is in this book, as a part of the organism rather than simply the principle or law of its behaviour, there are no plant souls. For plants (to all appearances) are not conscious; and hence there is no argument of the kind which I gave for animals and men, for supposing that they have such a constituent part.

assumption is, to say the least, slender. We know that certain areas of the brain need to function if subjects are to have sensations of certain sorts (e.g. auditory sensations); and, as I argued earlier in the chapter, we know that the brain needs to function if subjects are to have mental events at all, but the assumption of one–many correlation is an assumption for which no one has ever produced any detailed evidence. The assumption of one–many mind–brain correlation would follow from the assumptions that every event has a cause, and that all mental events are caused exclusively and instantaneously by brain-events. But I have argued against the latter assumption in Part I and I shall argue against the former assumption in Chapter 13.

However, solely to facilitate subsequent exposition, I shall make the assumption of one–many mind–brain correlation for humans, animals, and any other conscious beings there may be; and show that even with it, central theses of mine about the structure and causal efficacy, and yet ultimate inexplicability, of the soul still follow.

It is often popularly supposed that Darwin's Theory of Evolution by natural selection has given a largely adequate account of animal evolution. While not wishing to deny any claims which Darwin made, I do not think that his theory gets us very far in understanding the process of evolution.

Darwin said that animals had offspring with characteristics varying in various ways from those of their parents. Some giraffes grew taller than their parents, some grew shorter; some grew greener, and some grew browner. Some of these characteristics gave their possessors an advantage in the struggle for survival (e.g. the taller giraffes might be able to reach food more easily than the shorter ones; and the greener giraffes might be more visible to predators than the browner ones). Those giraffes were more likely to survive and so produce offspring. Those offspring would have characteristics varying around a new mean, those of their parents. And again those variations from that mean which helped survival were selected. Hence the evolution of animals with characteristics best adapted for survival in various static or changing ecological niches. The story of animal evolution is the story of the natural selection of those random variations which gave their possessors an advantage in the struggle for survival.

The past hundred and twenty-five years have of course seen

many details added to Darwin's theory. Neo-Darwinism tells us the mechanism of variation (in the sense of which changes in sperm and egg cells produce changes of observable characteristics); reassortment of chromosomes, transfer of genes between chromosomes, mutations of individual genes, and so on; and it has suggested that occasionally such processes may lead to large differences in the characteristics of offspring from those of their parents. And recent work has suggested a large chance element (known as 'genetic drift') in the genes which survive to the next generation. But with such filling-out, Darwin's basic structure remains. The crucial thing to notice about Darwinism is that natural selection is not a method of evolution at all; it is a method of eliminating the less satisfactory variants among those which have evolved. And it will not even eliminate all of those—there are characteristics which, to all appearances, give no advantage in the struggle for survival but which are presumed to survive because they are brought about by the same gene, or complex of genes, as brings about some characteristic which does have such an advantage.

The other determinant of evolution, however, is all important— whatever mechanism it is which determines which variations occur. For, although evolution has been going on for a long time, it has not been going on for an infinite time; and there are many possible variants which evolution has not yet thrown up (even if subsequently to eliminate). Why did no organisms develop with four wheels made of skin and bone, or organisms which eat coal, or organisms with built-in catapults to fire stones? And so on. And so on. The answer must be that DNA or other relevant molecules do not readily mutate to produce genes for such characteristics, but they mutate more readily to produce genes which give rise to organs sensitive to ordinary light-waves, to normal sound-waves, and so on. And why are certain characteristics which give no evolutionary advantage controlled by the same genes as ones which do give such an advantage, while others which give no evolutionary advantage are not so controlled? Again the answer must lie in the chemistry of the genes. So, even as regards normal physical characteristics, at least half (and I would suggest, a great deal more than half) of the explanation of why we have the animals we do lies not in natural selection but in the chemical properties of genetic material which make it more prone to throw up certain variants than others. The major task of explaining why organisms have the physical characteristics they do lies no longer with the theorist of natural selection but with the biochemist.

Given all that, what of mental properties? Take the simplest such property—sensations. There can be a physico-chemical explanation of how an animal's genes cause his nervous system to have a certain structure, and how a mutation in a gene can cause the nervous system of his offspring to have a different structure. It can explain how an animal comes to have organs differentially sensitive to light of this and that range of wavelengths, sensitive to temperature or bodily damage; sensitive to these things in the sense that it responds differently to light of this wavelength from the way it responds to light of that wavelength, and so on. But what physics and chemistry could not possibly explain is why the brain-events to which the impinging light gives rise, in turn give rise to sensations of blueness (as opposed to redness), a high noise rather than a low noise, this sort of smell rather than that sort of smell—why sodium chloride tastes salty, and roses look pink. And the reason why physics and chemistry could not explain these things is that pink looks, high noises, and salty tastes are not the sort of thing physics and chemistry deal in. These sciences deal in the physical (i.e. public) properties of small physical objects, and of the large physical objects which they come to form—in mass and charge, volume and spin. Yet mental properties are different properties from physical properties; and even if there is one–many correlation between mental events and brain-events, physics and chemistry cannot explain why there are these correlations rather than those correlations, and that is because mental properties fall outside the subject matter of physics and chemistry.

But could not physics and chemistry be enlarged so as to become a super-science dealing with both physical and mental properties, and providing explanations of their interactions? I do not think so, for the following reason. To give a scientific explanation of why some event occurred you have to show that, given the previous state of affairs, the laws of nature are such that it had to occur. You explain why the planet today is in this position by stating where it and other heavenly bodies were last month (the initial conditions) and how it follows from Newton's laws of motion and gravitational attraction that those initial conditions would be followed a month later by the planet being where it is today. To provide a scientific explanation you need laws of nature. Laws state what must happen of natural necessity[5] to all objects with certain properties; that is, they will claim, that some generalization 'all As are B' (e.g. have certain properties or do so-and-so) holds of natural necessity. And what will be the evidence that some such generalization does hold of natural necessity? First, of course, no As must have been observed to be not–B; and secondly, normally,[6] many As must have been observed to be B. But that is not enough. All ravens so far observed have been observed to be black. But that is quite inadequate evidence for supposing that 'all ravens are black' is a law of nature. We need evidence to suppose that all ravens so far observed being black is no mere accident of local conditions (i.e. caused by the chance that there hasn't actually occurred any mutation to produce a gene for whiteness in the genotype of raven), but that there could not be a black raven; however molecules were arranged, they could not give rise to a black raven. To show this of some generalization 'all As are B' we need to show not merely that the generalization holds universally, but that it fits neatly into a scientific theory which is a simple theory with few simple purported laws, able to predict a vast range of phenomena. The grounds which men had in the eighteenth century for believing Newton's 'law' of gravity—that all material bodies attract each other in pairs with forces proportional to the product of the masses of each and inversely proportional to the square of their distances apart—to be indeed a law of nature, was that it was a very simple law which fitted into a theory with four 'laws' in all, the others being equally simple, which together were

---

[5] There may be laws, such as those of quantum theory, which state only natural probabilities of things happening, not necessities. See Chapter 13 for further discussion of this. Such natural probabilities as ultimate determinants of the behaviour of objects are, however, to be distinguished from mere long-term frequencies of observed correlations (every A having an in-built propensity of 0.9 to become a B, to be distinguished from ninety per cent of observed As being B). Similar points to those made in the text against the suggestion that discovered mind/brain correlations might be ultimate laws of nature apply whether it is suggested that the laws are laws of natural necessity or laws of natural probability. For the distinction between natural probability (there called 'physical probability') and other kinds of probability (there called 'statistical probability' and 'epistemic probability') see my *An Introduction to Confirmation Theory*, Methuen, London, 1973, chs. 1 and 2.

[6] I write 'normally' because a generalization 'all As are B' deducible from a theory well established by the criteria about to be discussed is reasonably believed to hold of natural necessity, even if no As have been observed.

able to predict a vast range of phenomena. The law of gravity ($F = mm'/r^2$), is simple because the distance is not raised to a complicated power (e.g. we do not have $r^{2.003}$), there is only one term (e.g. we do not have $mm'/r^2 + mm'/r^4 + mm'/r^6$), and so on. The law is also simple for the reason that, given this law and only given this law, the total force exerted by a body on a hollow sphere of given uniform thickness and density centred on the body remains the same, whatever the inner radius of the sphere. The theory with four such simple laws was able to predict with great accuracy the behaviour of bodies of very different kinds in very different circumstances—the motions of planets, the rise and fall of tides, the interactions of colliding bodies, the movements of pendula, etc., etc. Einstein's laws of general relativity are of course more complicated than Newton's, but Einstein claimed for them that they had great coherence and great mathematical simplicity and elegance, at any rate in comparison with the complexity of the data which they were able to explain. I conclude that the evidence that some generalization is a law, as opposed to a mere generalization (holding only perhaps in a limited spatio-temporal realm, or by accident or coincidence), is that it fits into a simple coherent theory which predicts successfully a vast range of diverse data.

Now a scientist, I have assumed, could compile a very, very long list of the correlations between brain-events and sensations, stating which sensation occurs (e.g. a blue elliptical image) when a given brain-event occurs. These correlations would be generalizations, stating that all brain-events of this kind occur at the same time as sensations of that kind (i.e. correlations of the form 'always whenever this brain-event, that sensation'). The correlations would be established by noting the brain-states which occurred when observers reported having some sensation and not otherwise. In order to get exceptionless lists scientists would suppose that on some few occasions to mislead the scientist, or through inadequate grasp of sensory vocabulary or through misobservation (as illustrated on p. 32), observers misreported their sensations. Thus scientists would have applied the principles of simplicity and credulity in arriving at their list of correlations. But to explain those correlations we need by our principles to establish a much smaller set of purported laws, from which it follows that this kind of brain-event has to be correlated with a red sensation, that one with a blue sensation; this one with a high note, and that one with a low note. The purported laws would need to fit together into a theory from which we could derive new correlations (e.g. predict some totally new sensation to which some hitherto unexemplified brain-state would give rise). If our purported laws could do all that, that would be grounds for believing them to be indeed laws and so for believing that we had got a scientific explanation of the occurrence of sensations. Then we would be able to say why sodium chloride tastes salty rather than sweet in terms of the brain-event which tasting sodium chloride normally causes, having a natural connection (stated by our theory) with a salty tang. Mere correlation does not explain, and because it does not explain, you never know when your correlations will cease to hold. Because you have no explanation of why all ravens are black, you may reasonably suspect that tomorrow someone will find a white raven.

The list of correlations is like a list of sentences of a foreign language which under certain circumstances translate sentences of English, without any grammar or word-dictionary to explain why those sentences are under those conditions correct translations. In the absence of a grammar and dictionary you do not know when those translations will cease to be accurate (maybe 'blah blah' only refers to the sovereign when the sovereign is male). Nor can you translate any other sentence.

But why should not the scientist devise a theory showing the kinds of correlation discussed to be natural ones? Why should he not postulate entities and properties from whose interactions, the laws of which are simple, it would follow that you get the correlations which you do between brain-events and sensations? Although it is theoretically possible that a scientific theory of this kind should be created, still the creation of such a theory does not look a very likely prospect. Brain-events are such different things qualitatively from pains, smells, and tastes that a natural connection between them seems almost impossible. For how could brain-states vary except in their chemical composition and the speed and direction of their electrochemical interactions, and how could there be a natural connection between variations in these respects and variations in the kind of respects in which tastes differ—say the differences between a taste of pineapple, a taste of roast beef, and a taste of chocolate—as well as the respects in which tastes differ from smells and smells from visual sensations? There does not seem the beginning of a prospect of a simple scientific theory of this kind and so of having established laws of mind–body interaction as opposed to lots of diverse correlations; which, just because they are unconnected in an overall theory, are for that reason not necessarily of universal application. If we cannot have scientific laws we cannot have scientific explanation. The scientist's task of giving a full explanation of the occurrence of a man's sensations seems doomed to failure.[7] For a scientific theory with proposed detailed laws could not be a simple enough theory for us to have reasonable confidence in its truth (i.e. universal application).

The history of science is, it is true, punctuated with many great 'reductions', of one whole branch of science to another apparently totally different, or 'integration' of apparently very disparate sciences into a super-science. Thermodynamics dealing with heat was reduced to statistical mechanics; the temperature of a gas proved to be the mean kinetic energy of its molecules. Optics was reduced to electromagnetism; light proved to be an electromagnetic wave. And the separate sciences of electricity and magnetism came together to form a super-science of electromagnetism. How is it that such great integrations can be achieved if my argument is

---

[7] In his influential paper 'Mental Events' (in his *Essays on Actions and Events*, Clarendon Press, Oxford, 1980) Donald Davidson argued for the identity of the mental and physical by means of an argument which took as one of its premisses that causation involves law; that is, that one event can only cause another if there is a law of nature which lays down that events like the first in some crucial respect necessitate events like the second in some crucial respect. That, I suggest, is false. One event may cause another event without that causal process exemplifying any law-like succession. (On this see G. E. M. Anscombe, 'Causality and Determination', University of Cambridge Inaugural Lecture, reprinted in (ed.) E. Sosa, *Causation and Conditionals*, Oxford University Press, 1975.) We can understand the notion of a 'one-off' causal process, which was not repeated in similar circumstances. In my view, we would not know that a succession of one event by another was a causal succession, as opposed to being a mere accident, unless successions of that kind were fairly common, so that there was a frequently efficacious recipe for bringing about an event similar to the second event—viz. to bring about an event similar to the first event. Such regularity would indicate that there was natural necessity at work. Yet there might be no law (let alone discoverable law) which lays down exactly when such causality operates, or exactly what is the respect in which events have to resemble the first event in order to cause events similar to the second event. The causality in question might be a temporary and not fully reliable feature of some particular spatio-temporal region. It follows that brain-events may cause mental events, and conversely, and be known to do so, without this causality operating in virtue of some natural law.

correct that there cannot be a super-science which explains both sensations and brain-events?

There is a crucial difference between the two cases. All other integrations into a super-science, of sciences dealing with entities and properties apparently qualitatively very distinct, was achieved by saying that really some of those entities and properties were not as they appeared to be; by making a distinction between the underlying (not immediately observable) entities and properties and the phenomenal properties to which they gave rise. Thermo-dynamics was concerned with the laws of temperature exchange; and temperature was supposed to be a property inherent in an object, which you felt when you touched the object. The felt hotness of a hot body is indeed qualitatively distinct from particle velocities and collisions. The reduction was achieved by dis-tinguishing between the underlying cause of the hotness (the motion of molecules) and the sensations which the motion of molecules cause in observers. The former falls naturally within the scope of statistical mechanics—for molecules are particles; the entities and properties are not of distinct kinds. But this reduction has been achieved at the price of separating off the phenomenal from its causes, and only explaining the latter. All 'reduction' of one science to another dealing with apparently very disparate properties has been achieved by this device of denying that the apparent properties (i.e. the 'secondary qualities' of colour, heat, sound, taste, etc.) with which one science dealt belonged to the physical world at all. It siphoned them off to the world of the mental. But then, when you come to face the problem of the sensations themselves, you cannot do this. If you are to explain the sensations themselves, you cannot distinguish between them and their underlying causes and only explain the latter. In fact the enormous success of science in producing an integrated physico-chemistry has been achieved at the expense of separating off from the physical world colours, smells, and tastes, and regarding them as purely private sensory phenomena. The very success of science in achieving its vast integrations in physics and chemistry is the very thing which has made apparently impossible any final success in integrating the world of the mind and the world of physics.

So there is little prospect for a scientific theory of the origin of sensations. But, given that, by some means or other, genes gave such a structure to brains that there occurred brain-events of a kind which did give rise to sensations, can natural selection explain why animals with the capacity to have sensations survived? What evolutionary advantage does the capacity to have sensations give to a creature? If epiphenomenalism were true, there would be no evolutionary advantage in having sensations. For the having of sensations would never make any difference to the animal's behaviour. The capacity to have sensations would have to be the inevitable by-product of some process which did have evolutionary advantage. However, I have argued in earlier chapters that epiphenomenalism is false. It is my pain, not the brain-event which causes it, which causes me to cry out. But this system of ours in which sensations are causally intermediate between stimulus and response will clearly have no evolutionary advantage over a mechanism which produces the same behavioural modifications without going through sensations to produce them. It looks as if there can be mechanisms of the latter kind—are not the light-sensitive, air-vibration-sensitive machines which men are beginning to make, just such machines? Maybe there is a discoverable physico-chemical explanation of why there cannot be (or is not very likely to be produced) a set of genes which will give rise to such a machine, or maybe an organism with sensations has a less cumbersome process for modifying its behaviour (e.g. in response to bodily damage) than such an unconscious machine, and for that reason has an evolutionary advantage. Along one of these lines there are possibilities for a Darwinian account of why organisms with a capacity to have sensations have an advantage in the struggle for survival. But there cannot be, we have seen, a discoverable physico-chemical explanation of the origin of such organisms.

What about a physico-chemical explanation of mental events of other kinds—purposings, desires, beliefs, and thoughts? There is exactly the same difficulty in the case of all of these. There is not the ghost of a natural connection between this brain-event and that thought, so that we could understand how a change of this electrochemical kind would give rise to a thought that $2 + 2 = 5$ as opposed to a thought that $2 + 2 = 4$, the thought that there is a table here rather than the thought that there is no solid object here. There is a vast qualitative difference between thoughts with their in-built meanings (their intrinsic propositional content) and mere electrochemical events, so that it seems impossible to construct a theory in terms of which the various correlations between brain-states and thoughts follow naturally, which was simple enough for us to expect to make successful predictions about which new thoughts would be correlated with hitherto unexemplified brain-states. Only if this was done would the theory be one which we would be justified in believing to provide true explanations of the occurrence of thoughts. And what goes for thoughts goes also for desires, purposes, and beliefs which also have intrinsic propositional content. But given that there are certain connections between brain-events and these mental events, what natural selection advantage is possessed by organisms who have these mental events, e.g. a belief (a mental state of which the organism may become aware, expressible as a thought) that there is a table here, as opposed to a mere disposition to avoid bumping into the table and to put things on it (such as presumably are possessed by robots). What advantage is there in the mental awareness as opposed to the unconscious disposition? The corresponding question can be asked with respect to mental events of other kinds. As with sensations, we can sketch a possible answer—maybe organisms with beliefs, etc. will have less cumbersome processes for reacting to their environment than organisms without a mental life who react in the same way, and for that reason the former have greater survival value. (Robots perhaps need more bits and take up more space.) Or maybe it is not possible to have a set of genes produced by recombination of DNA molecules (as opposed to a silicon chip) which will give rise to an organism with complicated abilities to react to the environment, without the organism having beliefs about it and other mental attitudes towards it.

So we have noted one crucial all-important question which is utterly beyond the powers of Darwinism or apparently science itself to answer—why do certain brain-events give rise to certain mental events—and one question on which there are possibilities for a Darwinian answer. There is a third question, to which Darwinism can provide a clear and obviously correct answer as regards beliefs, purposes, desires, thoughts (and perhaps also sensations). This is the question—given the existence of mind/ brain correlations, and given that organisms with a mental life will be favoured in the struggle for survival—why are the brain-events which cause and are caused by mental events, connected with other bodily events and extra-bodily events in the way in which they are. Take beliefs. Why is the brain connected via the optic nerve to the eye in such a way that the brain-event which gives rise to the belief that there is a table present is normally caused to occur when and only when there is a table present? The answer is evident—animals with beliefs are more likely to survive if their beliefs are largely true. False beliefs, e.g. about the location of food or predators, will lead to rapid elimination in the struggle for survival. If you believe that there is no table present, when there is one, you will fall over it, and so on. Those in whom the brain-states which give rise to beliefs are connected by causal chains to the states of affairs believed, are much better adapted for survival than those whose belief–brain-states are not so connected and who in consequence tend to have false beliefs. Many animals have a built-in mechanism for correcting in the light of experience any tendency to acquire false beliefs by a certain route—e.g. finding frequently that an object of a certain kind which looks like food is really not food, they cease to acquire the belief that there is food in front of them when they receive visual stimuli from an object of that kind. Such animals are more likely to survive and produce offspring. A similar account can be given of why the brain-events produced by purposes give rise to the movements of body purposed. If, when I tried to move my foot, my hand moved instead, predators would soon overtake me. Similarly, given that I am going to have desires caused by brain-events, there are evolutionary advantages in my having some under some circumstances rather than others under other circumstances—e.g. desire for food when I am hungry rather than when I am satiated.

So then, in summary, the evolution of the mental life of animals (i.e. animals having souls with certain mental events) is a matter of (1) there existing certain physical/mental connections (certain physical events causing certain mental events, and conversely); (2) animals with brains, whose states are connected to mental states, having survival value; (3) evolution selecting animals whose brains are 'wired in' to their bodies in certain ways. Darwinian mechanisms can explain quite a lot of (3), and possibly some of (2); but neither Darwinism nor any other science has much prospect of explaining (1). The origination of the most novel and striking features of animals (their conscious life of feeling, choice, and reason) probably lies utterly beyond the range of science.

I conclude that the process of animal evolution, apparently so regular and predictable, is yet in the respect of those all-important properties of animals (their mental life which makes them, like humans, deserving of kindness and reverence, and which makes them also interact with ourselves) not scientifically explicable. The gradual evolution of the animal soul is a mystery, likely ever to lie beyond the capacity of science to explain. That need not inhibit science from describing this process in all its detail; and indeed trying to explain it. It is simply very unlikely to succeed in explaining what it can most illuminatingly describe. And if science cannot explain the evolution of animals *a fortiori* it cannot explain the evolution of men.

My argument as to the inability of science to provide a well-justified theory containing lawlike statements (i.e. purported laws) which would explain why men and animals have the mental events they do when they do, will also show that we cannot explain why, connected with some brain-events, they have mental events at all. For there is not the ghost of a simple connection between the electrochemical properties of some as opposed to other brain-events, with conscious awareness or propositional content. In other words, scientists will not be able to explain why men and animals have souls which function when they do and how they do. We have good reason to suppose that they do have souls which operate under certain physical conditions, but why they operate under those conditions and hence the limits to those conditions (whether the soul would function under such-and-such unrealized conditions) remains a mystery. There may be some natural law concerning when and how soul and body interact, but my argument suggests that there is not (because our present evidence would count against any suggested law) and in consequence scientists are unlikely to find one. There are reliable correlations between the functioning of the brain and the functioning of the soul in general and in detail. We can predict with justification that very similar brains will have connected with them very similar souls, and similar states of the former will give rise to similar states of the latter. But the source of these correlations remains a mystery. And we do not seem able to produce a well-justified scientific theory; we cannot say what it is about the brain which gives rise to mental events; nor what it is about the soul which requires a brain to sustain it as far as we know; and so we do not know whether some material object quite different from a brain can sustain a soul, nor whether a soul needs any material object to sustain its functioning. And what applies to souls as such, applies to individual souls. We saw in the last chapter that some brain keeps some soul functioning; but, lacking a theory of how this happens, we do not know how much of that brain is needed for that soul (as opposed to some-soul-or-other) to continue to function, or whether (under conditions very different from those with which we are familiar) a given soul can function without the brain which originally made it function, either with a totally new brain or without any material object to keep it functioning at all. Lacking a theory of what it is about the brain which keeps a soul functioning, our ignorance about how and when the soul can function is profound.

Martians, Robots, and Synthesized Animals

There are grounds for supposing animals to have a mental life of varying degrees of richness, but what of organisms who might be found on other planets, made of very different kinds of molecule from animals on this planet (let us call them 'Martians'); and what of organisms which are brought into being, not by normal sexual processes, but are put together in a laboratory on this Earth, made either of similar molecules and similar construction to animals (let us call them 'synthesized animals') or of very different molecules and construction (let us call them 'robots')? Suppose that they show similar sophistication of behaviour, which can be explained by a simple theory of their purposes and beliefs, to ourselves. Are they conscious or not?

The difference of construction of robots and Martians from ourselves, means that we no longer have the crucial grounds for attributing consciousness to them that they have brains similar to those which produce consciousness in ourselves. In such a case we do not have enough grounds to be confident that the sophistication of their behaviour is produced by conscious purposes and beliefs rather than by unconscious physical processes. It would be different if we had a well-justified general theory of consciousness, a super-science of the physico-mental that explained which physical processes of kinds currently unknown give rise to which mental events (because it followed from the integrated laws of such a theory that they would do so). Then we could examine the

Martians and robots to see whether their physical processes were of a character to give rise to mental events, i.e. were similar to our own in whatever respects the theory had identified as crucial for this. But I have argued that we are most unlikely ever to get such a theory. And in the absence of such a theory, any view we might have about whether the construction of these organisms was sufficiently similar to that of animals to give rise to consciousness would be an ill-justified guess.

This issue will prove to be a very important one when Martians are found or robots constructed which show a similar sophistication of behaviour to our own, and not merely a theoretical issue but a crucial issue of practical morality. If they have a mental life like ours, we must obviously treat them differently from the way in which we treat machines. And yet, even if our evidence is not adequate to enable us to discover it, there is a truth here—that some organism does or does not suffer pain when we tread on it. Any Martians or robots who are conscious are, by our earlier arguments, to be said to have souls in our sense.

With synthesized animals, the situation seems different. Here there will be the similarity of physical brains which justifies us in ascribing similarity of mental life. But the similarity of physical brains would have to be very considerable, since, in the absence of a super-science of the physico-mental, we cannot know exactly which features of our brains are necessary for consciousness. By my earlier arguments, synthesized animals, having considerable similarity of brain to ourselves, are justifiably believed to have souls. There is no reason to suppose that souls will come into existence only through the normal sexual processes. Laboratory synthesis which produces the same physical organism should produce the same mental life.

We saw in Chapter 8 that there may be already in existence a different way in which new souls are produced, other than the way of sexual reproduction. It is possible that a new person is produced within the same body as the former person when the *corpus callosum*, the main nerve-link between the two cerebral hemispheres is severed. It is however disputable, as we saw there, whether this is the correct account of what happens in cerebral commissurotomy, and much more scientific work is required before a well-justified conclusion on this issue can be reached.

APPENDIX

I have argued that science cannot explain the evolution of a mental life. This is to say that, as far as we can see, there is no law of nature stating that physical events of certain kinds will give rise to correlated mental events, and, conversely, there is nothing in the nature of certain physical events or of mental events to give rise to connections. Is there any other way of explaining this correlation?

I have argued elsewhere[8] that to explain some event or regularity as brought about by an agent intentionally (i.e. purposing so to do), that is personal explanation, is in effect a very different way of explaining from the normal scientific explanation, which finds some passive event which causes the subsequent event or regularity in virtue of some law of nature, which is found to connect events of the former kind with events of the latter kind.

In the terms used in this book (which are different from those which I have used before) the difference is that purposing is something which (see Chapter 5) must be viewed by the agent as his (intentionally) contributing causally to the occurrence of the event, and normally it must be so viewed by others as well. There is no independent description of purposing other than the description of its intended causal contribution. The hotplate getting hot is the occurrence of something independently describable which causes the oil in the pan to melt; my purposing to move my finger just is my (intentionally) causing the finger to move. So if we cannot give a normal scientific explanation of how brain-events cause mental events and conversely, we should seek a personal explanation.

Invoking a personal explanation in this case involves invoking God, a power behind nature, who intentionally keeps the laws of nature operative (i.e. conserves those natures which are causally effective, in substances which have them) and also brings it about that there is linked to the brain of an animal or man a soul which interacts with it in a regular and predictable way. God, an omnipotent, omniscient, perfectly free and perfectly good source of all, would need to be postulated as an explanation of many diverse phenomena in order to make his existence probable. But the ability of God's actions to explain the otherwise mysterious mind–body connection is just one more reason for postulating his existence.

The suggestion is that God has given to each animal brain and each human brain a limited nature, as it were; a limited nature such that in the circumstances of normal embodiment it keeps a soul functioning in predictable ways—without the brain having that nature deriving from any

---

[8] I summarize in this paragraph much of the argument of my book *The Existence of God*, Clarendon Press, Oxford, 1979. The need for God as an explanation of consciousness is discussed in ch. 9 of that book.

general law of brain/mind connection, stating in general under what circumstances souls function and have the particular mental events they do. God, being omnipotent, would have the power to produce a soul thus interacting, to produce intentionally those connections which, we have seen, have no natural connection. And God would have a reason for so doing—to give to the souls of men beliefs, thoughts, and sensations caused in regular ways by brain-states, and purposes, and desires which cause brain-states in regular ways, allow man to acquire knowledge of the world and to make a difference to it by choice—good things which allow men to share in the creative work of God himself. That there be animals who also acquire some true beliefs and make some choices, and interact with each other and with men in so doing, is also a good thing which an omnipotent God would have reason for bringing about.

A God would have the ability and a reason for bringing about such connections. There is available to explain the existence and mode of functioning of souls (under the limited conditions of embodiment in bodies with brains) the explanation in terms of divine action for what otherwise is likely to remain a total mystery.

That the human soul is not something which develops naturally from the genetic material, but is something created on each occasion by God and linked at each new birth to the developing embryo is an old theological doctrine known as Creationism. (See St Hilary: 'Though flesh is always born of flesh, every soul is the direct work of God.'[9]) The alternative doctrine, Traducianism or Generationism, is the doctrine that men derive their soul from their parents (or perhaps from only one parent). An extreme form of this doctrine as of so many other doctrines, is to be found in Tertullian who held a sort of ectoplasmic view of the soul; the soul of the child was a detached fragment of the father's soul. On this view, as N. P. Williams comments,[10] every human being is in a very literal sense 'a chip off the old block'. One can make Traducianism a little more plausible, as other writers did, by supposing it to assert not that souls are divided in procreation, but that natural processes produce souls from genetic material without any need for special intervention by God. However I have argued against Traducianism and in favour of Creationism,[11] the creation of each human soul anew by God who gives one to each embryo able to receive it. Indeed I have passed beyond the orthodoxy of Creationism to affirm the same in respect of animal souls.

[9] *De Trinitate*, 10. 22.
[10] N. P. Williams, *The Ideas of the Fall and of Original Sin*, Longmans, London, 1927, p. 236.
[11] Creationism is the orthodox Catholic view, though not one on which there have been any allegedly infallible pronouncements. Augustine is ambivalent between Creationism and Traducianism. (See Williams op. cit. pp. 367 ff.) Aquinas argues in favour of Creationism in *Summa Contra Gentiles*, 2. 86–9.

PART III

THE HUMAN SOUL

11. LANGUAGE, RATIONALITY, AND CHOICE

ANIMALS have a mental life of sensation, thought, purpose, desire, and belief, and so they have souls. But there are differences between the mental lives of animals and men, and so between the capacities of their souls;[1] and in this part I shall bring out what these differences are and consider how far we can understand their evolution. Two of the differences are fairly obvious ones—that human thought has a complexity and logical structure to it which is lacking in animal thought; and that humans have moral concepts. I shall discuss the first in this chapter, and the second in Chapter 12. But there are also, I shall be claiming, further differences which are not at all obvious—that human actions are not predetermined by brain-states (and so that in a crucial sense, humans have free will); and that the human soul has a complex, continuing structure to it, a character which does not arise solely from the brain-state to which it is linked. For these differences I shall be arguing in the two subsequent chapters.

Language and Rationality

I suggested in Chapter 4 that we have no grounds for attributing to animals without language thoughts other than those which manifest concepts which occur in the animal's beliefs which provide satisfactory explanations of its public behaviour. Maybe some animals have thoughts of a complexity which go far beyond such thoughts but we have no grounds for supposing that they do. We only have reason to suppose that a languageless animal such as a cat can have the thought 'the door is square' if it can have beliefs about doors and things being square; and this can be shown if it can be shown that its behaviour is sometimes most plausibly explained by its having a belief that some door has some property

---

[1] My contrast is of course between the souls of adult animals and adult men. The soul of an infant man obviously lacks some of the capacities of the adult, but equally obviously it is able to receive them as it and its sustaining brain develop.

and by its having a belief that some object is square. By its sensitivity to the presence of doors and square shapes it can thus, I shall say, manifest in its behaviour the possession of these concepts. I argued in Chapter 7 that we are justified in ascribing to an animal that system of beliefs and purposes which will explain its behaviour, and which accords with the principles of simplicity and charity better than any rival system of explanation, i.e. a simple system which attributes to animals purposes and principles whereby they structure their beliefs in accord with evidence, which are as similar as possible to those which we humans have. The only beliefs which, for a given purpose, are immediately manifest in action are means–end beliefs. The cat, having the purpose of getting food, goes through a certain kitchen door. Thereby it manifests the means–end belief 'if I go through the kitchen door, I will get food'. But animals often show many different means–ends beliefs by which they seek to realize the same given purpose. If that kitchen door is shut, and if we suppose in accord with the principle of simplicity that the cat's purpose of getting food does not disappear, it will do one or more of various other actions which manifest other means–ends beliefs about how the food is to be acquired—e.g. it will go through a different kitchen door, or a window into the kitchen, or mew at the kitchen door, thereby manifesting such means–ends beliefs as 'if I go through the other kitchen door, I will get food' or 'if I go through the kitchen window, I will get food'. Now it is simpler to suppose that an animal which has certain means–ends beliefs has also a theoretical belief from which they all follow and which in consequence explains why it has just those means–ends beliefs, than to suppose that it is a mere coincidence that it has certain means–ends beliefs which all follow from a theoretical belief which it does not possess. And if we can explain how the animal came to acquire such a belief (by a simple method of belief-acquisition similar to ours), the simplicity and explanatory power of attributing to an animal such a theoretical belief (which would be manifest in its manifestation of the various means–ends beliefs) provides strong justification for doing so. Hence we attribute to the cat the more theoretical belief 'there is food in the kitchen'. (Its having the theoretical belief explains its having the various means–ends beliefs because they are contained in it, in the sense that it couldn't have the theoretical belief without having many of them. The cat—logically—couldn't have the belief 'there is food in the kitchen' without having some belief about where the kitchen is and how to get there.)

I follow Jonathan Bennett's book *Linguistic Behaviour*[2] in allowing that organisms without language could still manifest in their behaviour a very wide range of important concepts. We could have grounds for ascribing to an animal general beliefs, e.g. 'normally crocodiles are dangerous', particular beliefs about the future, e.g. 'it will rain soon', and particular beliefs about the past. It would not be shown that a certain animal had a certain belief about the past simply because some past event influenced its behaviour. It would be shown by the particular belief about the past providing a necessary part of a simple set of beliefs and purposings which explained a number of the animal's present actions. To take Bennett's example,[3] its belief 'a bone was buried here' might be used in explanation not merely of a dog digging in some place, but of its trying to uproot a sapling in that place which in normal unloosened soil it could not budge. This belief, we could reasonably believe, provided part of the explanation of the dog's actions, if the obtaining of bones and the uprooting of saplings were among those purposings which could explain much other dog behaviour. The sapling example is, as Bennett admits, a little 'fanciful' and what perhaps that shows is that although languageless animals could exhibit beliefs about the past, typically they don't. Most languageless animals show by their actions only beliefs about where things are now (viz. 'the bone is here'), not where they were. We often need only to postulate beliefs about the present (caused no doubt by past experience) to explain behaviour, not beliefs about the past.

However, animals not merely can, but sometimes do, have beliefs about the future, and general beliefs, as well also as conditional beliefs ('if I do this, that will happen'), and disjunctive beliefs ('either this or that will happen'). For an animal's possession of such a belief could often make a difference to his non-verbal conduct. An animal can even have the concept of evidence—footprints on the sand of varying shapes being evidence that animals of various kinds have been present. For in fleeing

---

[2] Cambridge University Press, 1976. See ch. 4. He argues here against the view of his earlier book *Rationality* (Routledge and Kegan Paul, London, 1964) that languageless organisms cannot be credited with general beliefs or beliefs about the past.

[3] Op. cit., p. 107.

away from the direction in which footprint *A* points and in going in the direction in which footprint *B* points, the animal shows (given certain other actions) that he regards the first footprint as evidence of the presence of a predator and the other footprint as evidence of the presence of prey in the directions pointed.

There are indeed some quite complicated beliefs which could be manifested by animals without language, but it seems fairly evident that the beliefs possessed by such animals are of a much simpler kind even than they need be in the absence of language, and that it was the origin of language which gave to animals the powers of complex belief and so thought (including many such powers which they could have developed without language) and began to turn them into men.

I understand by a language in the broadest sense any system of devices for communicating claims that things are so, questions whether things are so, or requests for things to be so. Language no doubt arrived on the evolutionary scene in small steps—maybe, to begin with, a ten-symbol language, then a hundred-symbol language, then a thousand-symbol language, and so on. At first the symbols would have represented sentences rather than words, the symbol 'stone' being used only to express the command 'Bring me a stone' rather than being used as a component of sentences indicative, interrogative, and imperative which express different claims or commands or questions about stones. But as language developed, there developed separate symbols for separate objects, properties, and relations, for past, present, and future, symbols which are combined to make whole sentences, the meaning of which is a function of the component symbols. Once speakers came to use sentences whose meaning is a function of their component symbols, and to understand them (i.e. to have in thought the propositions which are expressed by them), they then came to use the component symbols to form sentences to talk with comprehension about absent states of affairs. When a speaker hears such sentences as 'There is the moon', 'This man is old', uttered in the presence of states of affairs which they describe, he comes to understand how the meaning of a sentence is affected by the presence or absence of words such as 'man' and 'moon' in different places in the sentence. Only then will he come to understand the sentence 'Once upon a time there lived a man on the moon'.

Animals do not have a complex language in the sense of a structured language in which symbols can be put together in new and different ways to form new sentences, and which is modestly rich in the kinds of objects and properties about which it can make declarative (i.e. indicative), not merely imperative, utterances. By these criteria all those so-called natural 'languages' which animals use for communication (without being taught them by humans) do not count as complex languages. Many animals have devices for warning or attracting, but ones without the structure of a composite sentence. The animal performance which most resembles a complex language in having structure remains the bee-dance. Von Frisch[4] discovered that bees who find a source of food return to the hive and do a dance whose features vary with the distance and direction of the food, and the concentration of sugar in it; and the features which correlate with distance and direction correlate also with the distance and direction of the subsequent flight of any bee who has observed the dance. But in his book *Rationality*, Jonathan Bennett argued that bee-dances hardly formed a 'language', i.e in my sense a complex language, because bee dancing possessed no concept of denial (one bee cannot 'deny' any proposition made by a fellow bee; indeed the language has no distinction between indicative and imperative), no way of adducing evidence for a claim, no distinction between past and present, no ability to talk about anything else than food. But although no group of animals has a natural complex language, that does not mean that animals cannot be taught such a language; and there are of course several programmes currently being pursued for teaching a complex language to apes (and also to dolphins). There is evidence that apes can acquire a vocabulary of a hundred or more signs and sometimes put signs together to form new concepts. But it is disputed whether these combinations of signs which they produce are anything more than imperatives, i.e. whether they can make indicative sentences which make statements about the absent and unrealized. The interpretation of what has been achieved is highly controversial, and it would be foolish to be too dogmatic about the matter at this stage. But it does seem that the chances of any animals learning a language of any sophistication are fairly remote.

[4] K. von Frisch, *Bees: their Vision, Chemical Senses and Language* (Reprinted, Cape edition, London, 1983).

Some time, however, in the tens of thousands of years BC there evolved, no doubt very gradually, among age-related hominids, a complex language and with that language a capacity for complexity of thought and reasoned argument which is the first of our four marks distinguishing the mental life of man from that of the animals. I commented that languageless animals could have more complex thoughts than they do. But there are certain kinds of belief which their non-verbal behaviour would never justify us in ascribing to animals; they thus involve concepts which could never be manifested in non-verbal behaviour, and for the manifestation of which language (and in most cases, as will be seen, a fairly complex language) is needed. Languageless animals cannot, for example, show understanding of the distinction between universality and mere normality—e.g. between 'all crocodiles are dangerous' and 'normally crocodiles are dangerous'. The same behaviour of fleeing from crocodiles will result, and for each belief the hypothesis that the animal has that belief has the simplicity to give an integrated account of this behaviour; either belief could result, by principles of inference with humans use, from sensory stimuli. Hence we cannot attribute to animals our concept of universality (which is so sharply distinct from mere normality). Next, languageless animals cannot apparently have the crucial concepts of truth and negation. You cannot in your behaviour show that you regard something as true or false unless you treat something as a communication, a message from somebody and so something expressed in the signs of a language, however primitive. But once a subject has acquired these concepts, he can comment on his own private thoughts, that some are true and some are false, and form the thought that certain things are not so. Thirdly, an animal with a structured language can come to form beliefs and so thoughts about aspects of the world which are such that for his purposes, they make no difference to his non-verbal behaviour. He can have thoughts about those aspects of the absent and the invisible which make no difference to the present and the visible, and so make no difference to the way in which he behaves non-verbally in his environment. This is because he can use words learnt from their occurrence in sentences to describe the present and the visible put together in a new way to describe the absent and invisible. He can form theories of ancient history or distant geography, or other worlds which he can never visit. Also, having the concept of negation, he can tell stories which he does not believe and does not intend his hearers to believe; for he can preface them with the claim that things are not as he will say.

One kind of belief which we would never be justified in attributing to animals, Bennett argues, is logical belief—e.g. a belief that p entails q, or is compatible with r. For the possession of such beliefs rather than beliefs involving no logical modality, would make no difference to any animal's non-verbal conduct. We would never need to invoke its possession of a logical belief to explain such conduct. We could, let us suppose, explain its conduct by its having the belief 'all crocodiles are dangerous', or by the belief 'this is a crocodile' or by the belief 'this is dangerous'. We could perhaps even explain some aspect of its behaviour by postulating its possession of the belief 'if all crocodiles are dangerous and this is a crocodile, then this is dangerous'. But it would behave in exactly the same way if it believed that the belief just cited was a contingent truth as is 'if all crocodiles lay eggs, and this is a crocodile, then this is dangerous', as if it believed that it was a necessity of logic. Beliefs that things are necessarily true, compatible, or mutually entailing generate the same public non-linguistic behaviour as beliefs that things are true, or not-both-true, or either-both-true-or-both-false-together. Non-linguistic behaviour cannot show beliefs about logical modalities. Yet once speakers have a language, they can draw up lists of necessarily true sentences, and distinguish them from contingently true and contingently false sentences, and show by their different linguistic attitude towards the groups of sentences and the subsequent classification of sentences as belonging to one or other group, their possession of logical concepts.[5] Once speakers recognize how the meaning of a sentence is generated by its component symbols, they can go on to distinguish in meaning between two sentences which are such that they must be true together, belief in which will manifest itself in the same behaviour—e.g. 'there are 2 + 5 apples in the box' and 'there are 3 + 4 apples in the box'. Non-linguistic behaviour could never evince recognition of a difference between two beliefs which mutually entail each other. And among sentences which mutually entail each other, speakers can dis-

---

[5] For the distinction between the analytic (logically necessary) and synthetic (logically contingent) sentences, and how it can be taught, see my 'Analytic/ Synthetic', *American Philosophical Quarterly*, 1984, **21**, 31–42.

tinguish those which are synonomous (have the same meaning as each other) from those which are not. Only to a subject with language are we justified in attributing belief about truth and meaning, entailment and self-contradiction.

Humans produce arguments externally in words which express their thoughts, or internally in private thoughts. They deduce from this thought that thought, from that thought a third thought. The limitation on the kind of thoughts which, our evidence suggests, languageless animals can have leads to an obvious limitation on the logical reasoning which such animals can perform. Their behaviour perhaps can show a succession of beliefs which are logically connected—e.g. one piece of an animal's behaviour may evince the belief 'there are two apples in the box', another piece may evince the behaviour 'I put two more apples in the box' and a third piece may evince the behaviour 'there are four apples in the box'; and therefore the animal can have the corresponding private thoughts. And, as we have seen, animals can have thoughts which they regard as providing evidence for other thoughts. But what they cannot do is regard a sequence of sentences which in fact forms a deductively valid argument as forming such an argument. For, lacking the concept of entailment, they cannot conceive of a succession of thoughts as a valid argument. Put another way—they cannot distinguish between deduction and induction. Nor can they understand *why* some sentence is evidence for some other sentence; for that understanding would involve a grasp of some general principles of confirmation (what is evidence for what) which would inevitably bring in principles of deductive logic. Hence, they cannot challenge the details of arguments. Nor, lacking the concepts of 'true' and 'false' can they challenge arguments by challenging their premisses.[6]

Once such concepts as I have been discussing have been developed in public language, they would have been internalized so that there occur to the subject thoughts on these matters to which he gives no public expression. These thoughts would at first be mediated by images of the public words, but later perhaps, as I suggested in Chapter 4, such images may be dispensed with.

---

[6] 'It is the knowledge of necessary and eternal truths which distinguishes us from mere animals and gives us *reason* and the sciences, raising us to knowledge of ourselves and God'—G. W. Leibniz, *Monadology* 29 (translated by Mary Morris in Leibniz, *Philosophical Writings*, J. M. Dent, London, 1934).

The advantages which language confers in the struggle for survival should be evident—powers of reasoning and communication will give to groups of animals which possess them great advantages in pursuing their various goals in difficult circumstances. If a capacity to use language appeared it would be selected, but whether it will appear will depend (as regards its public aspects) on the likelihood of mutations of various kinds, and (as regards the mental aspect that the spoken words be understood by speakers) on a process not susceptible to physical, or probably any scientific, explanation—for the reasons which I gave in the last chapter.

One thing which language made possible was theorizing about the origin and destiny of the world and of man within it. One naturally thinks of such activity as something which men do in universities when freed from cares about earning their daily bread; but knowledge of primitive peoples does not bear out that natural suggestion. Myths of origin and destiny are there long before much thought about economics. Towards the end of the Old Stone Age, men began to bury their dead with food and other things in the grave, presumably with the belief that they would be of use to the dead man in the world to come. Palaeolothic man had a theory of the afterlife. Man, unlike his animal ancestors, had a theory of origin and destiny, a capacity for reaching out to a God in the world to come.

Language and Evaluative Choice

On a more down-to-earth level, language gave to man the capacity for choice of what he believes worth while. An agent without language could perhaps set before himself in picture images the alternative actions open to him, and their different consequences, and perhaps state to himself how likely some action was to have some consequence (perhaps by the thought in picture, of that consequence being in a Humean way more 'lively'[7] than the thought of some other consequence). But what, I shall argue, an agent lacking a complex language could not do is to contrast the worth of one action or one set of consequences with that of another, and choose on that basis. This is because an animal cannot express by behaviour alone the contrast between what he desires most and what he thinks most worth while. Hence, we are

[7] See ch. 7 n. 1.

justified in supposing, he cannot make in thought the contrast between the desired and the desirable. Animals of different species have different goals (to incubate a nest, or build a dam, say) for longer or shorter periods of their life. Many of these goals are altruistic in that they are goals of the well-being of their families or others of their species. The pursuit of these goals comes naturally and instinctively to an animal, i.e. he pursues them because he desires to pursue them. But humans seek goals for two reasons—that they believe them most worth doing and that they desire them most. Yet the same behaviour of goal-seeking will result from desire for the goal and from belief that it is good to have. An animal's behaviour does not allow us to distinguish a belief in worth from a desire and so we have no grounds for attributing to it that distinction. To have the concept of goodness we need the concept of a property inhering in an object, whatever on a given occasion some agent does about it. That could only come to an agent who possessed a language which enabled him to talk about the properties of objects independently of subjects' reactions to them. A complex language allows men to talk about the absent and invisible which makes no difference to behaviour, allows them to talk about good states of affairs which they do nothing to bring about, and duties which they do not fulfil. Similarly, they come to talk about desires to which they do not yield.

A complex language, as we have seen, allows us to formulate propositions about states of affairs which are different in a way which would not show up in a difference of characteristic behaviour towards them. We can derive a concept of desire from situations where we feel natural inclinations to do certain actions (including situations where we do not act on those inclinations), and a concept of goodness from situations where we see some actions as more worth doing than others (including situations when we do not do those actions). We can name the results of those actions by words 'overall best' and 'most desired', which we can then use to describe two very different kinds of results 'best but not most desired' and 'most desired but not best', towards which we do not have any typical characteristic response, and so ones between which we cannot distinguish by mere behaviour. Language allows us to have this conception of worth which contrasts with desire, and so opens the possibility of pursuing what we believe best or most worth while despite contrary desire, or yielding to temptation in doing what we desire most despite a belief that it is not good. Yet, although the development of language allows us to make the contrast, humans do tend to believe that in general what they most desire is most worth pursuing—until they are faced with experience or argument which leads them to have a different view about particular cases.

Language containing such words as 'good' and 'desired' allows the contrast to be made publicly; and humans have the capacity to think the thoughts privately which can be expressed publicly by those words (and some human, perhaps by accident, took the first step towards making language express that distinction). That capacity is no doubt due to some feature of the human brain. But why a particular feature of the human brain should give to humans the capacity to have those particular thoughts remains the mystery which all such correlations between brain-state and thought are.

Animal owners sometimes claim that their animals can make this distinction between what they desire and what they believe good. A dog-owner may complain: 'My dog has a conscience. He knows right from wrong. You can see that by the look on his face when I catch him stealing meat.' Now certainly dogs can have desires both to eat the meat and to please the mistress, and like all of us they try to arrange things so that all their desires get satisfied. They do this by putting themselves in a situation where the satisfaction of one desire does not inhibit the satisfaction of another one. Dogs try to eat the meat when the mistress is not there (and so won't be displeased). And like all of us they are unhappy and show it when their desires are suddenly frustrated. The way of showing unhappiness varies with the unhappiness to be shown. You snarl when threatened, bite when attacked, look sad when finding a sick child. And there is no doubt a characteristic way for a dog to show its unhappiness when it has displeased its mistress. But to describe its belief as the belief that it is has given in to a tempting desire and done what it believes is wrong is hopelessly anthropomorphic. All the evidence suggests that it couldn't think in that way without a complex language.

The language which allows us to make a contrast between what we believe most worth doing and what we most desire gives us a conception of the goodness of things as an objective feature of them distinct from the way in which agents react to them. There may be some philosophical error in supposing that actions are good, or worth doing, independent of human attitudes towards them. Nevertheless, almost all human beings (even philosophers quite a lot of the time) consider questions about whether some action is worth doing, some state of affairs good, in the same objective way as they consider any question about obvious matter of fact; they bring arguments and adduce reasons. They have beliefs about the goodness of actions, whether or not what they believe evinces some philosophical error. This not being a book on moral philosophy, there is no space to consider whether or not there is a philosophical error here.[8] For simplicity of exposition, I shall make the common-sense assumption[9] that there are truths about what things are good (and, in due course, about what things are morally good), which humans try to discover and about which they have true or false beliefs. Nothing turns on this assumption. Those who do not share it can easily rephrase what I have to say in this chapter and the next about beliefs about goodness in terms of the growth of a psychological propensity to talk and think in a certain way rather than in terms of growth of awareness of truth.

Men may believe actions to be good for a whole variety of reasons, self-centred and idealistic. I shall be arguing in the next chapter that only some of those reasons deserve the name of 'moral', and that the recognition of the goodness of actions as having a moral dimension represented a new stage in human evolution. I shall wish to distinguish a moral reason for an action as a universalizable reason, i.e. one which sees an action as good because it is of a certain kind which can be described in general terms—e.g. not because it gives pleasure to me or to you but because it gives pleasure to a human being or to a lonely child or to someone to whom the agent has made a promise. Yet when our ancestors first became conscious of conflict between desire and believed goodness, they must initially have had a very limited conception of goodness in terms of benefit or harm to individuals,

---

[8] My own view is that there are indeed objective truths about goodness, and especially moral goodness. See my 'The objectivity of Morality', *Philosophy*, 1976, **51**, 5–20.

[9] J. L. Mackie, who thought that there was no objective goodness, brought out well in his *Ethics* (Penguin Books, Harmondsworth, 1977) how people normally think that there is; he attributed this tendency of people to what Hume called the mind's 'propensity to spread itself on external objects', to regard its attitudes as called forth by properties in the objects.

independently of whether those individuals had properties which made them deserve benefit or harm.

Any agent, *qua* agent, sees an action which he performs as a good thing to do. Yet an agent need not rank actions in respect of goodness; but among those actions which he regards as good to do, he may simply slip into doing one of them. It follows from my account of desire in Chapter 6, that what such an agent does is what he desires most to do (for he has no beliefs about worth to restrain his strongest desire), and what he desires most to do he will do. Let us call such an agent a wanton. The wanton knows no conflict between his desires and his beliefs about the relative worth of actions. He has not made enough spiritual progress even to show weakness of will.

My argument above has shown that languageless animals are wantons, and it is plausible to suppose that very young children are also wantons during the initial stages of their acquisition of language. It follows from the last paragraph that since purposes and desires first appeared in evolutionary history among languageless animals, they must have evolved simultaneously.

Kinds of Evaluative Understanding

There are various degrees of understanding in terms of such benefit or harm to individuals, which may be had by an agent without his having a fully moral understanding. Among those who do know the conflict between desire and belief about relative worth, but have no conception of moral worth, there are first those who are purely self-centred in seeing the worth of an action solely in terms of the enjoyment which it will bring to the agent. Among such self-centred persons let us begin with what I shall call the egoist. The egoist believes an action to have worth solely in virtue of the fairly immediate pleasure which doing the action or having its consequences will bring to him (i.e whether he will desire to do the action as he does it, or desire to have the consequences when he gets them); and so he believes that actions are more worth while in so far as they give greater pleasure. However, a man may desire to do an action before he begins to do it, although he does not believe that he will enjoy doing it as he does it or enjoy the consequences thereof. And he may desire to do less some action which he believes that he will enjoy doing when he does it. Consider a man like those discussed in Chapter 6, who desires to commit suicide so that the public knowledge of what he has done may hurt his relatives. He does not believe that he will enjoy the process of committing suicide (for it may be almost instantaneous) nor does he believe that he will enjoy the consequences (for he does not believe that he will see the consequences). And he may believe that if he stays alive, there will be actions which he does which he will enjoy doing; but he may desire to stay alive less than he desires to commit suicide. A less 'black' example is that of the man who desires to stay at home rather than go to a party, while believing that he would enjoy the party more than staying at home. Now if these men are egoists, they will believe that the only actions worth doing are those which they will enjoy—e.g. staying alive or going to the party. They then face a conflict between their desires and what they believe worth doing. An egoist has no sense that it is in any way deeply important that he do the action which is overall better; he will not think the worse of himself if he does not. So we cannot really dignify his conflict by calling it a struggle between *conscience* and desire. Still, there is a conflict; and it seems right to say of the egoist that if he does yield to desire in a case where he judges it best not to, he shows weakness of will.

The egoist does not plan for the future; he is concerned only with fairly immediate pleasure, and he ignores the fact that some actions which give short-term pleasure give long-term pain. And that point brings us to a more thorough kind of self-centred man, whom I will call the prudent man. For him, as for the egoist, the only considerations which affect the worth of actions are the satisfaction of desire and the obtaining of future pleasure (i.e. the satisfaction of future as well as present desire). But he is concerned with the long term as well as the short term; and this brings in new considerations about the worth of actions, which are likely to lead to more conflict with desires. There is, for example, the totally self-centred student, concerned only for his own pleasure, when the latter consists in loafing around doing little. He believes that he will be able to have a more pleasurable life after graduation if he gets a good degree, and that the only way to get a good degree is by doing some work. So he concludes reluctantly that, for the sake of long-term pleasure, it is today better to work than to idle. He may or may not actually do the work, but so long as some consideration other than the satisfaction of desire and the immediate pleasure which actions will produce enters his assessment of his actions, he has passed beyond simple egoism to prudence.

The prudent man, however, has, like the wanton, no standard for assessing the actions of others other than their contribution to his own happiness (i.e. the satisfaction of his own future desires, as well as his present desires). Nor does he have any sense of the deep importance of his doing the overall best action. Although of course he thinks that *in a sense* it matters that he should do the action which is overall the best (for believing that an action is overall the best carries just that implication), he does not feel anything analogous to guilt if he fails to do the best action. He has not 'let himself down'. The importance of doing the best action lies for him *only* in the subsequent pleasure, not in exercising his strength of will, in overcoming desires for lesser goods.

But then we come to the man who like the wanton and the prudent man, is totally selfish in that he is concerned solely with himself. Like the prudent man he seeks to satisfy his desires, and to obtain pleasure in the short and long term. But, unlike the prudent man, he thinks it deeply important that he should do the right thing, that he should not yield to desire where he believes it better that he should pursue long-term pleasure. The considerations by which he weighs which is the right action to do are the same as those of the prudent man—but once the judgement as to which is the right action is reached, he invests the doing of the action with an importance which the prudent man does not find in it. He has a pride in himself as a selfish pursuer of pleasure; and would feel shame at yielding to desires which conflict with this pursuit. I call such a person a narcissist. Examples of narcissists include the girl who seeks to make herself beautiful and admired, by a rigorous programme of slimming and avoiding cream cakes; and *minds* that she 'get the most out of life'. Or the politician who seeks power and fame and is prepared to go through the hard grind of being nice to unpleasant people which the pursuit of this goal involves; and who is proud of his single-minded pursuit of this power and fame.

The wanton, the egoist, the prudent man, and the narcissist are all self-centred in that, whether or not they in fact pursue their own subsequent enjoyment, no consideration other than their own enjoyment affects their beliefs about which actions are worth doing. But there are others, let us call them particularists, who see actions as having worth not because of the enjoyment they bring to the agent, but because of the enjoyment (i.e. satisfaction of desire) they bring to some other particular person (e.g. an individual who is the agent's favourite child, whether the agent even believes that that individual is her child), or the hurt (i.e. frustration of desire) they bring to some other particular person (e.g. someone who, in fact, has caused pain to the agent, again whether or not the agent believes that of him). Like their animal ancestors, men have natural affections for particular individuals, caused by genes and circumstances; and natural antipathies to other particular individuals—which they have before and quite apart from believing those individuals to deserve benefit or harm more than others do. It is a further stage for the agent with natural affections and antipathies to believe that the loved ones deserve benefit and the hated ones deserve harm more than do others. It is a yet further stage to believe that those individuals deserve benefit or harm in virtue of their possessing some universal characteristic (e.g. being 'a child of the agent' or 'someone who has inflicted undeserved harm').

We may approve highly of altruistic behaviour and disapprove of antagonistic and selfish behaviour, yet it has in common with them an instinctive character and a conferring of benefits apart from the perceived worth of the beneficiary, as a person satisfying a certain general description. Altruistic love may have the consequence that a parent benefits one of his children and harms another, although he does not believe that the former has any universal characteristic in virtue of which he merits preferential treatment. Yet once the altruist or antagonist acquires beliefs about the relative worth of benefiting or harming particular individuals (other than ones dependent on universal characteristics which those individuals possess), they may, like self-centred men of different kinds, feel the conflict between desire and believed worth. A man, tired of battle with his enemy and desirous of sleep, may feel nevertheless that he ought to take some opportunity open to him to hurt the enemy—not because the enemy in some sense deserves it, but just because he is Joe Bloggs. Or the woman, desirous to look after her family, may still feel that she ought to visit Henry with whom she feels much involved, but not for a reason such as that he is a friend who needs company or love, or any other general reason.

In describing in this section four kinds of evaluative under-standing—egoism, prudence, narcissism, and particularism—I do not in any way wish to suggest that the evolutionary development of man took him through these kinds in that order. Altruistic behaviour is a central feature of animal behaviour[10] (and so altruistic desires are central to many animals' desire systems) and once an agent has a concept of good he will readily believe that the well-being of others of his kin is in general a major good. It is unlikely that many primitive men or many human children were egoists before they were particularists; most probably passed from being wantons to being particularists before they came to acquire moral views. It was, nevertheless, worth distinguishing the logically distinct stages of development through which some creatures might pass and to which some men certainly regress.

[10] See M. Midgley, *Beast and Man*, Harvester, Brighton, 1979, especially ch. 6, for her emphasis on this point, and on the point that intentionally caring for one's children is not intentionally seeking to secure the survival of one's genes. The latter may often be a consequence, but it is not one intentionally sought.

12. MORAL AWARENESS

Moral Beliefs

AT the end of the last chapter we left man with a very limited conception of the good—as the satisfaction of his own future desire, or the desire of some one individual dear to him, or the frustration of the desire of some individual enemy. The next stage of evaluative understanding is when agents come to think of actions as having value (or lacking it) because of the universal properties which they possess. Most of us do think of acts as good or evil in virtue of being acts of a certain kind, where the description of the kind makes no reference to individual persons, only to persons of a certain kind. For example, we think an act to be valuable if it is *an* act of feeding *a* hungry person, or *an* act of saving *a* dying man. The 'persons of a certain kind' may be picked out by their relation to the agent, e.g. as the agent's child or parent or the person to whom the agent made a promise; and we think of acts as valuable if they are acts of 'educating one's own child' or 'keeping a promise made to a promisee'. By contrast, the self-centred man Jones thinks of an act as having value only in so far as it promotes Jones's ease, or achievement or popularity. And the particularist Smith may think of an act as having value because it promotes Brown's well-being, quite apart from Brown's having a universal property such as being a person or being related to the agent in a certain way (e.g. being his child).

Most of us believe that universal considerations sometimes outweigh other considerations in the value which they confer on an action—e.g. that it is on balance better that some action be done although it fails to satisfy one's own desire, because it makes *a* depressed person happy or fulfils *a* promise. I shall call beliefs about the worth of actions in virtue of their universal properties, of a kind which the believer believes to outweigh all other considerations in the value which they confer on an action, moral beliefs. In this chapter I shall be describing this phenomenon of moral belief, its arrival on the evolutionary scene and man's progressive understanding of morality.

My reason for grouping together beliefs of the kind which I described, and contrasting them with self-centred and particularist beliefs about the worth of actions, as *moral* beliefs is not merely their formal similarity in the respect described, but also the very considerable overlap in the universal properties which agents believe to confer positive or negative worth on actions. Of course people have different moral beliefs—some men believe euthanasia (in the sense of helping someone who wishes to die to do so) to be morally right, others do not, and so on. But most of those who dispute about particular moral issues agree that the considerations adduced by their opponents have some force; that is, would show the action (e.g.) right but for the considerations which they adduce on the other side. Thus the opponent of the euthanasia involved in helping a depressed man to commit suicide argues that such an act is wrong because of the sanctity and value of human life, the possibility of helping a depressed man to recover from his depression, the value of his overcoming that depression, and so on. The advocate of euthanasia argues that any man ought to be allowed to do any act which does not hurt others, and so that there is nothing wrong in helping an agent to do such an act. Both disputants appeal to considerations which their opponent will admit to have some weight, although they assess and apply them differently.[1] Also, many who disagree about one particular such issue will agree about many others. Most people in the world are such that I have many beliefs about the worth of kinds of action in respect of their universal properties in common with them. And many of those with whom I share few such beliefs will nevertheless have in common many such beliefs with many other people in the world. There is an overlapping and criss-crossing of beliefs about the worth of actions in respect of their universal properties. Finally, when agents do or fail to do the action which they believe most worth doing in virtue of its universal properties, they have similar reactions—of self-satisfaction, or shame and guilt, whatever the particular content of their universal beliefs. All of this

[1] W. D. Ross (*The Right and The Good*, Clarendon Press, Oxford, 1930, pp. 29 ff.) claimed that it was self-evident what are the prima-facie duties, i.e. what considerations tend to make an action obligatory to do or obligatory not to do, although not self-evident how these considerations were to be weighed against each other to determine what is a particular man's duty in particular circumstances. I am claiming only that it is often the case that disputants agree about prima-facie obligations.

makes it highly desirable to group together beliefs about the worth of actions in virtue of their universal properties, of a kind which the believer believes to outweigh all other considerations in the value which they confer on an action; and this I do calling them moral beliefs. This factor of 'universalizability' as a criterion of a moral consideration, was, of course, the hallmark of Kant's[2] account of morality and, in our time, has been a central feature of R. M. Hare's moral theory.[3] It is true that some views which we naturally call 'moral' views do hold that certain individuals or groups—the King, Parliament, the Pope, or God are entitled to special treatment. But my account does not debar these views from being 'moral' views when they hold (as they normally do) that the special treatment is due to the individual or group because of properties which he or it has—'having been elected by democratic suffrage', or being 'Bishop of Rome', or being 'the creator of the universe'—not because parliament is those people or the Pope is Karol Wojtyla.[4]

Because actions are valued for their universal properties, it follows that if someone has a moral view, he must have a view not only about what he ought to be doing but about what others ought to be doing. For if I think that it is important that I do not kill, because it is a case of one man killing another, I must hold a similar view about you killing me or you killing a third person. Morality, being universal, is also prescriptive.

Those of us who believe that there are moral reasons for actions, believe that we have discovered a kind of mattering, a sort of importance qualitatively different from, and superior to the kind

---

[2] See *The Groundwork of the Metaphysic of Morals.*

[3] See his *The Language of Morals*, Clarendon Press, Oxford, 1952, and *Freedom and Reason*, Clarendon Press, Oxford, 1962.

[4] In *Fear and Trembling*, Kierkegaard emphasizes that the ethical is the 'universal'; but claims that man's 'absolute duty towards God' which is a higher duty is not 'universal'. The exact content of this claim is none too clear. But if it is claiming that we have a duty towards God which does not depend on his unique possession of certain properties, it seems mistaken. It is surely because he is the creator of the universe (or omnipotent, or whatever) that we owe him what we do. Granted this point, Kierkegaard seems to me to be mistaken in holding that religion involves a 'teleological suspension of the ethical'. The grounds of religious obligation are of a kind with the grounds of obligations to humans—e.g. we owe worship to our creator, because there is a general duty to pay respect to benefactors, and so a duty to pay respect to human benefactors also. See. S. Kierkegaard, *Fear and Trembling*, translated by R. Payne, Oxford University Press, London, 1939, especially Problems 1 and 2.

of importance involved in satisfying our own desires, which exists independently of our awareness of it. A man's moral beliefs in my sense are not principles that he *decides* to follow; but convictions which nag at him and to which he often in part conforms. We who believe it wrong to torture children, believe it would still be wrong if we had been brought up to think otherwise. We who believe it our duty to help the starving, feel the force of a moral obligation from without. If we really were to believe that we had invented the 'moral obligation', we would believe that it had no objective force and so that we are equally free to jettison it, and so we would not regard it as a moral obligation at all. To believe that universal properties make actions good or bad, is to believe that these moral properties inhere in actions—badness in the action of torturing children, goodness in the act of helping the starving. (As I wrote in the last chapter, we may of course be wrong about this; I am not going into philosophical discussion of whether we are.)

My preferred use of the word 'moral' is, I believe, a normal one; but there are other uses among philosophers and non-philosophers.[5] For some, a belief about moral worth is simply a belief about which actions are important to do.[6] But that use would allow the narcissist, who thinks that is important that he promote his own happiness, to have a moral view, and so it would fail to bring out the distinction which most of us make among the considerations by which we judge the worth of actions, and which I argued to have such importance. For others, a belief about moral worth is a belief about the importance of actions in virtue of their universalizable properties of *a certain kind*—e.g. those concerned with sex or (more widely) those concerned with the promotion of happiness or unhappiness of other people.[7] On the latter account it would be a moral view that men ought to feed the starving; but not a moral view that men ought to worship God, or that artists who can paint great pictures ought to do so even if those pictures will be seen only by themselves. If you use 'moral' in this limited sense, you can say without contradiction 'I think that religion is more important than morality'; but on my preferred use it would

[5] See the Introduction to and the various views represented in (ed.) G. Wallace and A. D. M. Walker, *The Definition of Morality*, Methuen, London, 1970.

[6] See N. Cooper, 'Morality and Importance', ch. 6 of Wallace and Walker, op. cit. (Revised version of an article in *Mind*, 1968.)

[7] See, for example, G. J. Warnock, *The Object of Morality*, Methuen, London, 1971.

be self-contradictory to assert of anything describable in universal terms that it was more important than morality. A man's morality is (with the qualification that it be not centred on self or any other particular individual) what he believes most important. My grounds for preferring my use are that so many men's beliefs about which actions are important to do are supported or opposed both on grounds which concern the happiness and unhappiness of other people and also on other grounds (e.g. whether the action shows due loyalty, pays honour to whom honour is due, involves keeping a promise or telling the truth), that confining the term to the narrower use would obscure the overlap of grounds of the different kinds in leading to beliefs about overall worth.

The Origin of Moral Beliefs

In *The Descent of Man*, Darwin wrote: 'the following proposition seems to me in a high degree probable—namely, that any animal whatever, endowed with well-marked social instincts, . . . would inevitably acquire a moral sense or conscience, as soon as its intellectual powers had become as well, or nearly as well, developed as in man'.[8] Disparaging as I have been about scientific explanations of the first occurrence in our ancestors of most mental features, I am inclined to agree with Darwin about the moral sense.

The first crucial phrase in what Darwin wrote is the phrase 'endowed with well-marked social instincts'. Darwin drew our attention to the altruistic behaviour towards their fellows of many animals, and the recent doctrine of socio-biology has seen this as the origin of ethics. Animals are prepared to take much trouble, and often to sacrifice their lives, to protect their children and close relatives, and help them to flourish. They are also prepared to help and co-operate with members of their own group (e.g. share food with them and defend them against predators). This kin altruism (doing good to your own kin) and reciprocal altruism (doing good to those who do good to you), and the associated punishment of those who do not show reciprocal altruism, have survival value. If mothers do not protect their children or the members of the group

---

[8] Charles Darwin, *The Descent of Man*, second edition, John Murray, London, 1875, p. 98.

do not help defend each other, a group of animals is unlikely to survive.[9]

Animals before they acquire language exhibit both selfish and altruistic behaviour. Once they acquire language, it will then be open to them to believe actions to have worth in so far as they promote the well-being in the short or long run of the agent or of others close to him, and so to be open to the conflict of reason with desire which I outlined in the last chapter. But then it will almost inevitably strike those whose 'intellectual powers had become as well, or nearly as well, developed as in man' (to use Darwin's second crucial phrase) that there are very considerable similarities in respect of their universal properties between those whom they believe it good to benefit (or harm, as the case may be) and those of whom they do not believe this. The altruistic man feeding his own hungry children and thinking it good to do so, will note that his neighbours' children are hungry too. There is obvious room for his concept of goodness to expand so as to apply to all actions of feeding hungry children. And it will strike some members of the community who are sufficiently clever that it will help them to secure their goals if they draw the attention of others to such similarities. An aged parent who was not being helped by some child would draw the child's attention to the fact that helping him was in a universal respect (helping a parent) like helping the other parent whom the child did help and thought it good to help. And those who shirked fighting for the community could have their attention drawn to the fact that their fighting for the tribe would be like certain others fighting for the tribe, which they regard as a good thing, in the respect of 'able-bodied member fighting for the tribe'. The moralist deploys general terms which stimulate to action by drawing attention to universal properties. If genes produce men with thoughts that actions are good or bad, and a proneness to do altruistic as well as selfish actions, the society of such men has the capacity and proneness to develop moral concepts. Culture naturally fosters morality. There seems no need to postulate in man a special capacity for moral thought; it seems to arise naturally from his exercise of his other capacities.

The reader will regard this process, if he is a subjectivist about

[9] For a fuller explanation of the survival value of kin and reciprocal altruism, see P. Singer, *The Expanding Circle*, Oxford University Press, 1983, ch. 1, 'The Origins of Altruism'.

morals, as a process whereby some men (and especially the weak) deceived the community into believing that moral considerations possess an importance which really they lack; if he is an objectivist, he will regard the process as one whereby some men discovered and revealed to the rest of the community the moral truths which, like mathematical truths, were waiting to be discovered (as well as some moral propositions falsely believed to be truths and later perhaps discarded). Either way, moral talk would seem a natural acquisition for a community of partly altruistic and partly selfish agents with evaluative concepts and considerable intellectual capacities. But, as I wrote in the last chapter, I shall—for the sake of simplicity of exposition—phrase my description of the process of acquisition of moral talk in objectivist terms (i.e. as the process of acquiring beliefs that there are certain truths, and changing and extending one's system of beliefs, in the light of reason).

The core principles of the morality, whose origin can be explained in this way, are the principles of altruistic behaviour towards kin and members of your group. And, much though social anthropology has taught us about the diversity of moral codes, they surely all have a core of this kind.[10] The considerable diversity of moral codes has perhaps in part a genetic explanation (in terms of certain tribes having genes which favour the development of different moral beliefs); but it is more plausible to suppose that it has a largely cultural explanation in terms of certain tribes whose genes are not greatly different from those of other tribes being exposed by accident to certain moral teaching which is then transmitted culturally. But, again, knowledge of the causal story which accounts for men having certain beliefs—be they moral beliefs, scientific beliefs, historical beliefs, or whatever—leaves open the further issue of whether those beliefs are true or false.

While it is clear that the prevalence of certain moral beliefs (e.g. in reinforcing kin and group altruism) has survival value, other moral beliefs would seem to convey considerable evolutionary disadvantage for groups who possess them—e.g. the belief that weak children ought to be fed and not exposed to die. How, then, have human beings managed to survive, lumbered with moral beliefs conferring a disadvantage in the struggle for survival? The

[10] See Singer, op. cit., ch. 2.

answer must be that these latter beliefs go with the power for sophisticated and logical thought and other moral beliefs which together convey such an advantage in the struggle for survival that they outweigh the disadvantage conferred by some moral beliefs. But why should these go together? Would not a hominid community which had all and only moral beliefs which conveyed an advantage in the struggle be even better adapted for survival? And of course within the human race there have been sub-communities which cultivated an ethic of principles with survival advantage, e.g. Nazi Germany with its ethic of the moral superiority of strength and race-loyalty. The trouble is that humans regard morality (rightly or wrongly) as having its inner logic. You do not simply hold on to moral beliefs with which you are born or indoctrinated. You see them, either for yourself or if it is pointed out to you in ways which I shall describe shortly, as open to various sorts of criticism—which leads you to change them in various ways. A human race which is clever enough to have a morality will be too clever to have for long that apparently incoherent morality which will give the best advantage in the struggle for survival. It will, however, be clever enough to survive despite its more coherent morality being less than perfectly suited for survival.[11]

It was T. H. Huxley, Darwinism's most persuasive and powerful advocate, who urged so powerfully in his 1893 Romanes Lecture that moral goodness and fitness for survival are two quite different concepts which do not automatically go together. Moral goodness both helps and hinders the survival of a society, as I have described; but it ensures that within a society the weak survive as well as the strong. 'The practice of what is ethically best', Huxley wrote, 'involves a course of conduct which, in all respects, is opposed to that which leads to success in the cosmic struggle for existence.'[12] But of course Huxley did not wish to deny Darwin's claim that moral truth is a natural discovery for thinking man.

Morality's Inner Logic

So, almost inevitably, sophistication of thought led human communities to adopt moral beliefs—despite the dubious advantage

[11] For a similar view, see Singer, op. cit., pp. 139 ff.
[12] 'Evolution and Ethics' in his *Evolution and Ethics, and other Essays*, Macmillan, London, 1894. See pp. 81 ff.

of this step in the struggle for survival. But moral beliefs change and develop, like all other beliefs, under the pressure of reason and experience. In the different fields such as science, mathematics, or history, about which men have beliefs, there are criteria of truth and methods of investigation; and men pursue investigations to discover new facts, new arguments which will show which if any beliefs are true. And so it is in the moral field also. As in science and history, so also in morality, children are told how things are—that the world began in 4004 BC, or that every child ought to obey its parents. But they are also taught, or find out for themselves, many other things which are superficially in conflict with, or raise questions about, what they are originally taught. Then they can begin to assess views for themselves, or at least assess the relative competence of those who are proclaiming rival views. In morality men are exposed to arguments for and against this, that, or the other moral view; and arguments for and against the view that there are such things are true moral beliefs. Arguments have a role to play in changing a man's moral beliefs for the reason that men's moral beliefs overlap so much. As we have noted, two men may disagree about a particular matter (e.g. the morality of euthanasia or abortion), but share so much else (e.g. beliefs about the value of human freedom and the sanctity of human life). In consequence of this, one man can try to show another that his belief about the particular matter fits ill with the general understanding of moral worth implicit in his other moral views.

Thus, a man may hold that lying and deceit is always wrong; and also that it is always wrong to kill in war innocent civilians (as by using a weapon of mass destruction, such as an atomic bomb, on a city); yet also hold that, although such bombing would be wrong, there is nothing wrong in threatening to bomb—if this serves some great purpose, such as preserving democrative freedom. An opponent may manage to show such a man to be inconsistent—by helping him to see that threatening to do an act which you have no intention of doing is deceitful. Thus the moral believer will, under pressure of argument, alter his moral beliefs, abandoning the one of which he feels least confident (e.g. that deceit is always wrong) in order to make his set consistent.

Further, a man exposed to different moral views may recognize the moral principles of others as linked coherently together by principles possessing a unity and apparent truth, which his own lacks; while the principles of the others nevertheless justify those of his own moral beliefs of which he feels most sure. The fact that some moral belief fits well with a system into which fit other moral beliefs of which a subject feels confident is grounds for adopting the former belief, for the former belief then draws support from principles which themselves seem evident because they are exemplified in the latter beliefs.

The pursuit of coherence in one's moral beliefs often leads to a widening of their application. Early moral codes tend to commend duties of certain kinds towards members of one's own tribe, and not towards foreigners. Reflection on such codes inevitably leads the thinker to ask what is it about members of his tribe which entitles them to such privileged treatment. And he will often come up with the conclusion that with regard to certain duties it is arbitrary to confine them towards members of his tribe. The duty not to rape a woman, for example, is arbitrarily confined if it is limited to members of one's own tribe. It is respect for persons as persons which can alone make sense of this duty. By contrast it is not physically possible for a man to care lovingly for all men, and hence plausibly there is a duty to care for those who are involved with him in business, friendship, and ancestry in a way in which there is no such duty to care for all men.

On a more general level, many men have seen utilitarianism as providing a coherent moral code, with its great principle 'Always act so as to forward the greatest happiness of the greatest number' able to justify many but not all of their own previous miscellaneous set of moral views. Others have seen Jesus' summary of the Law and the Prophets, 'Love God and love your neighbour as yourself' as providing coherence to many of their previously held diverse views, and so to be their foundation and so to be preferred to some of their previous moral views where in conflict with that summary.

Finally, of course, experience does and should modify all moral views. Men change their moral views by seeing what it is really like when somebody lives by a certain code (e.g. by seeing the depth of pain caused by, or the inflexibility of attitude implicit in, that code).

In these ways men come to modify their moral views, and so make moral progress. Although at a given time some individual aware of a certain range of past experiences, and a certain range of arguments which he has heard, cannot help his moral beliefs; what he can do is choose whether to seek out (by reflection and talking to those with different views) moral truth, or not to bother, or he can even suppress half-thoughts that some view has 'got something' lest that view take him over.

Such are the kinds of reasoning by the pursuit of which men can grow in their grasp of moral truth. Who can deny that six or so millennia of civilization have seen great progress in moral belief? Think of the practices once so common and morally approved, and now morally condemned and so rare—child-sacrifice, exposure of infants, suttee, trial by ordeal, duelling, slavery, the worship of emperors; and think of the practices, now so frequent and morally approved, once so rare—vast quantities of food and medicine sent to help the starving in distant lands, schemes (voluntary or government-sponsored) to educate all and to care for the medical needs of all. And so on.

13. THE FREEDOM OF THE WILL

HUMANS have the capacities for logical reasoning and moral choice, and I have argued that it was the development of language which gave to our ancestors these capacities. I shall now argue that humans have free will, in the sense that they are not causally necessitated to do the actions which they do by brain-events or any other events. I discussed in Chapter 6 how humans find themselves with desires which make them slip naturally into doing some actions, and make it hard for them to do others. But my thesis is that humans have the power to choose between desires of equal strength, and the power to resist desire and do what they believe more worth while, and that their choice is not necessitated by brain- or other events. Although I cannot show this conclusively, I shall argue that the substantial balance of evidence favours that view; and that, although other animals may also be free of necessitation to make the choices they do, there is a crucial feature of humans which makes it much more likely that they have (in this sense) free will than that animals do.[1]

I argued in Chapter 5 that when a man performs an intentional action, his purposings (to achieve some goal) and his belief that a certain bodily movement will causally forward that goal, cause that bodily movement. An agent's purpose to open the door and his belief that pulling his hand holding the handle towards him will cause the door to open causes the hand to move towards him. So if his intentional actions are causally necessitated, this will be because his beliefs and purposings are causally necessitated. In so far as there are causes which influence what a man believes and what he purposes, almost certainly they all operate through the brain. The stimuli which land on the sense-organs or stimulate the peripheral nervous system and make humans more likely to have

[1] I believe that it follows from this and from the fact that humans have beliefs about what is morally good to do and what is morally wrong to do, that they can properly be praised for doing what they believe good to do and blamed for doing what they believe wrong to do; and so are morally responsible. Animals, lacking moral beliefs, are not morally responsible. However, I do not argue these theses here.

certain beliefs and desires, and so purposes, all act through the brain. I shall assume the absence of any telepathy or any other influence of one soul on another, which does not operate via the brain; anyone who does not accept this assumption will need to qualify my conclusion.

Hence, if men are causally necessitated to act as they do, the process works as follows. Brain-states causally necessitate a man's beliefs and purposings. The beliefs and purposings together causally necessitate other brain-states which in turn causally necessitate bodily movements. We will ignore the latter process, assuming it to be as deterministic as most physical processes, and concentrate on the mind/body processes. I argued in Chapter 10 that there was no reason to suppose that there were any general laws of such processes, from which one could derive special laws for men, for other animals, for robots, etc., and from which one could derive laws about the consequences (e.g. in the form of new kinds of sensations) of tampering with brains in various ways. There are at most regular correlations between the brain-states and subsequent mental states, between the mental and subsequent brain-states. (I did earlier, perhaps very rashly, assume one–many mind–brain correlations for simultaneous states; that the brain always constitutes a map from which the mind can be read off. The issue here is whether the processes of change are deterministic.) Are there internally reliable processes in humans, even though their source is a mystery, of the form $(B \rightarrow K)$, $(B \rightarrow P)$, and $((K + P) \rightarrow B)$, where B ranges over human brain-states, K over human belief-states and P over human purposings, or are such processes merely probabilistic?

I shall, to begin with, consider whether purely physical processes are deterministic, to see if we can reach a reasonably justified conclusion by analogy about psychophysical processes (even though we know of no law which explains their occurrence). I shall argue that we cannot; we need to look in detail at the processes themselves. We have little empirical information about the extent to which these processes are regular; and for the reasons given in Chapter 10 we are unlikely to have an overall theory of these processes, and so any empirically established generalizations could not be relied on to hold in slightly different circumstances. Then I shall consider whether a study of the evolutionary processes by which animals come to have a particular brain and a range of possible brain-states, as causes and effects of their mental states, suggests that evolution is likely to select brains whose states are correlated with mental states either in deterministic or in indeterministic ways. I shall argue that evolution will tend to favour indeterministic brain/purpose processes. Finally, however, I shall suggest that the phenomena of human counter-suggestibility tilts the balance decisively in favour of human purposings not being predetermined.

I begin by considering how far purely physical processes are deterministic.

Empirical Arguments for Physical Determinism

I understand by determinism the thesis that every event has a cause in the sense of a prior event which causally necessitates its occurrence in all its detail, and I understand by a process being fully deterministic that this is so of all the events which are the outcome of the process. Arguments given in the past in favour of determinism have included philosophical a priori arguments, as well as empirical arguments (i.e. arguments from experience, inductive a posteriori arguments). But since today few people think any of the former to have any worth I shall concentrate on the latter.[2]

I shall understand by physical determinism the thesis that every

[2] It has been argued that any argument for determinism would be self-defeating. For suppose a scientist discovers an apparently cogent argument for determinism. He will conclude that he has been caused to believe that his argument is cogent. But when we discover of people that they are caused to hold beliefs—e.g. as a result of the way they were educated, or of subjection to drugs—we do not regard them as having a rationally justified belief. To be rational in adopting a belief we have to do so freely, i.e. uncaused, the argument goes. So no one can ever be justified in believing determinism to be true. For one who believes determinism to be true must believe his belief to be caused and so unjustified. (There is a statement of this argument, subsequently retracted, by J. B. S. Haldane in his *Possible Worlds*, Chatto and Windus, London, 1930, p. 209. For references to other statements of it, including one by Epicurus, and discussion thereof, see K. R. Popper and J. C. Eccles, *The Self and its Brain*, Springer, New York, 1977, pp. 75 ff.) This argument has, I believe, no force at all. The mere fact that our beliefs are caused is no grounds for holding them unjustified. Exactly the reverse. I argued in Chapter 7 that to the extent that we regarded them as uncaused or self-chosen, we could not regard our beliefs as moulded by the facts and so likely to be true. The point is rather that if we see some belief to be caused by a totally irrelevant factor (e.g. a belief that I now am being persecuted being caused by something irrelevant in my upbringing) then we rightly regard it as unjustified. But a belief that determinism is true could be both caused and justified, if caused by relevant factors, e.g. hearing relevant arguments.

physical event (which does not have a mental event as part of its cause) has a cause, a prior event which necessitates its occurrence in all its detail. I thus understand physical determinism as a thesis about the physical world in so far as it is free from interaction with the mental.[3] Is physical determinism true?

Quite clearly there are many events which happen, of which we do not know the cause. We do not know why the rain started at exactly 2.00 p.m. rather than at 2.05 p.m., why the light bulb failed today rather than tomorrow, why this man died of the disease and that man survived, why this seed germinated and that one did not, the earthquake occurred today in San Francisco rather than tomorrow in Los Angeles. Why should anyone suppose that these events of which we do not know the cause, do in fact have causes? Why not suppose that they are simply random uncaused events?

There are two reasons why people have supposed that all physical events have causes, even if, for some events, we cannot currently discover those causes. The first is that provided by the argument from the success of science. I now set out this argument in a moderately rigorous form.

Physical determinism (PD), which concerns the causes of effects, follows from a more general principle, which I shall call the principle of spatio-temporal predetermination (STP), which concerns the effects of causes. STP states that for any sphere of any radius r centred on any point P, and for any smaller sphere of radius $(r - \triangle r)$ also centred on P, there is a (small) time interval $\triangle t$ such that the state of the larger sphere at t fully determines in all its detail the state of the smaller sphere at $t + \triangle t$. Put more loosely, the state of the universe over any region determines the state of a smaller region within the larger region at a slightly later time. STP entails PD. For every event is part of the state of a smaller sphere which lies within a larger sphere, and so will have some event which causes it in all its detail.

PD however does not entail STP. Given PD, STP will only be true given a third principle, the principle of action by contact in a wide sense, which I shall call AC. AC states that all physical causes are linked to their physical effects by spatio-temporal chains. If E

---

[3] Physical determinism in its strongest and most natural form is the thesis that every physical event has a physical event which necessitates its occurrence in all its detail. But if I am right in supposing that mental events have bodily effects, as I argue in Chapter 5, this thesis is mistaken. The physical world is not a deterministically closed system.

causes *F*, it causes *F* by causing an event *G* spatio-temporaily contiguous to *E*, which causes an event *H* contiguous to *G* which causes . . . etc., until we come to *F*. If we allow as events states of gravitational, electromagnetic, etc. fields of forces, which are after all not states inferable only from remote causes and effects but states detectable by instruments at the place and time of their occurrence; and if we ignore any quantum effects (such as the jump of an orbiting electron from one radius to another);[4] there is abundant empirical evidence for the truth of AC (viz. for any random sample of events, to the extent to which we have knowledge of causes and effects, we find that AC applies). If a distant sun causes the Earth to move, it does so via affecting the gravitational field in the intervening space (whether the effect is propagated with infinite velocity, as Newton claimed, or finite velocity, as Einstein claimed), as can be seen by putting test-bodies along the Sun–Earth line. And if an animal's past performance in solving the maze influences its present behaviour it does so via affecting the animal's brain-state in the intervening time. Despite the enormous knowledge which scientists have acquired of causes, they have no evidence of causes which jump.

Together with AC, PD entails STP. For if every event does have a cause, *and* causes are spatio-temporally contiguous to their effects, then there will be a cause of any state of the universe in one region lying in a slightly larger region which surrounds it (without their boundaries touching) and so within *any* such region at some earlier time. Hence the state of the universe in any region will predetermine the state of the universe in any smaller region within it.

For STP, it is claimed, there is empirical evidence for the success of science. (It is because it is easier to set out that evidence than to set out the evidence for PD directly, that I use the derivability of PD from STP.) For take any area of enquiry—the movements of planets and comets, the flux of electric current, the movements of tides, the interactions of simple inorganic liquids and gases to form new liquids and gases, and so on. Within such areas, scientists have sought for the laws of nature, laws which tell us which

---

[4] We can, I suggest, ignore quantum effects, partly because in this respect they affect only the very small scale—there is no way of magnifying quantum jumps—and partly because PD is doomed anyway once we take quantum theory into account, as I shall argue later.

preceding states bring about which subsequent states in the respects concerned (position, temperature, or whatever). A theory with universal laws states how a given initial state physically necessitates a later subsequent state within the region. A theory with statistical laws states only how the former physically probabilifies the latter. Scientists seek universal laws for preference. A theory is confirmed (i.e. shown likely to be true) to the extent to which it has simple laws which make accurate predictions. The more accurate its predictions, the more likely it is that the theory is approximately true; if its predictions are perfectly accurate over a wide range and a long period that is good evidence that it is completely true, that that is how nature is.

Now four thousand years ago, there were no areas in which scientists had well-confirmed theories. But between then and now, scientists have produced fairly well-confirmed theories for an ever increasing number of areas. And once they have a fairly well-confirmed theory in some area, they have often progressed towards producing better confirmation of that theory (by showing that it predicts more accurately than at first they were able to show) or have produced a better-confirmed theory (normally by amending the previous theory). Many of these theories today are universal, although originally the areas in question had only statistical theories. These theories concern the future development of variables within some field, subject to boundary conditions (e.g. of temperature or position, or genotype within some region, subject to non-interference from outside). This increasing success of science in predicting more accurately in more areas is, the argument goes, evidence that if we go on investigating, science will eventually predict to any desired accuracy we choose in all areas and so vindicate STP for all areas. Hence it will show that every physical event has a cause.

This general argument from the success of science is, alas, a bad argument. Increasing accuracy of prediction in more and more fields is only good reason for supposing that we will eventually reach prediction as accurate as you desire in all areas if there is a well-confirmed law of how that accuracy will increase (i.e. in which areas predicition to which degree of accuracy will be achieved when) which has that consequence. There needs to be a simple formula which yields predictable regularity in the accuracy achieved in different areas. For otherwise there is no reason to suppose that science will continue to make progress in covering ever new areas, as it has done so far, or to suppose that if it does it will eventually reach an accurate prediction to any chosen degree of accuracy (for one could go on predicting more and more accurately forever without getting anywhere near to being as accurate as one desired).

Consider an analogy. The North Sea is cut up into squares for drilling purposes (see Fig. 2). After drilling one hundred feet in all squares oil companies find oil in one square; after drilling two hundred feet in all squares they find oil in another square; after drilling three hundred feet in all squares they find oil in a third square. Does it follow that if they drill indefinitely they will find oil in all squares? Not at all. They could only conclude this if there was a well-confirmed formula correlating depth of discovery of oil with location of square, such that they can predict the depth at which oil can be found in any square, which has yielded successful predictions in all squares tested so far. So, too, with science. Only if there was some well-confirmed formula which states after how much work scientists would achieve successful predictions in any field could we reasonably infer (if it follows from the formula) that they will obtain successful predictions in all fields if they work hard enough. There is no such formula. In its absence we must affirm that increasing success does not indicate future total success.

Much stronger than this general argument from the success of science is the following argument. All physical events are states or changes of state of physical objects. All physical objects consist of subatomic particles interconnected in various ways. All human bodies, for example, are made of protons, and electrons, muons, neutrons, etc. We have found that individual subatomic particles are governed in their behaviour by the four forces (gravitational,

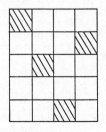

Fig. 2

238 The Human Soul

strong, weak, and electromagnetic). Hence, conglomerations of such particles are so governed. This argument has, I think, some force. Theories of the operation of the four physical forces have indeed had significant success in predicting the behaviour of free particles, or interactions within, say, the hydrogen atom. But such particles might behave differently when bound together tightly in large molecules of a solid. We need rather more evidence of the behaviour of particles within somewhat larger-scale systems before we can extrapolate with justification to the scale of medium-sized objects. I believe, however, that we are well on the way to getting this evidence, since a lot of current work in physics and theoretical chemistry is beginning to show that our laws of a more macroscopic kind (phenomenological laws about observables) follow from fundamental laws of the four forces.[5]

However, the laws which we find to operate on the subatomic level are subject to the overall limits on accuracy of prediction imposed by the laws of quantum theory, the guiding theory of the subatomic realm. I shall now argue that nature is deterministic only to within those limits.[6]

[5] See Additional Note 3.

[6] Popper has argued that physical determinism cannot be known to be true for a reason quite other than that provided by quantum theory—see his *The Open Universe*, Hutchinson, London, 1982, *passim*. This is that we cannot *pre*dict all events, in the literal sense of 'foretell their occurrence', *before* they happen. He claims that even classical mechanics is in an important sense not a deterministic theory, because while it claims that physical events are followed by other states in accord with universal laws, for some types of cause it is physically impossible to find out whether the cause C_1 occurred, and make the calculation to predict an effect E_1, until E_1 has itself occurred. In that case, E_1 would not in the strictly literal sense be *pre*dictable. In particular, neither people nor computers nor societies of people or computers, can predict their own future states before they happen.

But such impossibility does not seem to be relevant either to physical determinism or to STP which entails it. These are claims about events having causes or effects, and would be evidenced by the calculability of those causes or effects; whether or not the calculation can be done before any event predicted occurs is not relevant. When I write in the text of scientific theories predicting some event E_1, I mean only that its occurrence follows from the theory and the occurrence of some prior state of affairs, whether or not the calculation that E will occur can be made in advance of the occurrence of E.

On pp. 77–81 of *The Open Universe*, Popper attempts to meet the suggestion that, according to a theory such as classical mechanics, although many future events might not be *pre*dictable in advance, 'every physical system is predictable in the sense that *at least after the event to be predicted has occurred*, we can see that the event was determined by the state of the system, in the sense that a sufficiently full description of the system (together with natural laws) *logically entails* the prediction'. Popper claims that 'There is every reason to believe that we cannot

The Quantum Limits to Physical Determinism

I begin with a more general argument. Suppose that in some field of enquiry we have a theory T_1 better confirmed by evidence than is any other theory. However, T_1 does not predict the future development of the field with perfect accuracy, either because it does not claim to do so (having merely statistical laws, or being concerned only with certain ranges of variables) or because its predictions are in fact only of limited accuracy. In general, of course, showing that on T_1 we cannot predict the future development of the field, is not showing that there are no deterministic processes at work in the field; it is only showing that if there are such processes, T_1 is inadequate to reveal them.[7] However, the observations which confirmed our current theory T_1 are evidence against any rival theory T_2, rival in the sense of making predictions conflicting with those of T_1. For the evidence in favour of T_1 is evidence in favour of the predictions of T_1 and hence evidence against the predictions of T_2 and hence evidence against T_2. They are therefore evidence against the confirmability of any rival theory which claims to predict the future development of the field with perfect accuracy (i.e. any degree of accuracy you care to choose). The observations, however, are not evidence for or against the confirmability of any more fundamental theory T_3, from which the predictions of T_1 would be a deductive consequence. T_3 would not be a rival to T_1, for it would predict whatever T_1 predicted, but it would predict in the same field more than T_1. It might thus predict with perfect accuracy the characteristics of individual states, while T_1 only predicted overall patterns. Since, *ex hypothesi*, the evidence at present confirms T_1 better than any other rival or more fundamental theory, we would need additional evidence to confirm T_3, but that (unlike evidence to support T_2) would be evidence as to the occurrence of which in general T_1 would be indifferent. Hence, if we are to show that not

collect enough data to *entail* the solution of our prediction-task because we do not know what data will be needed for our prediction'—e.g. that we couldn't collect enough data about the state of the car before the crash to entail that there would be a crash. That might be. But Popper gives no argument for his 'there is every reason to suppose'.

[7] Some of the points made in the rest of this section are contained in an earlier article of mine, 'Physical Determinism' in (ed.) G. N. A. Vesey, *Knowledge and Necessity*, Macmillan, London, 1970.

merely have causes for all physical events not been found, but do not exist, we would have to produce evidence that an overall theory T_3 from which perfect predictions of all events could be made, could never be confirmed; that is, could never have evidence produced in its favour which was not simply evidence for T_1 but evidence which would give grounds for going beyond T_1 and adopting T_3. The evidence of observations from which T_1 was constructed would have, in this case, to be evidence that no more fundamental theory than T_1 predicting events with greater accuracy could be confirmed. Then we would have evidence that T_1 provided the most fundamental explanation of observations. For if a certain theory in some field is confirmed by observations better than any other theory, we are only justified in supposing that its laws are not the most fundamental laws, governing phenomena in the field, if we are justified in suspecting that one day some more fundamental theory will be confirmed better. We may have strong or weak reasons for the latter belief—e.g. that our theory was established merely on the basis of data of some peculiar kind. But if we have evidence that in some respect no more fundamental theory will ever be established, we must surely take the laws of the theory which we have in that respect as the fundamental laws governing phenomena. Evidence that a theory with statistical laws predicting events to different degrees of probability provides the most fundamental explanation of phenomena would be evidence that some events do not have causes.

What kind of evidence could show that no such fundamental theory of the field T_3 with universal laws making perfect predictions of all events could ever be confirmed? Clearly it would always be logically possible to *construct* a theory T_3 from which— for certain postulated empirical circumstances—the predictions of T_1 could be derived, T_1 having merely statistical laws and T_3 having universal laws which predict all events with unlimited accuracy. Thus suppose that the current theory T_1 is statistical and includes such laws as that there is a ninety per cent probability of an A turning into B. This explains such observations as that ninety per cent of As observed in large samples do turn into Bs. We then postulate that ninety per cent of As have an unobservable characteristic C, while ten per cent of As lack this characteristic. We then propose the theory T_3 which includes the laws that all As which are C turn into Bs, and no As which are not C turn into Bs. The predictions of T_1 are then deductive consequences of T_3 for the postulated empirical circumstances, and we have as yet no grounds for believing that these do not hold. What would have to be shown if we are to rule out the deterministic theory is that we could never have any evidence for the truth of such a theory which was not merely evidence for a statistical theory. We could show this if the current scientific knowledge embodied in T_1 showed reason for believing that a theory going beyond T_1 and explaining its operation, would have to be of a certain form, but that theories of that form consisting of universal laws could never be confirmed in such a way as to justify our going beyond a statistical theory and adopting it. Thus, the evidence could show that certain kinds of parameters ought to enter into such a theory, yet measurements of these parameters could never be made in such a way as to get evidence in favour of the theory which was not merely evidence in favour of a statistical theory. In our simple example, T_1 might show that C was an unobservable characteristic, such that there were no means of checking whether an A had that characteristic apart from seeing whether the A turned into a B and then retrodicting that it must have been C. But that is quite inadequate grounds for postulating the characteristic C. We have no good grounds for going beyond the statistical law, borne out by observation, that ninety per cent of As turn into Bs. Our T_3 makes claims of a detail which it is unable to substantiate. In such a case we would have evidence that our well-confirmed current theory which only predicted individual physical events with a certain probability could not itself be further explained by a theory which predicted with certainty. The evidence would thus show that T_1 provided the most fundamental explanation of phenomena and hence that initial conditions do not fully predetermine the subsequent development of the field, and so that STP is false. It would then follow, given AC (viz. that there are no causes acting from outside the set-up, e.g. at a distance without producing effects at the boundary), that physical determinism is false; not all events have causes which necessitate their occurrence; at most, causes which make probable their occurrence.

If my analysis of what would be evidence against STP and so (given AC) against physical determinism is correct, then modern science gives good grounds for believing that at the subatomic level determinism is false. For quantum theory is a very well-substantiated scientific theory which accounts for a whole host of physical and chemcial phenomena at that level, and, I suggest, on present evidence, better than can any rival theory. The occurrence of these phenomena is thus strong evidence against any rival theory which predicts more accurately. The laws of quantum theory are statistical in predicting future values of many physical states only with some degree of probability. Thus, given a light source emitting photons, an intercepting screen with a slit in it, and a plate beyond the screen, the laws of quantum theory predict only to a certain degree of probability whereabouts on the plate a photon emitted at a given distance will arrive. To explain the operation of these statistical laws we could construct a more fundamental theory consisting of universal lawlike statements which explained the subsequent destination of photons by properties which they possessed on leaving the source, their possession of which made inevitable their destination. Yet we have evidence that such a theory could never be confirmed. The evidence is that the whole of mechanics and electromagnetism which is taken over by quantum theory indicates that free subatomic particles such as photons travel along continuous paths and hence that in order to know their subsequent positions, we need to know, as well as the surrounding circumstances, their present position and their momentum (which way they are moving and how fast). Yet it is a consequence of quantum theory that the position and momentum of a particle cannot be measured simultaneously to joint accuracy of greater than $h/4\pi$, where h is Planck's constant. ($\triangle p. \triangle q \geqslant h/4\pi$.) This result, the Heisenberg indeterminacy principle, follows from the basic structure of quantum theory,[8] and is well confirmed

---

[8] This is because if we could know the simultaneous values of position and momentum of a sub-atomic particle, then statements about it could not be written as statements about a wave packet, in which case if it were subsequently put into circumstances where it behaved like a wave, this wave-like behaviour would be a mystery. Wave packets are bundles of waves which interfere so as to cancel each other out except in a small region. Photons and other subatomic particles behave, as is well known, in some circumstances as particles and in some circumstances as waves. There are well-established relations between particle parameters and wave parameters which enable us to predict the wave behaviour from knowledge of particle parameters and conversely. ($E = h/4\pi \; \omega$ and $\mathbf{p} = h/4\pi \; \mathbf{k}$, where E is the energy and $\mathbf{p}$ the momentum of a particle, and ω the angular frequency and $\mathbf{k}$ the propagation vector of the corresponding wave.) It is a consequence of these relations that the narrower the wave packet (viz. the smaller the region in which the waves of the bundle do not cancel each other out), the wider the range of the

independently—we can show for any instrument which may be proposed for detecting position or momentum, that using it to detect one of these rules out the simultaneous use of that or any other instrument to detect the other.

It follows that given the truth of quantum theory, no theory consisting of universal laws about the exact paths followed by particles could ever be confirmed by observation. For the evidence is that the theory must take the form of claiming that particles with such-and-such initial positions and momenta move in certain ways. But since initial positions and momenta cannot ever be measured simultaneously any theory which predicts behaviour in virtue of these characteristics could never be confirmed. This is because the evidence which we could have in its favour could not be evidence about the paths taken by all particles having such-and-such position and momentum, since to the accuracy to which we could measure these, particles having any given position and momentum would always take very different paths, and hence their behaviour would only support a mere statistical theory. Nor can there be indirect evidence of the position and momentum of a particle from the measurement of other subatomic parameters (e.g. energy), for a similar indeterminism affects their measurement. Hence, the evidence is not, and cannot be, strong enough to justify our going beyond a merely statistical theory and postulating universal laws. And, as I say, what goes for particle motion goes for various other phenomena covered by quantum theory. Just as you cannot measure position and momentum simultaneously, so you cannot measure the energy of a particle and the time at which you measure it, except to within the limits of Planck's constant. If you measure precisely a particle's energy, there will be a vagueness about the time at which the particle had that energy. *All* subatomic phenomena are infected by quantum indeterminacy, predictable only within certain limits. Among the phenomena which in consequence we cannot predict more accurately than within a certain range is the time at which a radioactive atom will decay— all we can say of any given such atom (e.g. an atom of radium) is that it has a certain half-life (e.g. 1,700 years), i.e. that there is a probability of ½ that it will decay during the next 1,700 years.

propagation vectors and so of the momenta of the corresponding particles. Hence, the more precisely we know the position, the less precisely we know momentum. If we could know both simultaneously for a particle, we could not translate our knowledge into statements about the frequency and propagation vectors of waves.

In this way the very form of quantum theory, as well as ruling out rival theories also rules out any more fundamental theory explaining by universal laws. The evidence in favour of quantum theory with its statistical laws making possible only probabilistic predictions of physical states is thus evidence against any theory with universal laws ever being substantiated. It is thus evidence in favour of a theory with statistical laws providing the most fundamental explanation of observations. Quantum theory has the exceptional characteristic among statistical theories of ruling out more fundamental non-statistical theories.

Quantum theory is a theory extremely well confirmed by observations of small-scale phenomena. It has always proved better at predicting observations than innumerable deterministic theories which have been constructed as rivals to it. Despite this, it just may happen that one day it will be shown to be false and replaced by another better-confirmed rival theory. But at any stage of science we must draw conclusions from the evidence which we have and not that which we guess we might one day obtain. Next century's theory may explain the physical and chemical phenomena which quantum theory purports to explain today in a way entirely different from that of quantum theory. By it a light source may cause a plate to be illuminated without emitting photons which cross the intervening space. But until such a theory is substantiated by evidence, we must reach our conclusions from the best-confirmed theory which we have.

In general the quantum effects which manifest themselves so evidently on the subatomic scale will not, according to quantum theory, manifest themselves much on the macroscopic scale of medium-sized objects. The indeterminacies in the behaviour of individual particles generally more or less cancel each other out, so as to produce virtual determinism on the macroscopic scale. Thus, although of an individual atom of radium we can say only that it has a 50% probability of distintegrating within the next 1,700 years, we can say of a medium-sized block of radium that there is a 99.99 chance that virtually 50% of the block will disintegrate within the next 1,700 years. But although normally small-scale indeterminacies more or less cancel each other out, this does not always happen. There are mechanisms which make the occurrence of a large-scale effect depend on the occurrence of some subatomic event, when the probability of its occurrence or non-occurrence is no near certainty. Thus, Ernie, the machine which produces on a medium-sized screen the numbers of premium bond winners, has been so constructed that which numbers it produces is determined by subatomic processes with probabilities of occurrence close to neither 0 nor 1. One could make a hydrogen bomb, the explosion of which depends on whether an atom of some radioactive substance decayed within some period. Quantum theory can tell us only the probability of such decay, which needs to be close neither to 0 nor 1.

Let us call any system (temporarily isolated from outside causal influences) an averaging device if only a very large number of significant independent divergences from the most probable values of the subatomic states will make any observable difference to later large-scale states. Almost all naturally occurring chunks of matter are like the block of radium, averaging devices. Take a stone falling from a height on a still day. Whether it falls in a straight line will depend on the average horizontal momentum of the particles which compose it. The most probable value of the horizontal momentum of each such particle is zero; and although that momentum may vary in case in undetermined ways within the quantum limits, the probability of the average momentum of the particles diverging to a significant degree from its most probable value and so making the stone diverge to any observable extent from its straight line fall, is very, very close to zero. There is a probability of ½ perhaps that such a thing will happen once in a million million million years. The probabilities are so high that we can talk of a virtual determinism, a causal probabilifying to all intents and purposes as good as causal necessitation. Call a device a multiplying device if whether the large-scale observable states occur depends crucially not on a very large number of independent subatomic states, but only a few, and, in the extreme, only one such state. The hydrogen bomb which I have just described would be a multiplying device. A divergence from the most probable value of one or a few subatomic states will make an observable difference; and such divergence is quite probable. So, if the only source of indeterminism in the physical world is quantum theory, its extent and influence will depend on the frequency among systems of multiplying devices. No doubt this is small, but any device of great complexity whose large-scale behaviour depends on small-scale goings-on will be a candidate for being such a device. In consequence the brain is an obvious candidate. That it is such a device was first defended in detail by Sir John Eccles in lectures of 1947 published as *The Neurophysiological Basis of Mind*;[9] but he is not now too convinced about his argument there. However, in favour of the supposition there is the fact that stimulation of a single neurone can produce gross bodily movements; and the firings of such neurones may well on occasion depend on the quantity and timing of the release of transmitter substances at synapses within the quantum limit. However, we just don't know enough from the neurophysiological side to know if the brain is a multiplying device or not. If it were a multiplying device it would follow that even if mind–body causation were not crucial in the production of human actions (and I have been arguing that it is crucial), still human actions would not be causally necessitated by prior events.

My conclusion to this section is that quantum theory shows that there is a substantial limit to physical determinism; on the subatomic level there is nothing like determinism. On the larger scale quantum theory allows that earlier states probabilify later states with such high probability that we can talk of virtual causal necessitation—so long as they are states of averaging devices, not of multiplying devices.

Application to Psychophysical Determinism

So what does all this suggest about psychophysical processes? It has been evident since Descartes that the three such processes which concern us—the production by brain-states of purposings and of beliefs, and the production of brain-states by purposings and beliefs—are totally different from any physical process—whether a process of a kind hypothesized by Descartes, or of kinds hypothesized by Einstein or Heisenberg. For, as we have seen in detail, beliefs and purposings are intrinsically propositional; they possess in-built meaning, something totally lacking to physical processes.

The fact that these processes are so totally different from any physical process has the consequences that even if all physical processes were totally deterministic there would be little reason for supposing that the body–mind and mind–body processes were similarly deterministic. However, the evidence of quantum theory

[9] Clarendon Press, Oxford, 1953.

is that physical processes are only deterministic within certain limits.

Given that, analogy offers little guidance about what to expect about the extent to which mind–body and body–mind processes are deterministic. We would need to reach a justified view on what is the natural analogue in the mental world of those differences in the physical world which are of quantum significance—is the difference between purposing to go to London and purposing to go to Moscow like a difference in length of 10 cm. or like a difference in length of 10^{-13} cm.? Analogy suggests no answer; and that is why any conclusion which we might reach about the level on which the physical world is indeterministic will suggest very little about the amount of indeterminism outside that world.

Perhaps, however, a detailed study of the three psychophysical processes in question will suggest an answer as to whether the processes operative in humans are deterministic. A start would be to consider how far there are uniform correlations between kinds of brain-states and resultant beliefs, kinds of beliefs-and-purposes and resultant brain-states, and kinds of brain-states and resultant purposes. (Note that our concern here is with correlations between mental states and prior brain-states, and conversely; whether the development of the mental life is correlated with the prior development of the brain. I have already assumed a one–many correlation between the mental and simultaneous brain-states— see pp.183 f. The issue here is concerned with the predictable development of the mental, whether or not that development is reflected simultaneously in a developing brain; and conversely with the predictable development of the brain.) In the way of establishing such correlations there is the very considerable difficulty that the subject is better positioned than outsiders to know about his mental events, including his purposes and beliefs; and, even if he seeks to be honest, he may not mean by the words by means of which he describes them the same as others mean. There will, therefore, always be some doubt about the extent to which various correlations have been established. But let us ignore this difficulty and suppose that we can trust absolutely speakers' descriptions of their purposes and beliefs. Given that, there is evidence of much uniform correlation between kinds of brain-state and kinds of subsequent beliefs. Since our beliefs about the state of the world around us often have a high degree of correlation with the states of the world around us, and the latter operates on our sense-organs to cause the brain-states connected with our beliefs, that shows that there must often be a high degree of correlation between kinds of brain-state and kinds of subsequent belief. Similarly, there is evidence of much uniform correlation between kinds of purpose to effect some goal and beliefs about which bodily movement will effect that goal, and kinds of resulting bodily movements (when the beliefs about the necessary bodily movements are of a certain kind—e.g. to move a whole finger rather than a finger-nail—that is, the movements are those which lie within the agent's capacity to produce). That shows that there must often be uniform correlations between beliefs and purposes and the brain-states which cause the bodily movements. But of course these correlations do not always hold—sometimes men acquire false beliefs or cannot move the limbs they purpose to move. And there is little evidence of uniform correlations between kinds of brain-state and kinds of subsequent purpose. Of course people habitually do certain things in certain circumstances, but when people have to make choices, there is little certainty about how they will choose. This may be either because different people in similar circumstances have different brain-states or because the brain-state–purpose correlations are far from uniform, or both.

If we did have good evidence that the $(B \rightarrow K)$ and ($(K + P) \rightarrow B$) connections were deterministic, that would provide some weak evidence by analogy that the $(B \rightarrow P)$ connection was also deterministic. The analogies however are weak. Purposings are active states, things that agents do, whereas beliefs are passive states, things that happen to them—and so one might well expect beliefs and not purposings to be caused; and the efficacy of the mental ($(K + P) \rightarrow B$) is, because it involves active intentional choice, very different from the efficacy of the physical.

Our next kind of evidence comes from the fact that humans, like other animals, have evolved by natural selection. Organisms ill-adapted for survival would have been eliminated. In order to survive, an organism with beliefs and purposes needs largely true beliefs about its environment, and largely efficacious purposes. A species of animals whose beliefs about the presence of food, predators, mates, etc. were largely false would not survive for long—and the same goes for a species whose attempts to avoid predators and secure food and mates were always frustrated by their purposes to move one limb causing the movement of a different limb. In order to have such largely true beliefs, animals need to have brains 'wired in' to their bodies in the right way and also to have largely deterministic connections between brain-states and beliefs, e.g. the presence of a predator must normally cause via a sense organ a brain-state, which causes the belief that the predator is present when and only when the predator is present. If mutations produce animals whose brains are wired in the wrong way, they will be eliminated. Similarly if mutations produce brain-states which cause certain beliefs only probabilistically, not with any high degree of necessity, they, too, will be eliminated. A mutation cannot cause a given brain-state to have an effect other than its normal one, but it may be that a given belief (K_1) can be produced either by B_1 or B_2, but the ($B_1 \rightarrow K_1$) connection is invariable while the ($B_2 \rightarrow K_1$) connection only operates with a moderate degree of physical probability. Natural selection will favour animals which have brain-states connected deterministically rather than only probabilistically to a given belief; only in such animals can their beliefs be fully sensitive to how things are. A similar argument shows that evolution favours animals in whom there are deterministic belief-and-purpose/brain-state connections; only such animals can achieve their purposes. If there are alternative sets of ($B \rightarrow K$) and (($K + P$) $\rightarrow B$) correlations available, then evolution will favour the evolution of animals with brains having brain-states governed by the more deterministic processes. Evolution gives no indication as to the particular forms these deterministic processes must take; it merely insists that whatever the brain correlates are, they must be 'wired in' in the right way.

What of the ($B \rightarrow P$) processes? There are certain restrictions upon them needed if organisms are to survive. Organisms need to have the purpose of escaping predators (whenever they believe that there is a predator present) and the purposes of eating, drinking, and mating—from time to time. (Perhaps also the purpose of lying down where it is convenient to sleep.) Or rather, what is necessary if a species is to survive is that, in general, organisms of that species shall have such purposes; the processes which produce such purposes must give quite a high probability to their occurrence. This would be the case if brain-states gave rise to an ever-present desire to escape predators, and the desires to eat, drink, etc. when eating, drinking, etc. are good for survival; but the organisms might choose sometimes for good reason to resist the latter desires. The species will still survive so long as most members yield to such desires after a time, and yield immediately to the desire to escape a predator believed to be present. But, that said, there are many ways of escaping predators, eating, drinking, etc., and many other things to do between morning and night. There would seem to be no evolutionary advantage for the organism to be determined in these respects. On the contrary, there would be an evolutionary advantage in the process being indeterministic. For purposes which are not determined cannot be predicted, however sophisticated the predictor, and if the details of an organisms's behaviour are not predictable, he will be able to escape his predators and those who seek to control him. If for a given purpose, there were two brain-states, one of which produced the purpose deterministically and one which produced it only with a moderate degree of physical probability, there would be an evolutionary advantage for an organism which had a brain-state of the latter type only.

Now the fact that there are evolutionary pressures favouring the selection of animals with brain-states connected deterministically or indeterministically, as the case may be, with mental states of certain kinds, is some small evidence for supposing that those animals which have survived do have brain-states of those kinds, that the $(B \rightarrow K)$ and $((K + P) \rightarrow B)$ processes are deterministic while the $(B \rightarrow P)$ processes are indeterministic. Of course we do not know whether alternative deterministic and indeterministic processes of these kinds were or could be thrown up for selection to operate upon. But there are indeterministic processes in nature, and there are often alternative processes for achieving a given goal in different organisms, one of which may give the organism a selective advantage. So deterministic and indeterministic alternative processes of the $(B \rightarrow K)$, $((K + P) \rightarrow B)$ and $(B \rightarrow P)$ kinds could well have been available. I have suggested which such processes selection would have favoured; and that fact is some reason for supposing that in animals, as in men, nature has selected indeterministic $(B \rightarrow P)$ processes. The fact that quite a bit of human behaviour is currently unpredictable is compatible with, and indeed would be explained by, the $(B \to P)$ processes being indeterministic.

On top of the difficulties for brain-state/purposing determinism discussed so far in this chapter, there is the very substantial difficulty considered in Chapter 10, in supposing that any uniform mind/body or body/mind correlations which might be established have the status of deterministic laws. As we saw there, in order to have a theory with scientific laws of mind/body and body/mind, we need more than a list of well-authenticated correlations between events of one kind and events of the other. We need a theory with a few simple laws by which we explain why there is this correlation rather than that—why this brain-state is correlated with this belief and that brain-state with that belief, or (to taken an example of a different brain–mind connection, the brain-state–sensation connection) why the brain-events caused by tasting sugar give rise to a sweet taste, and those caused by tasting salt give rise to a salty taste, and so on. The theory would need to find intrinsic features of brain-events of different kinds which made natural a connection with mental events of different kinds. But how can brain-events vary except in electrochemcial properties and how can one set of such properties have any more natural connection with one kind of sensation or belief than another? Yet in the absence of such a theory we would not know why the correlations hold which do hold, and so would have some reasonable doubt whether they would continue to hold when circumstances change—e.g. when the brain environment was slightly different (e.g. in different people). We may attempt to bypass the mental and establish correlations between the brain processes prior to purposings and the brain processes which initiate bodily movements, or (for agents of normal capacity) the bodily movements themselves. However, any such regularities would be brought about by the operation of purposings and beliefs. If we were ignorant of these causal processes which brought about the observable physical correlations, we could have no well-justified theory of why there occur the correlations which there do; and in the absence of such a theory, we would have no strong reason for supposing that the observed correlations would hold in different environments (e.g. for different kinds of people).

The considerations adduced so far suggest that there is no adequate reason to suppose that brain-state/purpose links are deterministic. These considerations apply equally to animals, as to humans. And maybe in animals those links are indeed indeterministic. There is, however, one further consideration in the case of humans which, I suggest, decisively tilts the balance of evidence in favour of the view that humans have free will.[10] This is the phenomenon of human counter-suggestibility.

Human Counter-Suggestibility

As we noted in Chapter 11, humans seek theoretical truth. And when theories about the world are presented to them by others, they do not always take them on authority; they test them and thereby either show them to be false or confirm them better. Among the knowledge claims which any agent who seeks a well-justified understanding of the world will seek to test, is the claim of any hypothesis about the springs of human behaviour, and especially his own behaviour; above all if that hypothesis is well supported and taken seriously in the scientific community. Such agents need not be fanatical anti-determinists but simply seekers after truth on important matters, i.e. scientifically minded persons. I call such agents counter-suggestible, but I suggest that most humans are in this sense counter-suggestible. Counter-suggestibility, I shall now argue, makes it very unlikely that human purposings are determined by brain-states.

If, despite the difficulties outlined in the last section, there were a true deterministic account of the correlations between brain-states prior to the formulation of purposes and beliefs, and subsequent bodily movements, it would have to apply to agents who if they knew of the account, knew it to be well supported, and knew its prediction about their own behaviour, would sometimes put it to the test if they could do so easily. (I distinguish such an 'account' as a mere list of which brain-events cause which mental

---

[10] In *The Freedom of the Will* (Clarendon Press, Oxford, 1970), chs. 24 onwards, and elsewhere, J. R. Lucas has argued that humans have a different further characteristic which shows their possession of free will. He argues that there is a sentence of some language which is true and may be seen to be true by any human, but to which a human brain cannot be programmed to give assent; so there are rational judgements which men make although their brain-states do not cause them to make them. Lucas's argument depends on an application of Godel's Theorem. Lucas may be right. For criticism however, see David Lewis, 'Lucas Against Determinism II', *Canadian Journal of Philosophy*, 1979, **9**, 373–6; and Lucas's reply, 'Lucas Against Mechanism II: A Rejoinder', *Canadian Journal of Philosophy*, 1984, **14**, 189–91.

events, and conversely, without supposing the account to be backed by any scientific theory which explains why there are the causal connections which there are.) A counter-suggestible agent informed of the predictions of such an account that he would do some simple basic action, would sometimes clearly try to do the opposite, and would succeed since not doing such a basic action lies easily within his power. It follows that if there is a true deterministic account of human behaviour, scientists cannot get a counter-suggestible subject to know the predictions of that account about his immediate future basic actions.

The suggestion (often only implicit) in much writing is that the latter will always be the case with any account of human behaviour. The point is often made that if a scientist examines your brain-state at t_1, predicts on the basis thereof what you will do at t_4 and then tells you at t_2 his prediction, this will alter your brain-state in such a way that the prediction no longer follows from the scientist's account. But what is at stake is whether the scientist can get you to know what his account predicts about your behaviour when your brain-state is that resulting from your having been given his prediction. I know of no discussion in the literature of whether this can be done. I wish to show that whether it can be done depends on the processes in accord with which beliefs are caused by brain-states, depends on what are the $(B \rightarrow K)$ processes, and that for almost all logically possible such processes, this information can be transmitted. Only for $(B \rightarrow K)$ processes of a very narrow (and complex) kind can this not be done; and there are in consequence good inductive reasons for supposing that the actual processes are not of that narrow kind.

A deterministic account of the brain T, which bypassed purposes and beliefs, would show how brain-states were altered by input and were followed (after the formulation of purposings and beliefs—which it ignores) by bodily movements. The account would list which different brain-states $(B_1 \ldots B_n)$ plus which different input to the brain $(I_1 \ldots I_m)$ leads to which different bodily movements $(M_1 \ldots M_x)$. Let us hold constant all non-sensory input to the brain—e.g. keep the blood flowing at a constant rate with its chemical composition constant—or, if this is not possible, allow it to vary in a predictable way of which we can take account. Let us represent the different sensory input by $S_1 \ldots S_m$. The Ss represent not the sensations themselves (e.g. 'a red flash'), but the input along the sensory nerves which gives rise to sensations and also (or thereby), if the sensation is recognized as a means of transmitting information, to beliefs. Then the processes listed by the account will have the form:

$$B(t_1) + S(t_2-t_3) \rightarrow M(t_4)$$

showing for different B and S the different resulting M; t_1 represents an instant of time before the formation of the relevant purpose; t_2-t_3 represents the period during which sensory input is sent to the brain; t_4 represents the instant at which the bodily movement is complete. I stress that this account is concerned with relations between physical variables only. If determinism governs bodily movements, then there will be a list of such deterministic processes for any choice of intervals

$$t_1-t_2, \ t_2-t_3, \text{ and } t_3-t_4.$$

Suppose a scientist to have discovered an account T of the above type and to regard it as well confirmed. Take a simple basic action having as its result a simple bodily movement M_a, which is such that its occurrence is under the voluntary control of normal subjects, e.g. the movement of a subject's left arm so that it touches a switch at a certain time t_4. Equipped with various measuring instruments the scientist now examines the brains of many subjects, normal in the above sense, at t_1 and determines of which of two kinds is each subject's brain-state—$B(1)$ which is such that if the digit 1 is flashed on the screen in front of the subject causing S_1 to be propagated along his optic nerve during the period t_2-t_3, T predicts of him that his brain-state will cause M_a at t_4—or $B(\text{o})$ which is such that if the digit 1 is flashed on the screen in front of the subject causing S_1 to be propagated along his optic nerve during t_2-t_3, T predicts of him that his brain-state will cause a bodily state which does not include M_a—call it $\bar{M}_a$. Each subject is told beforehand that if he is found in a brain-state of kind $B(1)$, the signal S_1 will be transmitted to him to convey that information; if he is found in a state of the kind $B(\text{o})$, no signal will be transmitted. Call this latter method of transmitting information the use of code W. Many subjects are examined; such as are found to be in a state of kind $B(1)$ are sent signals S_1—they will then know that T predicts of them that they will bring about M_a. Being counter-suggestible, some of them show the account to be false by not doing so, by bringing about $\bar{M}_a$.

Suppose however that counter-suggestible subjects were never under these conditions found to be in a state of kind $B(1)$—i.e. were always found in a state of kind $B(o)$ and so the account could not be proved false by this method. In that case we might try a different system of transmitting information, which I call code X. If the subject is found in a state of kind $B(o)$, the signal S_1 will be sent as a means of transmitting to him the information that T predicts of him that on receipt of the signal he will bring about $\bar{M}_a$, i.e. will not bring about M_a. The scientist tells subjects this code before examining them. He then examines them, and sends signal S_1 to such as are found in $B(o)$. They will then know that T predicts of them that they will bring about $\bar{M}_a$. Being counter-suggestible, some of them bring about M_a and so show the account T to be false.

Since every brain-state is either of kind $B(1)$ or of kind $B(o)$, T could only fail to be shown false by use of one or other of these methods if the very process of informing subjects of the code, of which kind of brain-state they would be in if the signal S_1 was to be sent, would cause them not to be in a brain-state of that kind. That is, the sensory stimuli (the impinging on the subject's ear-drums of certain air-waves, or on his eyes of certain light-waves) which cause a subject to have a belief that a certain code will be used to signal to him the prediction of T about his behaviour on receipt of the signal if he is found in a brain-state of a certain kind, will cause him never to be in a brain-state of that kind. This would hold whether the information was transmitted orally or in writing and in whatever language. And not just for the two simple codes described so far, but for all of an infinite number of codes which could be used to signal to subjects the predictions of T about their behaviour on receipt of the prediction. Consider a marginally more sophisticated system of information transmission which I call code Y—a system using two digits—the digit 1 displayed on a screen, causing the stimulus S_1 to be sent along the subject's optic nerve; and the digit 2, causing the stimulus S_2 to be sent along the subject's optic nerve. Adopt the following system of labelling kinds of brain-states. As before, call those brain-states states of kind $B(1)$ which are such that according to T, if the subject receives S_1, he will bring about M_a, the arm movement described earlier. Of the remaining states call those states of kind $B(2)$ which are such that, according to T, if the subject receives S_2, he will bring about M_a. Call all other states $B(o)$. Then if the subject is informed of the coding and then found in a brain-state either of kind $B(1)$ or of kind $B(2)$ the scientist can send to him such signals as will enable him to defeat the predictions of the account. If T is to be true, it must be that the very process of informing the subject of this method of coding will put him into a brain-state other than one which can be utilized to send him information about his brain-state, viz. a brain-state of kind $B(o)$. And so on, for infinitely many methods of coding.

Codes can easily be devised which allow an informative signal to be sent to the subject if he is found in any brain-state other than a very small proportion of possible brain-states. Consider the effect of S_1, i.e. the sensory input caused by displaying digit 1 on the screen, on the subject, causing or not causing M_a. Either the majority of his brain-states will be such that according to T, if he receives S_1, he will bring about M_a, or the majority will be such that according to T, if he receives S_1, he will bring about $\bar{M}_a$. Label states of the majority class states of kind $B(1)$, and inform the subject that if he is found in any state of kind $B(1)$ he will be sent S_1; and then inform the subject what T predicts about him in that case. Now consider the remaining states—of the minority class. Either the majority of those brain-states are such that according to T, if the subject receives S_2 (i.e. the sensory input caused by displaying digit 2 on the screen), he will bring about M_a, or they are such that according to T, if he receives S_2, he will bring about $\bar{M}_a$. Label states of the majority subclass among this minority class states of kind $B(2)$, and inform the subject that if he is found in any state of kind $B(2)$, he will be sent S_2; and inform the subject what T predicts about him in that case. Continuing in this way with different signals S_3, S_4, S_5, etc., we can soon reduce to a very small proportion of the total the number of unlabelled brain-states, i.e. ones which are such that if the subject is found in them we do not have a signal whereby we can convey to the subject the predictions of T about his behaviour on receipt of the signal. Indeed if the total number of brain-states is finite, all brain-states could be labelled in this way. However, there is a limit on the viability of too complicated a code, provided by the ability of subjects to hold in memory the rules of too complicated a code—a limit no doubt itself arising from the size and construction of subjects' brains. Yet the point made in the first sentence of this paragraph remains, that there are very many simple codes which allow an informative signal to be sent to the subject if he is found in any of the vast majority of his possible brain-states, informative that is in telling the subject of the predictions of *T* about his behaviour on receipt of the signal.

It follows that if there is to be a true deterministic account of the above type, if *T* is to be true, then informing a subject by any means whatever of any code whatever for transmitting to him information about the predictions of *T* about his behaviour on receipt of the informative signal will put the subject in one of a very small proportion of possible brain-states where the code has no signal for this purpose.

So what we are being asked by the determinist to believe is that the brain-belief links are of this very peculiar character, which prevent the acquisition by a human of true beliefs of a certain sort—viz. any true beliefs about any well-supported predictions about the human's future behaviour which coincide with the predictions of a certain account *T*, by any language or any method of coding—and this, despite the fact that in general the human brain is so constructed that it can cause the acquisition of all sorts of other kinds of belief, including any belief of any other kind which any other human tries to convey to its subject. This feature of a belief acquisition system for beliefs of a certain kind would make such a system complicated (perverse, perhaps one should say) and one of a very small proportion of logically possible belief acquisition systems.

This can be seen by considering the brain-state–belief correlations on their own. Successfully informing a subject that a certain code will be used to transmit information to him does of course limit the number of his possible brain-states; they now all have to include a part which will sustain the belief that the code will be used. The subject's future brain-states have to include a part which is such that it gives rise to the belief K_1 that that code will be used. But there is no particular reason if we consider just the brain-state–belief correlations why every brain-state which included that as part should be such that it lies inside the narrow range for which the code provides no signal for signalling to the subject which brain-state is his. Why should informing the subject that code *W* is to be used automatically confine subjects to brain-states of kind $B(o)$—i.e. states picked out by what *T* predicts will be the effect of

S_1 upon them, that it will cause $\bar{M}_a$? There are so many logically possible sets of brain-state–belief correlations, which incorporate that information in other ways. And so on through all the vast number of possible codes. Granted that brain-state–belief correlations are deterministic, there is no reason a priori why they should have this very perverse character. It is very unlikely a priori that the set of deterministic brain-state–belief correlations should belong to this narrow and complex class.

If we had reason to suppose that the causal connections between brain-states and beliefs were created by a being who wished to prevent us acquiring certain sorts of knowledge, e.g. a Cartesian evil demon, then we would have reason to believe that the connections are of this kind. Or if we had prior reason for supposing brain-state–purpose correlations to be deterministic (and so there to be a true deterministic account such as T) we would have reason to believe the brain-state/belief laws to be of this narrow kind (for that is a necessary condition of the former being deterministic). But, we have noted, the situation is that on all the normal scientific evidence we have no prior reason for supposing brain-state–purpose correlations to be deterministic. The consideration that these can only be deterministic if the set of brain-state–belief correlations is of a narrow and complex class, which a priori is unlikely (in view of the vastly larger class of sets of different and simpler brain-state–belief correlations), counts against the brain-state–purpose correlations being deterministic. If it is equally likely that an A is B and that it is not B, and it is shown that it can only be not–B under very unusual and complex and so a priori unlikely conditions, the final judgement (the posterior probability) must be that it is likely that it is B.

The determinist is committed to holding that whatever power produced consciousness in men and animals ensured, when arranging for the operation of processes whereby brain-events would give rise to beliefs, that there were certain beliefs which agents could not acquire, by any means, however hard anyone tried to give them to them. Nature, as it were, already foresaw the evolution of counter-suggestible subjects and was determined to defeat their best endeavours. A more likely story is that there were available one or two different routes by which beliefs could be produced, deterministic and indeterministic. Natural selection favoured a deterministic route but not of the narrow kind which prevented agents from acquiring beliefs of the stated type. There were also available one or two different routes by which purposes could be produced by brain-states, deterministic and indeterministic. Natural selection favoured the evolution of organisms whose purposes were produced by a non-deterministic mechanism, because of the evolutionary advantages which would be possessed by organisms who tried to defeat the predictions of predators and those who would enslave them, the forecasts of experts and commands of authority! This very important characteristic of humans, their readiness to test the theories of the world put forward by others, which I have called counter-suggestibility, could have evolved *either* via deterministic processes including some very complex and perverse brain-state/belief processes, *or* via indeterministic brain-state/purpose processes. The probabilities suggested by the evidence stated above favour, I claim, the latter supposition. In this case anything known by anyone can be conveyed to a subject, including the predictions of any theory *T* about the subject's behaviour; but the subject will always be able to show *T* false, for *any* theory *T*.

I conclude that the phenomenon of human counter-suggestibility is strong evidence of indeterminism in the production of purposes and so intentional actions, because it would only be compatible with determinism on the assumption of an a priori very unlikely mechanism for the production of beliefs.

Once the force of the argument from human counter-suggestibility is granted, it will be seen to apply with equal force to any intentional action which some scientific hypothesis might attempt to predict. Humans have the power to act contrary to the predictions of any scientific hypothesis by performing intentional actions of any kind.

The Limits to Free Will

Men do, however, have a whole system of desires, no doubt ultimately causally dependent on their brain-states (though often arising in complicated ways, as we shall see in the next chapter), which lead to their slipping into doing certain actions, and they will only resist the onward movement of desire if they believe that it is good to do so and if they then make the effort (i.e. so purpose). Desire is like a stream which carries us onward unless we swim against it. And because desires are predictable, we find that much human action is predictable with quite high degrees of probability. Men get into habits of work and relaxation and response to circumstance, because they find themselves having certain desires to which they will yield unless they believe that it would be good not to do so; and not doing so requires effort.

A man will only resist desire if he believes it good to do so. Many men brought up in a narrow environment and not exposed to a range of moral argument, and experience of the nature and effects of possible actions open to them, naturally and unthinkingly follow their desires in almost all circumstances. They see no reason for doing otherwise. A major function of education in the widest sense (backed up, if need be, by some kind of psychotherapy) is to make men aware of the variety of possible actions which they can do and of the good and bad reasons for doing them. And education needs to teach a given man, not merely that such actions are possible for men in general, but that many such actions are within the capacities of that man (i.e. are such that if he purposed to do the action, he would succeed).[11] The education which brings before men new serious possibilities for action may either give men new and strong desires or give them good reason for acting contrary to their desires in some respect. It widens the range over which human free will may be exercised.

Humans can only resist desire in so far as they believe it good to do so. And if human beliefs are easy to predict, this will be a further reason making human actions easy to predict. But once humans are exposed to a wide range of reasons for actions, their beliefs become harder to predict; and, even given knowledge of their beliefs, how they will act in a conflict between desire and believed worth remains unpredictable from mere knowledge of the strength of their desires and beliefs. Human action is largely predictable because human desires are predictable and so are the paucity of occasions on which they will conflict with the subject's beliefs about what is worth doing, and so too are the beliefs which men have about which movements will forward their purposes. Hence we can predict the kind of sentence which a man will utter in order to express a certain opinion, and the kind of movements

---

[11] For a survey of recent psychological work on the effects of making people feel that they have a significant choice between alternatives, on their exercise of that choice, see H. M. Lefcourt, *Locus of Control*, Lawrence Erlbaum, Hillsdale, NJ, 1976.

which he will make in order to get to work. But all of this casts no doubt on the indeterminism and so unpredictability of actions in which desire conflicts with believed worth, or the subject has two desires of equal strength, or beliefs that two actions are equally worth doing. Education widens the class of such actions.

When did men acquire free will? It is, as I have stated, possible that few or many animals have it. The possession of free will by animals would mean simply that when they have desires of equal strength to do two or more actions, their brain-states do not allow predictions of which they will do. Alternatively, free will might not have arrived until men began to challenge scientific hypotheses including those which make predictions about their own behaviour. However, counter-suggestibility is the habit of resisting a very pervasive human desire which all young children exhibit, the desire to conform—including the desire to conform to what scientists predict that we will do. My suspicion is that the indeterministic brain-state/purpose links which constitute human free will arose in connection with the resisting of desire generally, whether through a stronger desire or through a belief that the action desired is bad.

14. THE STRUCTURE OF THE SOUL

In this chapter I argue for a final characteristic of man—that his soul has a structure. I shall not deny that some sort of structure is present in the souls of the higher animals also; my point is only that there is a far more complex, rigid, and lasting structure to all human souls. What I mean by claiming that the soul has a structure is very roughly that the determinants of change of belief and desire are in part soul-states, not mere brain-states; and that if body and soul were separated, some character would remain with the soul.

As we have seen in earlier chapters, which action an agent will do is limited and influenced by his system of beliefs and desires, his continuing mental states. He will do the action which, he *believes*, will, most probably, attain his goals; and he can only choose some goal if he believes it in some way a good thing to do or bring about that goal. Other things being equal, he will choose to do that action (if there is one) which he believes to be overall the best of those open to him. But other things are not necessarily equal; an agent is also subject to *desire*; some actions come more naturally to him than do others. Whether to yield to desire or to pursue the best lies within the agent's free choice. An agent's system of beliefs and desires is a continuing one. Gradually beliefs change or are forgotten, but most beliefs continue for quite a while. Some desires are of short duration and for short-term goals (e.g. for a drink now), but there are many desires which are long term and long lasting. Agents thus have a continuing system of beliefs and desires subject only to gradual change. We will in due course discover the reason for this continuity.

The Integration of a Belief–Desire Set

Every agent's belief–desire set is necessarily an integrated one in the sense that each belief and desire requires many other surrounding beliefs and desires to give it meaning and justification. There are logical limits to the possibility of an agent having beliefs and desires isolated from the rest of the set, or not having beliefs and desires which follow naturally from other members of the set. Quine[1] taught us that our beliefs form a net which impinges on experience only at its edges. To put his point in my way and my terminology—the beliefs at the edge are the beliefs about our mental life, including beliefs about our apparent experience of the external world—that I seem to feel the edge of the table or hear a loud voice or remember putting the book down here yesterday. Next to these beliefs lies a ring of beliefs about particular facts about the external world—that there is a table here, that someone is speaking loudly, that I put the book down here yesterday, that I am now in Keele, that this is 1984. Then comes a ring of beliefs about the history and geography of the physical world, and of the agent's more immediate environment (that Aberdeen is to the north of Edinburgh, that the Second World War ended in 1945). Then there come more fundamental particular beliefs—that I live on the Earth, that it is spherical, and millions of years old. Then come general beliefs about how the world works—that bodies on Earth fall to the ground, that dry twigs and paper ignite easily but water does not. And finally, close to the middle of the net, there are an agent's most general metaphysical beliefs—that there are other people who have feelings and thoughts, that memory is generally reliable, and that there is a public world.

The point of the metaphor of the net is that an agent's beliefs cannot be obviously inconsistent with his other beliefs, and must be rendered to some extent probable by those other beliefs. In consequence, if you give up one belief, you have to change, introduce, or abandon others; and the more central a belief is, the greater the difference to other beliefs a change in it will make. If I am to come to believe that the world began in 4004 BC, I have to give up thousands of beliefs about prehistory, about the respectability of geology and historical cosmology as academic subjects, about the nature of biblical revelation, etc., etc. If I am to come to believe that today is Monday, not Tuesday, some other beliefs have to go (e.g. that I always lecture in Aberdeen on Tuesdays, or that tomorrow is Wednesday) but not so many.

Quine's point is well recognized, but what is less generally appreciated is that desires interact with the belief network. You

---

[1] For the initial statement of this view, which he developed more fully in later writings, see W. V. O. Quine, *From a Logical Point of View* (first published 1953), Harper and Row, New York, 1963, pp. 42–6.

cannot just desire something; you need some beliefs about it in order to desire it. And any one desire fits well with some desires and beliefs and badly with others. To start with, as I argued in Chapter 6, to have a desire to do any action at all is to believe the doing of that action to be in some way a good thing. I can't desire to go to London if I believe that in all ways it is a very bad thing to do. Secondly, I cannot desire to do an action, unless I have beliefs about what doing that action consists in; and the more complicated the action desired, the more complicated the beliefs I need to have about it. I cannot desire to fly to London, unless I have some beliefs about what flying is (e.g. what aeroplanes are, what the difference between air and land is, what travelling is as opposed to resting somewhere) and some beliefs about what London is (e.g. that it is a great city; and to believe that I need to have some beliefs about what a city is and what constitutes greatness for a city). My beliefs about what there is in the world and what can be done in it give my desires a focus, and desires differ in complexity according to the complexity of the beliefs on to which they latch. I don't need to believe much about yawning in order to desire to yawn, but I need to believe a lot about geography and politics in order to desire to be President of the USA. Thirdly, I desire things because of certain properties which they have; normally many of its properties will be irrelevant to my desire for something, some will be positive (leading me to desire the thing) and a few negative (lessening my desire). If I desire to be President of the USA, it will be the applause, the power, the wheeler-dealing, the ceremony, the comfort, or some or all of these which will give rise to the desire. But in that case, that feature or features which attract in the Presidency will attract me in other posts—e.g. the Vice-Presidency—although those posts might have other features so that I did not desire them on balance. Still, it remains the case that one desire will be associated with others; other things being equal, I will desire similar things. Desires fit together as desires for things which the agent believes to be in similar ways good.

Desires, like beliefs, differ in their centrality. Those desires which need relatively little in the way of belief about the nature of the states or actions desired are typically connected with beliefs about the worth of those states or actions isolated from other beliefs about worth. Such desires are also typically short-lasting desires for short-term goals which have direct physical causes, i.e.

bodily states; such desires are often called urges or pangs. My desire for a drink now needs little in the way of belief to give it focus—I have to know what liquid is and what will contain it and how to consume it, but little more in the way of belief about the nature of the object of my desire. I believe it a good thing to have—but not normally because of some moral belief about the overwhelming importance of making philosophers as liquid as possible; the goodness of my drinking is seen as independent of its moral goodness. This desire is to do an immediate action and is set off by a parched throat, not by the acquisition of some new belief. My desire for a drink is thus, in the network metaphor, near the edge of the net; its connection with other desires and beliefs are few. Contrast it with some man's desire for a stable marriage. He needs many beliefs about what is involved in a marriage, and what its stability would consist in (e.g. what, if any, sorts of extramarital friendships, and intramarital disagreements, would be compatible with it). He will think it a good thing in virtue of some of these aspects (e.g. sexual activity or children), which will—other things being equal—lead him to desire those aspects in other circumstances (e.g. extramarital sex and the company of children other than his own). The desire for a stable marriage is a long-term and normally long-lasting one, and is not caused directly by some bodily cause.

Because in these ways a man's desires and beliefs put constraints on which other desires and beliefs he can have, all agents must have some minimum degree of integration in their beliefs and desires. No agent, animal or Martian or man, can suddenly acquire a desire isolated from his whole understanding of the world and what is good in it. Yet it is obvious that some men have belief–desire sets far more integrated than do others. As regards beliefs—some men have many particular beliefs about this or that fact of geography or history or mental life, that this act is wrong or right, without having very much in the way of general beliefs about the pattern of their environment, or the sequence of historical events, about physics, theology, metaphysics, or ethics into which their particular beliefs slot. Some men have two or more general systems of belief which the subject sees as having little connection with each other, while in other men systems of belief about similar matters are well integrated. There are men whose beliefs about religion and science seem to have little connection with each other;

and others whose beliefs about religion are dictated by their beliefs about science, or conversely.

A more serious case of lack of integration is where a man has a belief which, given his other beliefs, is (by his own standards of probability) unlikely to be true. The subject cannot believe that that is so, for (see pp. 126 ff.) if he believes a proposition, he must believe that it is likely to be true; but it may be so all the same. The extreme case is where a subject has beliefs which are inconsistent with each other. He cannot believe that they are inconsistent with each other. For if he believes p and also believes that p entails not-q, he will believe not-q (as being involved in what he believes); and in that case he cannot believe q. A subject may nevertheless believe inconsistent propositions, when ignorant of their inconsistency.

Integration of belief is a matter of beliefs giving each other support; integration of desire is a matter of the agent having desires which fit together in such a way as to minimize or eliminate conflict of desires. Desires conflict when they cannot be co-satisfied. Conflict is minimized when one of the two conflicting desires is greatly reduced in strength, so as not seriously to rival the other. We are almost all of us subject to desires for short-term goals in conflict with long-term desires or other short-term desires; the desire to stay in bed in conflict with the desire to get up and have breakfast and the desire to go to work. But some men have desires for long-term incompatible goals—for a stable marriage to Jane and an affair with Jill; or for ends which are difficult to realize together—such as doing a hundred and one different things, and not being tired and distracted. Not all men are in the latter predicament; some have desires to live a certain sort of life, within which there are no incompatible parts. Further, some men have desires as to how to deal with conflicting desires (and that means normally desires for short-term goals) when they arrive. A man may desire to indulge his sexual urge never, or only with his spouse; or to indulge his pangs of hunger only in so far as doing so is compatible with preserving his figure or with good manners. These long-term desires are second-order desires, for they are desires to resist or indulge other desires.[2]

---

[2] The importance of second-order desires, leading to an extrinsic/intrinsic distinction was brought out by Frankfurt. See H. G. Frankfurt, 'Freedom of the Will and the Concept of a Person', *Journal of Philosophy*, 1971, **68**, 5–20.

The stronger an agent's second-order desires compatible with his other long-term desires, the more they will reduce, take the sting out of, his sudden urges, and the more integrated will be the agent's system of desire. For short-term urges will then be kept in their place, and no longer pull the agent in conflicting directions. By contrast, an acute form of conflict arises when a subject has a second-order desire not to have a belief which he has, or a first-order desire which he has.

Some agents' desires are well integrated with their beliefs about moral worth, others not. As we have seen, in so far as an agent desires something, he believes it to have worth. But agents may desire much less that which they believe to have most worth, and in particular that which they believe to have moral worth. There is a conflict between what they desire to pursue and what they think worth pursuing. Where the conflict is between a complex long-term desire and a moral belief, the agent will have a whole little island of beliefs about the worth of aspects of his long-term goal, which is isolated from his moral beliefs. He desires, say, to be President of the USA and he regards as worth having various aspects of that life, and he sees those aspects—fame, power, organizing opportunity as valuable in that job and others. Yet his moral belief may be that it would be wrong for him to seek to become President, because of the unhappiness it would bring to his family, to whom he has an overriding obligation. He has a larger system of beliefs about the overall worth of goals which is in conflict with his sub-system of beliefs about the worth of fame, power, etc.

Some agents have long-term desires only for what they believe to be morally good; their desires and moral beliefs are integrated. Almost all agents who have moral beliefs have on occasion short-term desires in conflict with them. But even that conflict is not inevitable. Some men so train themselves, that they learn to only desire short-term goals to the extent to which they are not in conflict with their moral beliefs—they do not even want to satisfy hunger which would lead to another being deprived.

Philosophers sometimes distinguish between extrinsic (or external) desires and intrinsic (or internal) desires, the latter being

Frankfurt, however, like many other writers, unfortunately ignores the distinction between those actions which we do because we desire to do them and those which we do for other reasons.

those which the agent welcomes and the former those which he does not welcome.[3] We can make this distinction clearer by saying that a desire is extrinsic to the extent to which the agent believes that it would be overall bad (e.g. morally bad) to indulge it, or has a stronger desire more integrated with his other desires and beliefs which is in conflict with it; to the extent to which neither of these conditions apply, the desire is intrinsic. Thus the sudden sexual desire of the monk totally dedicated to chastity is fully extrinsic in that, not merely does the monk think it would be bad to indulge this desire but he desires not to do so; he has a stronger desire for chastity which arises both from his desire to follow the Church's general teaching (including teaching prohibiting sexual intercourse outside marriage) and from his desire that the pattern of his life should be the fulfilment of his monastic vows (including the vow of chastity). The sexual desire is unwelcome to the monk; it comes from without and he sees it as no part of himself. If it does manage to influence his conduct, he sees himself as having yielded to an alien force. Similar examples of an extrinsic desire would be the desire for alcohol of the teetotaller dedicated to its conquest, or the pangs of hunger of the hunger-striker. Fully intrinsic desires include our long-term ambitions which we see as worthy of pursuit, and short-term pangs which are not in conflict with our values and aspirations. The final stage of integration is where extrinsic desires are tamed, in the way I suggested in the last paragraph, so that (e.g.) the hunger-striker only desires food the taking of which will not constitute a breaking of his strike vow.

The moral beliefs of some men are themselves a highly integrated system of strong convictions and cover many aspects of life. To the extent to which this is so, those moral beliefs are close to the centre of the man's belief network. For others, their moral beliefs are few, weak, and disintegrated (i.e. consist of beliefs that this or that kind of act are wrong or right, without the agent having any more general theory of why those kinds of act are wrong or right). Their moral beliefs are much closer to the periphery of the network of belief.

A man's character is a matter of his beliefs about the worth of actions and their centrality in his system of beliefs; his strong, long-lasting and more intrinsic desires; and whether he has or lacks

[3] For commentary on this distinction see Terence Penelhum, 'Human Nature and External Desires', *The Monist*, 1979, **62**, 304–19 and the references cited there.

the desire to control the short-term desires which frequently occur. Put another way—it is a matter of what he thinks worth while, how he naturally directs his life, and how he is inclined to cope with his pangs and urges when they come. A man's character is a central element of his belief–desire set. Character does not determine an agent's choice, I have argued, but simply makes certain choices easy and others hard.

Change of Belief and Desire—Normal Processes

The way in which beliefs and desires require and sustain each other points to the mechanism of change of belief and desire. The normal procedure of belief change is of two kinds; one of an agent's beliefs changing through some initial non-rational change (i.e. one which does not involve other beliefs) and other beliefs rearrange themselves to fit in with the new belief; or the beliefs rearrange themselves to fit in better with each other, to make themselves a more integrated set. Changes, that is, occur through experience and through reflection. One point of Quine's metaphor of the net was to bring out that the beliefs which are subject to initial non-rational change are those on the edge of the net which concern particular present experiences of the subject. Sensory stimuli cause me to have beliefs about my present sensations and the present objects of my experience (that there is a table here now, etc.). Or rather, they cause them in interaction with the already existing belief system (which includes beliefs about what sort of things there are and can be in the world). If you show an Englishman a telephone, he will probably come to believe that there is a telephone there, but if you show one to a New Guinea tribesman, he won't acquire that belief (since he does not know that the thing before him is a telephone)—he will acquire perhaps simply the belief that there is a black thing in front of him. As we have seen, beliefs near the edge of the net affect beliefs closer to the centre. If a new belief is obviously inconsistent or believed to be inconsistent with an old one, then the weaker one (whichever it is) must go. If through experience I come to believe that I have seen a black swan, and I have a general belief that all swans are white, then one of these beliefs must go. Which will go depends on the firmness of my conviction that I saw a black swan, as opposed to my belief (based on inductive evidence) that all swans are white (i.e. my conviction based on the observable evidence of experience or the theoretical evidence of genetics that there cannot be an exception). Also if a new belief renders old beliefs improbable, and conversely, one or other has to go, or the subject's standards of probability (what is evidence for what) have to go. Changing the latter in one case could lead to many changes elsewhere in the system. Although normally more central beliefs come to be changed under the pressure of a lot of experiences on the edge of the net, the central beliefs of some people may be so strong that they interpret all experience in the light of their existing system of belief, so that the latter is virtually unalterable by experience. Some men are so convinced that there are ghosts or flying saucers that they keep 'seeing' them; and others are so convinced that such things do not exist that they never interpret any experience, however white or bright, as an experience of a ghost or flying saucer. Beliefs can change, not merely through experience affecting beliefs at the edge of the net, but through reflection on their internal consistency, and coherence (i.e. whether I have a simple set of more central beliefs which explain the beliefs caused by experience, or a complicated *ad hoc* set). Reflection on the content of my belief–set may lead to a shift in the more central members—e.g. in the way illustrated in Chapter 12 for moral beliefs. (One circumstance which may eventually lead to the rejection of a general belief under pressure of other general beliefs is when the subject has forgotten the particular beliefs about his experiences which originally sustained the former general belief.) Such is the normal procedure of belief change. Note that its crucial feature is that beliefs anywhere well away from the edge of the net change under the pressure of the agent *seeing* their logical relations (deductive and inductive) to other beliefs—under the pressure of the forces of reason, we may say; and beliefs on the edge, too, feel these forces, in that a man rejects a belief which experience would otherwise produce, if it is incompatible with any stronger more central beliefs.

While beliefs do not require desires to sustain them,[4] desires do require beliefs. There are, therefore, three sources of change of desire—a purely bodily source, a belief change, and a change of

---

[4] While beliefs may be influenced by desires, this is an irrational process and the agent cannot consciously allow this to happen. For, by an argument similar to that given in Chapter 7 with respect to the purpose/belief connection, if we recognize that we believe something because we desire to, we will recognize that the belief is independent of the facts, and so we will cease to believe it.

other desires. A change of desire initiated by a bodily change (without that change working first through a change of belief or other desire) will be most evident with regard to short-term desires. Let a man's hand come into contact with a stinging nettle and he will immediately desire to scratch. Certainly the desire involves beliefs—about what scratching consists in and that it is good to do it. But these beliefs can be created by the sting; they need not exist anteriorly to the sting. Next, there are bodily changes which create desires, only given an anterior belief about the kind of thing which will satisfy some state of mental unease in which the agent finds himself; such a belief will be a fairly peripheral particular belief, normally originating from an agent's own experience or the testimony of others. Take a man who knows what heroin is and has experience of its marvellous effects, and give him an injection of heroin; you will cause him (as its effects wear off) to desire more of it. But give such an injection to a man asleep who does not know that he has been given it and has no other knowledge or experience of heroin, then as the effect wears off, the man will become very uneasy but he will not desire heroin; for he will have no idea that more heroin will relieve his distress.

Desires for food, drink, sleep, etc. are triggered off by bodily changes, and disappear with other bodily changes. At least, they do so except in so far as the belief that the food, etc. are good things (to be had now rather than in general) is sustained by a web of further beliefs. The wanton who eats 'when he feels like it' does not regard food as good-to-be-eaten-now, except when bodily change promotes that belief. But the man in the habit of dining at 7.00 p.m. who believes that is is now 7.00 p.m., has a desire for food at 7.00 p.m. not at the mercy of the normal bodily causes of desire to eat. He sees the habit as good to indulge for many self-centred reasons. He values a regular life, and regards dining at 7.00 p.m. as one instance of it. But such a value system is a comparatively small island of values; the agent may regard the indulgence of such a habit as having no moral significance. Yet the man who believes that he has a moral duty to keep himself well, that regular eating promotes health, and that he has not eaten for a while, and also has a desire to keep himself well, has a whole system of desires and beliefs which sustains the desire to eat at a given time. The switching on or off of the normal bodily causes will not make nearly so much difference to the desire.

It is not only short-term desires which are switched on by bodily change. No doubt all desires have a source in bodily change. But in the case of the longer-term desires, the bodily change needs prior beliefs with which to interact in order to yield the desire,[5] and the desire once generated is likely to be sustained by such a wide web of beliefs and desires that it needs in some sense a total bodily collapse or alternatively many complicated changes in the web of belief and desire if it is to be removed. Examples are the desires for love, fame, or power. There are obvious bodily sources of the desire to be loved by those with whom we come into contact. But the desire could not exist without a web of factual belief—about which things surrounding us are persons, and what constitutes their expression of love (a child has to learn that a rebuke is not incompatible with love, and so on). And the web of factual belief is not created by the hormones or whatever bodily sources help to create the desire to love. Once the desire is generated, it involves regarding all sorts of things as good for interconnected reasons—kissing, hugging, giving things, asking one's opinion; and usually not merely good for the agent, but good for anyone, that is, morally good. These beliefs will remain and sustain the desire for love when its bodily origins subside. The same goes for the similar desires for fame and power. Such desires can be switched off, as we will see shortly, through changes in other beliefs and desires. But they can also be switched off through what I called 'total bodily collapse'. What I meant by this is that all desire can subside. A man can be drugged so that he is half-asleep or become so

[5] It is the plausible thesis of Mary Midgley's *Beast and Man* (Harvester, Brighton, 1979; see especially ch. 15) that human beings have a 'nature'. That is, they are so made that they come to have always or at certain periods of day or life or in certain circumstances, very similar desires to each other. These desires are continuous with the desires of our animal ancestors. They may be given form by our culture—for example, through acquiring various beliefs from our culture about what is ordinary and to be expected, we come to have beliefs about what is incongruous, and so the desire to laugh at the incongruous; and through acquiring beliefs about how you address strangers of different kinds, we come to have the desire to shake hands with various newcomers. Culture gives its particular form to a desire to laugh and greet, but we are so made as readily to imbibe from our culture a pattern of laughing and greeting, and so a desire to laugh and greet in certain circumstances. We are so made, she claims, that over a wide range of cultures, desires often take quite similar forms (e.g. the way in which the newcomer is greeted is not very different in European culture from what it is in Indian culture, and less elaborate than in ape culture). Subsequent to our acquisition of desires, our culture or we ourselves may set about modifying our desires, but our nature is there, formed by our genes, before it is given form or modified.

depressed that he does not desire anything very much. But bodily tampering will not change the relative strength of a longer-term desire, without change of belief or other desire; and the more wide ranging is the net of belief and desire which sustains a desire, the less effect will bodily tampering have on it.

Secondly, there is the role of belief in changing desire. There are various kinds of belief involved. First, there is belief about what will satisfy a certain unease—e.g. heroin. Then, there is belief about what will satisfy a general desire. I desire to appear on television because I believe that everyone on TV becomes famous (viz. is talked about by everyone), or I desire to be Vice-Chancellor, because I believe that Vice-Chancellors are powerful men. Clearly in these cases my desire will change as my belief changes. I may come to learn that the Vice-Chancellor has no power, he is a mere figure-head. Then I shall cease to desire to become Vice-Chancellor. Then there is belief about general desires that their objects have certain further qualities. I may desire to administer because I believe that administration will hold my attention. I find that it doesn't and so lose my desire to administer. Various objects and activities are thought of by me as valuable for their connection with each other in respects which I regard as good for me. I value power because doing the actions involved in exercising it will hold my attention, because I can make the world the way I would like it to be, the way it would be good for me to live in, the way I think it ought morally to be, and so on. And of course if I believe the goal of my activity to be morally good, that will sustain my desire, because inevitably I desire the morally good as such (even if I do not desire it very much in comparison with more limited goods). And, as I have emphasized, the more my beliefs connect my desire with other of my desires and with my moral beliefs, the more it is likely to continue when its bodily sources fail.

And there is the role of other desires in changing desire. My desire for fame is sustained by my desire for other things which I believe to go with it. Likewise, desire is weakened in so far as I desire other things which I believe to be incompatible with being famous. The pressure for integration of desire works in favour of a unified life-style.

This normal process of change of belief and desire can be initiated by the agent. As regards belief, as we saw in Chapter 7, an agent cannot there and then choose his beliefs, but he can choose which areas to investigate and so which things to have beliefs about. Also in so far as he does have some belief about which he is only mildly confident (because in his view although the balance of evidence supports it, it does not do so overwhelmingly), he will believe that (probably) more investigation will strengthen it—since if a belief is more probable than not, it is probable that the next piece of evidence will support it and so raise its probability. But only probable. Still a man may investigate some belief in order thereby to strengthen it. But the investigation will be honest only in so far as he is open to evidence pointing in either direction. In contrast, the agent can help the forces of reason along more directly in attempting to change the balance of his desires. He can act on the bodily sources of a desire which he believes wrong to indulge. Or as above, act on the beliefs which sustain the desire—either by investigating his beliefs in a way open to evidence, or by attempting to change them in a way which hides evidence.

For example, the monk seeking to eliminate his sexual desire may subject himself to certain bodily conditioning (e.g. fasting) known to lessen such desire. Alternatively, believing that indulgence would be wrong and unsatisfying, he thinks through his belief, believing that that procedure will make him believe more strongly (but of course running the risk that it won't). The monk may reflect that indulging sexual desire would involve developing an intense relationship with someone whom he would never see again. It might even involve going to hell. He gets himself to face up to the fact which indeed he believed but hadn't taken the force of—that there are many aspects of the relation which he simply doesn't want. Then he brings home to himself the immorality of the act, the deceit and cheapening of sexuality involved. All this taken seriously will weaken the sexual desire. Influencing belief in these ways will not eliminate the desire, because it is still sustained by bodily forces, but it will weaken it, and leave it without any tendency to persist in the absence of bodily forces.

Change of Belief and Desire—Abnormal Processes

I have been arguing that the normal processes of change of belief and desire operate through other members of a person's belief–desire set. The more integrated a person's belief–desire set, the harder change will be to achieve. A wide belief–desire set is obviously correlated with a wide base in the brain, an extensive brain-state, and hence whether it is the beliefs and desires themselves or the brain-states with which they are correlated which determine which new belief and desire will arise, there is more internal influence, the more integrated a belief–desire set, and so the harder change will be to effect. No significant change can be achieved by a single bodily stimulation. That change of belief and desire (except for the occasional short-term bodily desire of narrow focus) works through the existing belief–desire set is true also of the abnormal processes of change, resulting from self-conditioning of belief, psychiatry, drugs, brain surgery, and brain disease.

Among such abnormal processes there is a clear distinction between those which operate by operating at the edge of the body and those which operate within the body. Self-conditioning and psychiatry belong to the former class.

If someone tries to 'brainwash' himself, he tries to forget (by refusing to think about) certain things, and hammers home to himself (gets himself to take very seriously) other things. He gets himself to believe that dialectical materialism is true by exposing himself to Communist propaganda and trying to forget what he believes about the deceitfulness of such propaganda. But a whole host of other beliefs operates to determine what he comes to believe as a result of reading the propaganda—beliefs, to start with, about the meaning of words, and then beliefs about geography and history presupposed by the authors of the propaganda which he shares with them, and a belief that writers are generally trustworthy (and he forces himself to ignore his conviction that Communists are an exception). The propaganda will be effective to the extent to which it latches on to existing beliefs (e.g. that there are now many unemployed in Britain, that income tax for the rich has recently been greatly reduced, and so on) and draws consequences from them. Quite clearly, too, techniques of a counselling or Freudian nature utilize the existing belief–desire system—for they seek to effect behaviour change precisely by getting a man to take seriously his existing beliefs and desires, albeit sometimes ones suppressed from consciousness.

When we come to processes which start inside the body, clearly any very localized brain surgery, injury, or disease is not going to change belief or desire except in conjunction with the existing set. For, as we have noted, the existing set has a wide brain base. There is no one place in the brain where your belief that all bodies including human bodies are affected by gravity is stored. No one could get you to believe that gravity doesn't affect human beings simply by altering certain neurone connections. For suppose the surgeon began to achieve this, the emerging belief would immediately appear to contradict a host of past memories about the world (about people falling downstairs, always returning to ground after jumping, etc., etc.), as well as all sorts of beliefs about physics. The belief about gravity couldn't be inculcated without a much more extensive revamp of the brain.[6]

Yet the only processes currently available which affect large areas of the brain are 'ham-fisted' processes which inhibit or facilitate neural transmission in a non-selective way. Although these may have some effect on character, I shall now show that they do so by using the already existing belief–desire system; and I shall also show that they have progressively less effect on character, the more integrated that character is.

It is worth, to begin with, making the point that most brain disease and injury, most drugs and brain surgery affect capacity (give to agents the ability to do or not to do things), not character. They remove (or, if beneficial, restore), or make it difficult or easy for an agent to exercise, a capacity to perform certain bodily actions, or mental actions, or to have thoughts or chains of thought of certain kinds. Parkinson's disease prevents a man from moving his limbs as he chooses. Broca's aphasia prevents a man not merely from saying things out loud but even to himself. (It prevents him from expressing certain thoughts to himself.) And old age prevents a man from having complex mathematical thoughts.

Brain disease may not merely remove or make it difficult for an agent to exercise some capacity. It may at the same time cause to occur unpurposed movements of the kind which the agent has lost his capacity to bring about voluntarily. In consequence, observers may be deceived into supposing that the movements are voluntary, and the agent may even be unaware that they are occurring.

---

[6] The difficulty of 'writing in' a belief is well made in D. C. Dennett, *Brainstorms*, Harvester Press, Brighton, 1979, ch. 3, 'Brain Writing and Mind Writing', p. 44.

Epilepsy provides an obvious example where a whole pattern of bodily movement occurs quite uncontrolled by or unknown to the agent. But a more interesting example is provided by the form of aphasia known as Wernicke's aphasia. If you talk to a man with Wernicke's aphasia, he will reply to you naturally in smoothly phrased grammatical sentences, but it soon becomes apparent that these sentences have little meaning and little relevance. They are simply phrases which the agent has got accustomed to uttering, now occurring without his conscious control.

Brain disease may of course involve not just a loss of one capacity but a fundamental general loss of capacity—for all kinds of sophisticated action and thought. A patient may regress so that he cannot have any (or at any rate only the most simple) thoughts, and can only execute very short-term purposes; cannot carry through a plan for the future. Such is the plight of the victim of Alzheimer's disease. But if the sleeper does not lose his character, no more does the victim of Alzheimer's disease. He cannot exercise many capacities; but in so far as he can, he is guided by the system of desires and beliefs which formed his pre-disease character. Some general loss of motor and mental capacity is of course characteristic of normal ageing; and it is also characteristic of normal ageing that the 'individual, as he ages, is likely to become ever more entrenched in his habits and style of living',[7] i.e. in his character.

I have made the point that much brain disease, surgery, injury, and drugs affect capacity rather than character. They do, however, often affect character, but I now wish to make the point that the way in which they affect character is by bringing into operation the normal rational processes of experience and reflection, which utilize the existing belief and desire system to create a somewhat different one—in terms of the net metaphor, pressure on the edge of or from within the net leads to a change in the shape of the net. The first process occurs when drugs, surgery, or disease create experiences or eliminate memories of them; or create new bodily desires. This then has effects on the whole system through the way in which it rationally utilizes the more central existing beliefs and desires. Thus, various drugs and disease may make men more religious—epilepsy, for example, is often said to do this. What

---

[7] H. Gardner, *The Shattered Mind*, Routledge and Kegan Paul, London, 1977, p. 271.

obviously *doesn't* happen here is that some secular man who knows nothing of religion gets epilepsy and then acquires a deep conviction of the truth of the Nicene definition of the Trinity. But what may well often happen is that those who get epilepsy have certain experiences of wonderful sights and sounds, which if they already have some knowledge of the details of a certain religion and some prior belief that that religion is not too improbable, they then reasonably interpret in the categories of that religion, say as a vision of the Blessed Virgin or of the Sacred Heart. (In saying this, I do not here in any way wish to suggest either that the interpretation is true or that it is false. The effect of epilepsy is just as likely to be to open our eyes to what is there all the time, as to make us see what is not there.) The vision provides the subject with new evidence, which in a perfectly rational way then tips the balance of his belief strongly in favour of the truth of the religious system.

Conversely, certain forms of treatment, e.g. ECT, often lead to the suppression of recent memories. Subjects no longer remember certain recent events, and so the peripheral beliefs that these events occurred no longer influence their more central beliefs. These then come to be more under the influence of present experiences, as well as of the existing system of more general beliefs and desires. This provides a possible explanation of the fact that the patient becomes more sensitive to his environment and open to cognitive reorientation.[8]

For a very simple example of the creation of a new bodily desire, consider the electrical stimulation of pleasure centres in the brain. Such stimulation will give to the subject a desire to continue the stimulation. But whether that desire will lead to such action depends on its compatibility with his other desires and the degree of their integration into his belief-desire set. Whether the subject will do simply nothing, or whether he will grab the apparatus from you and go on stimulating himself—depends on his other desires and beliefs, his views about the morality of stimulating pleasure centres, and the kind of person he wants to be. You don't change the latter by stimulating isolated centres.

Disease and surgery also lead to change of character through their influence on more central beliefs. They may alter the net of

[8] On this, see E. J. Valenstine, *Brain Control*, John Wiley, New York, 1973, pp. 158–62.

belief by drawing a patient's attention to certain beliefs and desires and making him less mindful of others. They make some beliefs and desires more prominent than others. By beliefs and desires being more prominent I do not mean that they are stronger; I mean rather that they obtrude on a subject's thinking and influence his actions, even when barely relevant. More precisely, by beliefs being prominent I mean that the subject knows their remoter consequences (see p. 130) and so the belief is (via the other beliefs which the subject understands to be included in it) influential in determining a wider range of the subject's actions. (A belief is strong in so far as the subject believes it to be more likely to be true than some other belief; a belief is prominent to the extent to which the subject understands what is involved in it.) By desires being prominent, I mean that the subject looks for opportunities to indulge them, he seeks beliefs about how to satisfy them. (A desire is strong to the extent to which the subject acts on it rather than other desires when he believes that there is opportunity for so doing; a desire is prominent to the extent to which the subject seeks out such opportunities.) If a subject's desire to become President of the USA is prominent ('in the sun', we may say), then he calculates with respect to so many actions (e.g. accepting or refusing a minor invitation) whether or not it will forward his ambition. If the desire is less prominent ('in the shade', we may say), it will direct his actions when he is invited to stand for Congress, but not when he is invited to dinner with the local tax inspector.

Being influenced more by certain beliefs and desires than by others remains a perfectly rational process (in the sense that it is understood reasons which are at work). Our beliefs change in the light of those beliefs of which we are aware, and our desires give rise to actions in the light of our beliefs about how to fulfil them. And if we do not think things through very thoroughly we ignore those beliefs and desires which do not immediately occur to us as relevant. No doubt some individuals are so made genetically that desires and beliefs of certain kinds tend to become prominent in them; recent work on depression suggests that some individuals have an innate predisposition to depression.[9] But individuals who see reason for doing so can choose to try hard to give prominence to desires and beliefs of other kinds.

[9] See e.g. P. Gilbert, *Depression*, Lawrence Erlbaum, Hillsdale, NJ, 1984.

So brain change produces character change, but it does so by utilizing the subject's existing belief–desire system; and I now make the point that brain change is far more efficacious in securing character change, to the extent to which the agent does not have an integrated character. Any brain change will be effective in changing character only to the extent to which that change affects the brain correlates of certain beliefs and desires and not the brain correlates of other beliefs and desires. But to the extent to which the belief-desire system is an integrated system, there will be a pressure from the rest of the system to restore the missing or changed beliefs and desires. If, *in extremis*, every belief and desire was linked in an unforgettable way with a certain further desire and belief, the latter would be ineliminable except by rebuilding the character from scratch (viz. not by utilizing the existing belief–desire system). As an example of what I have in mind take the belief–desire system of a devout contemplative whose every belief which is not about God is sustained in part by a belief that God made things thus, and whose every desire is a desire to do something for the reason that it is pleasing to God. He believes that the sun rises daily because it seems to him that he has seen the sun rise a few times in the past and he believes that God is reliable and so that nature is regular and that what has happened will continue to happen; without the belief in God's reliability, he wouldn't believe that anything happens in a regular way or that his memory is reliable. He desires to eat cabbage because he believes that God wants him to eat what is in front of him and the only reason for doing anything is that God wants him to do it; without the belief in God, he would have no desire to eat, for he has conditioned himself to think of God's wanting things to happen as the only reason which makes things worth doing. It is not in the case of this contemplative, as it is with other religious people, that the desire to eat is largely kept in control by a different desire (to do the will of God), which latter normally wins if there is a conflict; but rather the former is simply a special case of the latter. In such a case no amount of brain tinkering can remove the central beliefs and desires; you would need to rebuild from the beginning.[10]

---

[10] One test of how integrated a personality a man has is, as Freud taught us long ago, his dreams. If in my dreams I yield to desires to which I would not yield in my waking life (do things which I would not dare to do while awake), then there are within me partly welcome to me, inconsistent desires, separate and unintegrated

Or, again, if my only desire is to forward the Revolution, if I have so organized all my other desires that I desire only that which I believe does forward the Revolution, if I desire to forward the Revolution because I believe that that is the one good in the world, you can't change that by switching several neurone connections (because so many beliefs and desires are involved). And if for a second you succeeded, all my other beliefs and desires would as it were conspire to restore it as that desire which alone gave them unity.

In an integrated system the subject's desires have clear boundaries to their application, and they form a whole; and beliefs which are relevant to other beliefs or to conduct are seen as relevant. A less integrated subject may have a desire to have a busy social life and a desire to become President of the United States, without each having clear boundaries—so that when the desires conflict (e.g. the subject believes that he needs to attend a committee rather than a social evening, if he is to forward his ambition), he is torn as to which to follow. Whereas the more integrated subject will have a desire, say, to lead a busy social life only to the extent to which it will not significantly lessen his prospects of becoming President of the United States. In the less integrated subject desires can fade into the shade, and be

---

with each other, of different strengths. If I act lovingly while awake but not in dreams, then my love has not become fully part of me. At least, that is so for the dreams of the lighter sleeper in which the dreamer performs intentional actions. He acts for a purpose, often trying hard; he resists temptation and tries to do the right thing. (Of course he does not achieve what he believes he does, for his purposes are to achieve public states of affairs.) He may try very hard to move out of the way of a car, or resist the attractions of the opposite sex. But there is also a kind of sleep—deeper sleep—in which the dreamer dreams that he does actions which, if he was awake, would be intentional actions; but over the occurrence of which in his dream he exercises no control. No purpose or assessment of the moral worth of consequences enters into his 'acting'—his apparent limb movements are viewed by him as events which just happen to him. The sleeper's awareness of what is going on is like watching a film; he is not an agent yielding to or resisting desires.

In the lighter kind of sleep, the agent may have particular factual beliefs wildly different from his beliefs when waking (since such factual beliefs do not depend very much on more central beliefs, some of them can change without much immediate change in the more central beleifs), and yet the agent's most general moral beliefs about right and wrong and his more general desires remain the same. Augustine has an interesting discussion of one's moral responsibility for the actions which one dreams one does. He claims that one is not morally responsible for them at all. I have sought to make a distinction between two kinds of such action. For valuable discussion of Augustine's views, see G. B. Matthews, 'On Being Immoral in a Dream', *Philosophy*, 1981, **56**, 47–54.

separated off from the system without affecting the rest of the system. But if one desire has clear boundaries to its application, it contains within it an understanding of the presence of the other desire, and the latter cannot be quietly forgotten. The sun/shade distinction has less and less application, the more integrated is the system.

Empirical evidence bears out my claims that change of character is far easier to achieve by brain tampering, the less integrated the character is. Drugs, brain surgery, etc., are in general only used upon those with psychiatric problems, and it is typical of those so classified that they do have highly *dis*-integrated systems of belief and desire. Their desires are pulling them in different directions, and in directions some of which they believe not good ones to follow. Most of those with psychiatric problems *seek* medical help, and that is because they desire or believe it good that they should not have certain aspects of character—and what is more indicative of a divided self than that? The man who feels suicidal and asks the psychiatrist for help has a desire not to have the desire to commit suicide (or the belief that it is bad to do so). It being thus already disconnected from the agent's general world-view, we would expect the brain correlations of the desire to commit suicide not to be connected too well with the brain correlates of other parts of the agent's character. Hence it is possible that drugs or surgery may cool down the suicidal desire without cooling down other desires so much. But there cannot be a drug which extinguishes *any* desire to commit suicide, as will be evident if you reflect on the fact that giving an antidepressant to a dedicated member of EXIT is not going to stop him from committing suicide when he suffers from an incurable cancer—for his desire to commit suicide is totally aligned to his world view; it arises from his belief about his situation, what kinds of life are worth living, and what kinds not, and so on.

One kind of lack of integration which a character can have is that its high-level moral desires are in tension with low-level desires for limited short-term personal goods. If we weaken the connection between parts of the brain, the low-level desires which have perhaps a more localized brain correlate may get out of hand. Take a very simple case, which really reveals what is going on in all other such cases—alcohol. I have a few drinks and I tell a scandalous story I wouldn't otherwise have told. The alcohol, as we say, has released my inhibitions. What is clearly the case, and is indeed revealed by the description 'released my inhibitions', is that I had at first the desire to tell the story and also the higher-level desire not to be a scandalmonger. The alcohol strengthened the former and/or weakened the latter, so that I failed to resist the pressure from the former. This process will have worked by 'bringing into the sun' beliefs associated with the desire to tell the story (e.g. 'it is good that truth be known', 'the victim had no reputation to lose') and putting other beliefs into the shade. The process operates through my existing belief–desire system. But the point is that the desires are separate; I have relatively intrinsic desires pulling in different directions. I hadn't thought through my desire to scandalmonger in such a way as to be unable to think of it except as a desire to do what is hurtful for the sake of being the centre of attention. If I come to see it as that sort of a desire, it will inevitably be cut off from my system of beliefs about worth, and be a desire on its own regarded as totally extrinsic. If I think through my desire so as inevitably to think of it in this way, a few drinks will have far less power to release it from captivity to the higher-level desire, for there will be no beliefs about the worth of indulging it to encourage me to do so, if the alcohol leads me to be less aware of other beliefs. The fact that such desires can be rendered fully extrinsic is indeed shown by the fact that there are some people who like telling scandalous stories but who have such strong desires not to scandalmonger that, however much alcohol you give them, they will never scandalmonger. Notoriously, alcohol takes different men differently. And what goes for alcohol, goes also for drugs which do the same kind of job, and for frontal leucotomy, and for the more sophisticated but similar forms of psychosurgery.

So the usual way in which brain change leads to character change is by utilizing the existing belief–desire system; and empirical considerations support my thesis that the more integrated a character, the harder it is to change it by tampering with the brain. That suggests that in the extreme case it will not be possible to change a character by utilizing the existing system. We would need to build the whole system from scratch by brain surgery. And, thank God, that is beyond present human capacities; there are some strong people whose central beliefs and desires even Soviet psychiatrists are unable to change.

So in abnormal as well as normal cases, the processes of change of belief and desire operate through the existing members of the belief–desire set, in that desires are moulded by the content of other desires and beliefs, and beliefs by the content of other beliefs; and the moulding is in the direction of some sort of at any rate minimal degree of rational integration in the sense that beliefs have to be consistent with other beliefs, and not (by the subject's standards) to make each other evidently improbable, and desires have to fit to some extent with other desires and beliefs about worth. But how the integration will be achieved—which beliefs will yield to others, and which desires will change to fit with others—will vary with the individual; and there may be some generalizations here which describe the processes of change in most human beings (e.g. that recently acquired evaluative beliefs are preserved in changes, much more than are less recently acquired factual beliefs). Psychologists have done significant recent work on this process of belief and desire change, much of it stemming from the theory of 'cognitive dissonance' put forward by Leon Festinger in 1957.[11]

Agents can attempt to make their belief–desire systems more integrated by testing the coherence of their beliefs and desires with each other (e.g. in the way described in Chapter 12 with respect to moral beliefs), thinking through their consequences and facing up to their conflicts; or they can try to ignore certain beliefs and thereby (albeit not intentionally) make their system less integrated. Agents who are informed (e.g. by the psychologist of cognitive dissonance) of the processes by which their beliefs and desires come to change may be forced to recognize inconsistencies in their own system, which itself will lead to changes in that system. (E.g. if I come to believe that some of my beliefs have been influenced by a desire to believe certain things rather than by weighing evidence in the way which I believe rational, I shall have to abandon those beliefs because I can no longer regard them as reflections of how the world is (see p. 127).)

The Locus of Desire and Belief

So much for the processes by which beliefs and desires are

[11] L. Festinger, *A Theory of Cognitive Dissonance*, Row, Peterson, Evanston, Illinois, 1957. For a survey of more recent work in the field, see R. A. Wicklund and J. W. Brehm, *Perspectives on Cognitive Dissonance*, Lawrence Erlbaum, Hillsdale, NJ, 1976.

changed. There are two possible accounts of what is happening here, according to one's view about the locus of desire and belief. We saw in Chapters 6 and 7 that a man's desires and beliefs are continuing mental states which exist while he is giving them no thought and they are not influencing his behaviour; but that there are two ways of understanding this continuing. On the dispositional account, it is simply the continuing of whatever brain-state of the man is responsible for the manifestation from time to time of the desire or belief in thought or action. On the categorical account, it is the continuing of an intrinsically propositional state of which the subject is from time to time aware and which influences his behaviour from time to time; by the argument of Chapter 8 it will be a state of his soul.

I now argue in favour of the categorical account. My arguments are concerned largely with beliefs, but in view of the role of beliefs in sustaining desires, it will be seen that what holds for the one, holds for the other too. I begin with two considerations not suggested by the previous arguments of this chapter. The first is that, as I pointed out in Chapters 6 and 7, when we become aware of our beliefs and desires, they come to us (often) as states of affairs previously existing on which the spotlight of our consciousness has lighted. We seem to find within ourselves attitudes to the world and longings to do things in it, which were not created by our awareness but were there prior to that awareness. All this may be an illusion; but the principle of credulity bids us suppose that things are as they seem to be, in the absence of counter-evidence.

Secondly, as we have seen, beliefs and desires are often manifested in actions, while the subject is unaware of them. My purposing to go home causes my legs to move in the direction of the left-hand road without my having the conscious thought that the left-hand road leads home. I do the action which I would do if I were to derive from the thoughts 'I purpose to go home' and 'the left-hand road leads home', which action I ought to do. My action would be understandable if I had used the thought that the left-hand road leads home in calculating what I ought to do. So it is natural to postulate something identical with that thought minus the subject's state of awareness, viz. an intrinsically propositional belief, as what together with the subject's purposing causally affects his behaviour, causes his legs to move as they do, whether or not he is aware of the belief. That is what the categorical theory does. The dispositional theory must allow that thoughts affect behaviour—e.g., for the reason given on p. 82 that thoughts lead to their public acknowledgement in speech; and so it will allow that if I work out how to get home in conscious thought, that will affect the route I choose. But it must claim that an entirely different mechanism (causation by purposing plus brain-states alone) affects my bodily movements when I do not express my beliefs to myself in thought. In view of the fact that awareness is a matter of degree and there is continuity between beliefs of which we are fully conscious and those of which we are only half-aware, it seems implausible to postulate that a quite different mechanism suddenly operates when awareness falls to zero. The categorical theory in postulating only one mechanism is by the principle of simplicity more likely to be true.

Both of these considerations in favour of the categorical accounts of beliefs (and similar considerations can be adduced for desire) are arguments not merely in favour of beliefs and desires as categorical states, but as causally efficacious ones. We can explain our awareness of belief and desire by their being states which cause us to be aware of them, and we explain actions by the causal efficacy of these states.

The main argument of this chapter has been that virtually all change of belief and desire is constrained by the subject's existing belief–desire system. On the categorical view beliefs and desires, as intrinsically propositional states of soul, limit new admissions to the system to beliefs and desires not obviously incompatible with existing ones. On the dispositional view, whatever brain mechanism causes the actions and conscious states whereby a belief or desire is manifested, prevents the occurrence of brain-states which cause actions and conscious states whereby an obviously incompatible belief or desire is manifested.

The process of belief change (and a similar argument would go for desire change) shows the influence of beliefs of which the subject is unaware at the time. We saw in Chapter 4 that thoughts often cause other thoughts, in part directly, not totally via the brain, in virtue of their content. This happens in particular when those thoughts are judgements, and we noted that background beliefs often play a role in determining which thought succeeds which other thought. I must now bring out more fully the role of belief in such a process. Consider again a piece of reasoning which a man does mentally, not this time deductive reasoning, but an attempt to solve a practical problem or to solve some murder mystery or problem of history. The man begins by expressing in thought his premisses (say, the evidence available to the detective) and then argues to each new step (e.g. many of the steps may state that this or that suspect can be eliminated), eventually working up to the conclusion 'Jones did the murder'. Each new step constitutes the expression in judgement of a newly acquired belief. What leads a man to acquire that belief is what has gone before. Yet in such a case and especially when the reasoning is not deductive, often each step would not have been taken but for other beliefs which the subject takes for granted but does not express to himself. Thus he may move from 'Smith said he was in Edinburgh on Wednesday morning and two people claimed to see him there' to 'He was not in London on Wednesday morning'. In the background are a number of beliefs which alone make this a reasonable step to take, e.g. 'Edinburgh is four hundred miles from London', 'trains take more than four hours to travel four hundred miles', 'Smith would not travel by air', etc. The previous beliefs, expressed and unexpressed, lead to the new belief. Now the subject looking back on the process will affirm that he came to acquire his new belief under the pressure of reasons, through seeing what was involved in the old beliefs, guided by beliefs which he did not need to express to himself; he was, it *seemed* to him, drawing out the consequence of the beliefs which he did so express. It *seems* clear to the agent that the new belief would not have been accepted but for the nature of his old beliefs, quite independently of any brain-states with which they might have been correlated. There is a naturalness and *simplicity* of connections between the propositional content of the beliefs which can be expressed by the rules of deductive and inductive inference which the subject is (in general) following; the beliefs 'follow from' each other. The principles of credulity and simplicity lead us to suppose that the acquisition of the new belief was caused by the old beliefs in virtue of their propositional content, rather than by their brain correlates.

Men do not of course always reason cogently in accord with correct rules of inference, but explanations can be given of why they argue incorrectly, which also depend crucially on the content of the beliefs from which and to which they argue. They may reach a conclusion which is not entailed or rendered probable by the premisses. But this will only be if their pattern of inference has some similarity to a correct pattern (but in a way which does not make it a correct pattern). They may for example generalize too widely on the basis of a very small or biased sample. This may happen either as a result of unthinking habit or in consequence of a desire to believe the resulting conclusion.[12] But in either case a major factor in our acquiring the new belief we do (the conclusion of the inference) is the content of the old beliefs (the premisses). For even if we desire to believe the conclusion, we cannot believe that any premisses whatsoever provide it with justification; the premisses have to have some connection with the conclusion.

The pattern of succession of beliefs and the inherent striving for consistency and integration of a belief–desire system is made comprehensible if we suppose that beliefs are stored with an intrinsic propositional content rather than being mere patterns of thought succession and action. While I do not wish to deny that there could be a conscious being which, as a result of quite different causes had the conscious episodes (e.g. judgements) and did the actions which men do as a result of their desires and beliefs, my argument is that the simplest explanation of human thought and conduct is that it is moulded by the intrinsically propositional states of belief and desire and for this reason it is to be preferred to the alternative explanation. I am not wishing to deny that the process of change of belief and desire in practice requires an active brain to sustain it, and that it is accompanied by change of brain-state—only to assert that beliefs and desires themselves are parts of the causes of other beliefs and desires.

I have argued against epiphenomenalism about mental events of various kinds. The view that where we speak of belief affecting thought or conduct, what is really going on, except when the belief is expressed in thought, is that a brain-state which on occasion causes us to express to ourselves a belief, affects thought or conduct is another example of epiphenomenalism about the mental. I call it epiphenomenalism of belief. The dispositional theory involves epiphenomenalism of belief.

---

[12] It is the thesis of the psychologists R. Nisbett and L. Ross that incorrect inference is caused almost entirely by unthinking habit and hardly at all by desire to believe the conclusion. See their *Human Inference: Strategies and Shortcomings of Social Judgment*, Prentice-Hall, Englewood Cliffs NJ, 1980.

So far I have simply been claiming that the balance of argument suggests that epiphenomenalism of belief is false. There is, however, the further point to be made that to the extent to which epiphenomenalism is true we would lack any justification for believing it. Consider first what I shall call the extreme theory that affirms both epiphenomenalism of belief and of thought, viz. that neither unconscious beliefs nor consciously affirmed beliefs are causally efficacious. If this theory is true, then our judgements will be caused by brain-states and these brain-states by other brain-states, and these ultimately by physical states outside the body. They will not be caused by other logically relevant beliefs (in virtue of their intrinsic propositional content) or formed by chains of cogent thoughts. Now, the belief that my belief B is formed through a causal chain as such in no way impugns my justification for holding B. Thus my belief that my belief B that there is a table in front of me is caused by a series of brain and then bodily and then extra-bodily causes in no way impugns my justification for holding B, since I will believe that among the causes of B is the table being in front of me; and so that I would not have held B but for B being true. But the belief that there are no mental items among the causes of B puts B into a certain category, the category of perceptual or semi-perceptual beliefs which are non-reasoned responses to the environment—beliefs which are not held because they are justified by other beliefs. Such beliefs form the foundations on which other reasoned beliefs are built—or so we normally think. But if the extreme theory is true, it will not be so; all beliefs—be they about cosmology, or quantum physics, logic . . . or epiphenomenalism itself—will be in the same category of intuitive responses to the environment, not grounded in other beliefs. Our belief in that case that the extreme theory itself is true will not be something which we hold because of reasons (for we would hold it just because the right brain-event occurred, whatever other beliefs we held), or which we can get others to hold by getting them to consider reasons. The epiphenomenalist's arguments, whatever they may be, play no role in the formation of his beliefs or those of anyone else. But although my belief that there is a table in front of me needs no arguments by which to justify it, my beliefs in complicated scientific theories or world-views—including epiphenomenalism itself—surely do, at any rate sometimes when they are the subject of serious dispute. The epiphenomenalist may react to this argument by abandoning the extreme theory and reverting simply to epiphenomenalism of belief; he may allow that thoughts affect other thoughts while denying that unconscious beliefs play any role in determining which thought follows which other thought. But, as illustrated a few paragraphs back, there are beliefs which justify our deriving one thought from another which are not consciously expressed; and almost any argument which influenced a thinker to adopt epiphenomenalism would take many beliefs for granted. But if epiphenomenalism of belief is true those beliefs would have played no role in leading the thinker to adopt his theory, and to that extent his adoption of it would be ill-justified. On the categorical theory unconscious beliefs also play their role in determining how thinkers draw conclusions, and so these conclusions have far more backing. The very practice of psychology as a science producing reasoned, justified, conclusions requires the assumption that its practitioners are affected in drawing their conclusions by the content of their beliefs.

I am not, I repeat, giving the old bad argument which has been deployed so often against determinism (see ch. 13, n. 2) that if our beliefs (e.g. that determinism is true) are caused, they are unjustified. Rather it is the argument that insofar as our beliefs which require reasons for their justification do not have acceptance of those reasons among their causes, they are unjustified.

But if we abandon epiphenomenalism of beliefs, we have to say that beliefs are held because of other beliefs in virtue of the propositional content of the latter; that is, they are held in their place by states possessing intrinsic meaning, not by mere brain correlates. Because of the close connection between belief and desire, the same applies to desire. Men have the desires they do because of their beliefs about the nature of what they desire and the worthwhileness of possessing it. Desires are not formed merely by brain-states. There is a structure of belief and desire with intrinsic meaning distinct from any brain structure which may help to sustain that belief–desire structure. The latter structure is a continuing structure, since it determines at different moments of time which new beliefs will be admitted to a subject's belief set. Beliefs and desire, as mental events, and like the intrinsically propositional thoughts and purposes, inhere in the soul.

An analogy will bring out the consequences which we have now

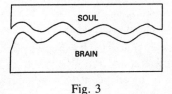

Fig. 3

derived from the categorical view of belief and desire. Consider an object with a complex shape whose contours are adjusted to those of a second object, so that their shapes fit together, as in Fig. 3. One object represents the brain; the other the soul. The shape of the soul represents its beliefs and desires; the shape of the brain its electrochemical network of the brain correlates of beliefs and desires. Now it could be that the soul was like a soft cushion, and the brain a hard object; so that the shape of the soul was entirely determined by that of the brain. The categorical view maintains, however, that the soul is not totally soft; it has to it some structure so that its shape in some parts is determined by its shape in other parts, and its shape to some extent determines that of the brain. The beliefs and desires inherent in the soul, to which the above is an analogy, that is, affect other beliefs and desires, conscious episodes, and behaviour. A particular belief, for example, is kept in place, not merely as a result of a certain brain-state, but by the presence of the other beliefs and desires. To revert to the analogy, some changes in the soul can be made easily by changing the brain's shape; but some attempts at changing the soul by changing the brain would be resisted by the soul—because it has a shape of its own.

On the dispositional view, by contrast, the only true states of the soul are conscious states. (Talk which leads us to suppose otherwise is a mere *façon de parler*.) The only structure belongs to the brain, whose shape as it were alone determines which judgements, awarenesses of desire, and other conscious episodes occur.

Different consequences follow for what would happen if it were possible to move a soul from one body controlled by one brain to another body controlled by a different brain, i.e. if it were possible to give to an agent a different body and brain. On the dispositional view the soul would automatically take over the beliefs and desires associated with the new brain which it is given. On the categorical view, the soul would take with it its own desires and beliefs (other than those directly dependent on bodily causes); if put in a body whose brain was not yet shaped to give rise to desires and beliefs, it would (to some extent) impose its shape upon the brain; if put in a body whose brain was shaped to give rise to different desires and beliefs, there would be a conflict as to which desires and beliefs the resulting person would have.

In this section I have argued in favour of the categorical view that the soul has a structure of intrinsically propositional beliefs and desires, while allowing that this structure is kept functioning by the operation of the brain.

The Unconscious

Once we have allowed the existence of the soul, as a separate immaterial entity, for the reasons which I discussed in Part II, there is no particular reason for supposing it to lack structure. I have now given positive reason for supposing it to have a structure of interconnected and (varying with the degree of integration) mutually supporting beliefs and desires. To the extent to which the system is less than perfectly integrated, there will be beliefs coexisting with other beliefs which the subject thinks of as having no connection with each other, and which may nevertheless (by the subject's own standards) render each other improbable; there will be desires coexisting with other desires which are hard to co-satisfy; desires for the non-existence of other beliefs and desires; and desires for goals believed undersirable. Subjects attempt to resolve such conflicts in ways which I have noted earlier; but, if conflicts remain, the various beliefs and desires may preserve some 'distance' from each other and affect behaviour and other mental events on different occasions. The various beliefs and desires may form two or more sub-systems, the members of each of which fit well together. In so far as the members of one sub-system are more prominent in their influence on the subject's behaviour and mental life, they are more 'in the sun'. Each sub-system may be highly integrated and yet the whole be highly disintegrated. Members of one sub-system may affect members of the other sub-system causally (as when a wish to have a belief helps to cause the belief), but in ways which the subject would recognize, were he aware of them, as being irrational. Each sub-system may be accessible to the agent in consciousness, but in that case the agent is likely to become aware of the relevance of members of each to the other (e.g. one belief rendering another improbable; or one desire being for the non-existence of another desire). In that case it becomes impossible or difficult for both sub-systems to be preserved, though it sometimes remains possible. (It is not possible for a subject to believe each of two propositions, and also to believe that each, given his other beliefs, renders the other improbable—see p. 263.) Hence one or other sub-system may be repressed from consciousness.[13]

Repression can be understood in different ways, but it is characteristic of a repressed belief or desire that in some sense the subject is aware of it and it influences his behaviour, but the subject will not acknowledge this fact even to himself (nor will he acknowledge the fact that he will not acknowledge it, etc.). Fingarette has described repression as a refusal to spell out to himself in thought what the subject is aware of.[14]

That some human behaviour needs for its explanation the postulation of subconscious beliefs and desires is surely a lesson which we have learnt from Freud—however materialistic his formal position, and whatever details of his psychology we have found too extravagant to take on board. No one pictured better than Freud the need to understand the human soul as a structure of interacting beliefs and desires, some overt and some repressed from consciousness; and in effect he pictured the suppressed beliefs and desires as having just the same nature as the manifest ones (i.e. being intrinsically propositional) except that they were repressed.

He saw that much puzzling behaviour could be explained by postulating systems of desires and beliefs, repressed from con-sciousness, which sometimes escaped from repression to give rise to intentional action—though intentional action which would not

---

[13] The need to postulate two (or more) separate sub-systems of belief and desire to explain much irrational behaviour and thought, is brough out by D. Davidson 'Paradoxes of Irrationality' in (ed.) R. Wollheim and J. Hopkins, *Philosophical Essays on Freud*, Cambridge University Press, 1982; see especially pp. 303 ff. These sub-systems, he emphasizes, may be functionally separate without either of them being subconscious. To postulate that one sub-system is subconscious is to take a further step, though one which may well be justified. This approach is developed at greater length in D. Pears, *Motivated Irrationality*, Clarendon Press, Oxford, 1984, ch. 5.

[14] H. Fingarette, *Self-Deception*, Routledge and Kegan Paul, London, 1969, ch. 3.

be acknowledged even to himself by the subject as such (errors such as slips of pen and tongue, and dreams) or for which the subject would not acknowledge his ultimate purposes (neurotic behaviour).[15] As an example of the former, consider this: 'Ernest Jones relates that he once allowed a letter to lie on his writing desk for several days for some unknown reason. At last he decided to post it, but received it back from the Dead Letter Office, for he had forgotten to address it. After he had addressed it he took it to post but this time without a stamp. At this point he finally had to admit to himself his objection to sending the letter at all.'[16] Here actions (leaving the letter on the desk, etc.) which the subject would not at the time admit as intentional at all, are explained as intentional movements or non-movements explained as guided by a purpose that the letter be not posted, arising from a continuing subconscious desire that it be not posted. As examples of neurotic behaviour, Freud described the lady who several times a day 'would run out of her room into the adjoining one, there take up a certain position at the table in the centre of the room' (near a great mark on the table cover so that when the maid came in, she could not help seeing the mark), 'ring for her maid, give her a trivial order or send her away without, and then run back again'. Freud gave a complicated explanation of the behaviour in terms of a belief that the lady's actions represented actions of her husband after their wedding night whereby he sought to avoid disgrace in front of a servant, and an intention of hers that thereby he should avoid such disgrace.[17] The continuing subconscious desire that the husband be not disgraced, and a continuing subconscious belief about how this could be achieved, gave rise intermittently to the intentional actions involved in attempting to prevent his disgrace. The lady repressed this ultimate purpose from her consciousness, and saw her actions as intentional only under the description given earlier.

Freud gave different pictures of the anatomy of the mind at different stages of his thought. The picture in the later (1933) *New Introductory Lectures*[18] is of three parts to the mind—the super-ego (or conscience), the ego (or person which actually performs

---

[15] See especially his *Introductory Lectures on Psychoanalysis*, translated by J. Riviere, George Allen and Unwin, London, 1922; Part I on errors, Part II on dreams, and Part III on neuroses.

[16] Op. cit., p. 44.

[17] For the detailed explanation, see op. cit., pp. 221 ff.

[18] Translated by W. J. H. Sprott, Hogarth Press, London, 1937, Lecture 31. Quotations are from p. 99.

the public actions), and the id (system of 'conative impulses' and 'impressions', i.e. memories). In the id 'contradictory impulses exist side by side without neutralizing each other or drawing apart; at most they combine in compromise formations'. The realm of the unconscious includes the 'pre-conscious', conscious states which can easily be uncovered (including, presumably, desires and beliefs of which the subject is not currently conscious, but can easily be made conscious), and the true unconscious, the mental life repressed (unconsciously) by the super-ego, which includes parts of the ego and super-ego as well as the id. The structure is a complicated one, but the main idea of interacting systems of desires and beliefs existing, and, while quite unacknowledged by the agent, explaining much human behaviour and mental life has proved an enormously illuminating one.

So the soul has a structure of interconnected beliefs and desires, integrated with each other to a greater or lesser degree, of which the subject may become aware and which influence his behaviour from time to time, some of them more 'in the sun' than others, and some repressed. When the subject is aware of his beliefs and desires in consciousness, as when he has other conscious events, he will be more aware of some than of others, i.e. his attention will be on some rather than others. Awareness is a matter of degree.

We saw earlier that no present-day brain surgery and other techniques of brain interference, neither microsurgery to a small area of the brain nor global brain-hacking are ever going to make much difference to a well-integrated charater. But I left open the issue of whether the next century's surgeons could change a character totally by doing a really systematic job on the brain, changing neurone after neurone in the brain, either by stimulating already existing circuits or by creating them by surgery. But if the arguments of the last few pages are correct, even this method *may* fail. Certainly the surgeon can readily alter those beliefs and desires which are not kept in place by other beliefs and desires, but have mere bodily causes. As we saw earlier, hunger and thirst can easily be created by tinkering with the nervous system; and so can beliefs about particular perceptual facts (e.g. that I am now seeing a table). But the more beliefs and desires are sustained by other beliefs and desires, the harder that will be. What my arguments have shown is that there are forces at work resisting alterations of the more central elements of a man's system of beliefs and desires, including those which form his character, other than mere bodily forces. The soul itself has a structure; and the more integrated the character, the firmer the structure. If the surgeon starts to change the brain correlates of some of a subject's beliefs, the subject will tend to resist this change—in the sense that his altered beliefs will return because of the pressure of his other beliefs. If the surgeon is determined and totally alters the brain, my model suggests that what will happen will depend on just how firm the soul's structure of belief and desire is. If a subject's beliefs and desires are very disconnected, the surgeon could win. But if they are firmly interconnected, the subject will die. For the set of beliefs and desires which sustain themselves despite neurone changes will no longer have the neuronal correlates which allow them expression. (In my analogical picture, the belief–desire set will no longer fit the brain which allows expression to the beliefs and desires). And that of course is what medical science suggests would be anyway the effect of too much brain surgery—for quite down-to-earth empirical reasons, there are limits to what the outsider can do to an integrated soul.

The Evolution of Structure

My argument for the soul having a persisting structure turned in large part on subjects forming judgements and desires because they are supported by other beliefs not all the time present to consciousness. Animals however do not often make judgements on the basis of other beliefs; nor do they often see beliefs as supported by evidence, and without language they cannot see beliefs as following deductively from other beliefs. Yet they do on the other hand do actions to fulfil purposes because guided by beliefs of which they are not at the time conscious. So although there is an argument for their having intrinsically propositional beliefs embedded in their soul, that soul will lack a structure of interconnected beliefs and desires which has some self-sustaining force. Their desires and beliefs are dependent much more directly on their brain-states.

What seems to have happened in the course of evolution is that when genetic changes gave to animals beliefs and desires, they were beliefs about how to attain fairly immediate goals and desires for those goals. The causal efficacy of those beliefs and desires was limited to causing actions in pursuit of immediate goals. But gradually our ancestors began to have more sophisticated beliefs and desires which came to form a structure, so that the causal efficacy of beliefs and desires now included causing other beliefs and desires. On this as on all the other topics which we have looked at in this book, those who rightly draw our attention to the animal origins of man and the inanimate origins of animals, often make the error of supposing that there is nothing new in what has evolved. As so manifestly the evolutionary process has thrown up consciousness and more sophisticated forms of consciousness, it would not be surprising if its products come to exert causal influences which did not exist before. That is what has happened, I suggest, with beliefs and desires. Gradually the soul has passed from being passive and structureless, to being structured and active—structured by causally influential beliefs and desires. Mutations of genes gave rise to organisms with brains which in certain environmental circumstances occupied states which gave rise to sophisticated and causally efficacious desires in the soul. The mechanism of this causality remains the mystery which we have seen the mechanism of production of all desires and beliefs to be. The continued possession of complex beliefs gave to the organism the ability to plan, and the continued possession of complex desires gave him the purpose to pursue plans over a continued period of time; and both of these features plausibly confer evolutionary advantage on their possessor.

That the human soul is not a bare particular, but a thing with structure which affects bodily conduct in virtue of its structure was affirmed by Aristotle with his slogan 'the soul is the form of the body'. But Aristotle's form could not exist apart from the body. Aquinas proclaimed the same slogan, but with an understanding of the soul as a substantial form which could exist apart from the body. The differences between souls, Aquinas thought, consist in the differences in the bodies which they fit[19] (as keys differ according to the different locks which they unlock); my soul can only be taken out of my body and put into another one if the other one has a brain fitted for the expression of my character. But although my model does indeed imply that souls have different structures from each other, I stress, what Aquinas did not bring out, that the differences between souls do not lie solely in their structures; two different souls can have the same character. They differ in soul-stuff, a category which Aquinas did not recognize; and that difference is the essential difference between souls.

[19] See his *Summa Contra Gentiles*, 2. 81. 8.

15. THE FUTURE OF THE SOUL

FOUR thousand million years of evolution produced man, a body and soul in continuing interaction. A human soul is more dependent for its development on its own states than is an animal soul, for it has complex beliefs and desires kept in place and changing in accord with other beliefs and desires. Other animals having only much simpler beliefs and desires are much more dependent for their continuing beliefs and desires directly on their bodily states. Can this complex evolved human soul survive on its own apart from the body which sustains it? I have argued so far that the functioning of the human soul (i.e. its having conscious episodes) is guaranteed by the functioning of the brain currently connected with it (connected, in that the soul's acquisition of beliefs about its surroundings and action upon those surroundings is mediated by that brain). I considered in Chapter 10 what it is for a man or his soul to exist unconscious, and I argued that that was a matter which required to be settled by definition. The definition which I suggested was that a soul exists if normal bodily processes or available artificial techniques can bring the man to be conscious, i.e. his soul to function again.

When the body dies and the brain ceases to function, the evidence of the kind considered in Chapter 10 suggests that the soul will cease to function also. For that evidence suggests that the soul functions only when the brain has rhythms of certain kinds, and at death the brain ceases to function altogether. If the soul does not function before there is a functioning brain, or during deep sleep, when the brain is not functioning at a certain level, surely it will not function after there ceases to be a functioning brain? However, there are arguments and evidence of less usual kinds which purport to show that things are different after death from what they are before birth.

Before we face the question of whether the soul can function without the functioning of the brain currently connected with it, we must consider the question of whether, after death, the brain which ceases to function at death can be made to function again and whether thereby the soul can be revived.

Can the Brain be Reactivated?

A crucial problem is that we do not know how much of the brain that was yours has to be reassembled and within what time interval in order that we may have *your* brain and so your soul function again. We saw this earlier in the split brain cases. If both half-brains are transplanted into empty skulls and the transplants take, both subsequent persons will satisfy to some extent the criterion of apparent memory (as well as the brain criterion) for being the original person. One subsequent person might satisfy the criterion better than the other, and that would be evidence that he was the original person; but the evidence could be misleading. The situation is equally unclear with possible developments at death.

Suppose you die of a brain haemorrhage which today's doctors cannot cure, but your relatives take your corpse and put it straight into a very deep freeze in California. Fifty years later your descendents take it out of the freeze; medical technology has improved and the doctors are able quickly to mend your brain, and your body is then warmed up. The body becomes what is clearly the body of a living person, and one with your apparent memory and character. Is it you? Although we might be mistaken, the satisfaction of the criterion of apparent memory (together with the—at any rate partial—satisfaction of the criterion of brain continuity) would suggest that we ought to say 'Yes'. So long as the same brain is revived, the same functioning soul would be connected with it—whatever the time interval. But what if the brain is cut up into a million pieces and then frozen? Does the same hold? Why should there be any difference? Suppose that the brain is reduced to its component atoms; and then these are reasembled either by chance or because they have been labelled radioactively. Again, if the subsequent person makes your memory claims, surely we ought to say that it is you. But how many of the original atoms do we need in the original locations? That we do not know. So long as the subsequent person had many similar atoms in similar locations in his brain, he would claim to have been you. So, the criterion of apparent memory will be satisfied. Total non-satisfaction of the brain criterion would defeat the claims of apparent memory (in the absence of any general failure of coincidence in results between these criteria). But it remains unclear and indeed insoluble exactly how much of the original brain is needed to provide satisfaction of the brain criterion.

This problem of how much of the original body is physically necessary when other matter is added to it so as to make a fully functioning body, in order that the original soul may be present and function, is a problem which concerned the thinkers of the early Christian centuries and of the Middle Ages. They considered the imaginary case of the cannibal who eats nothing but human flesh. Given that both the cannibal and his victims are to be brought to life in the General Resurrection, to whom will be flesh of the cannibal belong? Aquinas[1] begins his answer by saying that 'if something was materially present in many men, it will rise in him to whose perfection it belonged', i.e. that that part of the body which is necessary for a man being the person he is will belong to him in the General Resurrection. But what part is that, and what guarantee is there that the matter of that part cannot come to form the essential part of a different man who cannot therefore be reconstituted at the same time as the original man (given the operation of normal processes)? Aquinas goes on to produce an argument that the 'radical seed' (i.e. the sperm, which according to Aristotle formed the original matter of the embryo) forms the minimum essential bodily core around which a man could be rebuilt. But we know now, as Aquinas did not, that the sperm does not remain as a unit within the organism, and there seems to me no reason why all the atoms which originally formed it should not be lost from the body, and indeed come to form parts of original cells of many subsequent men. The atoms of the original cell are not therefore the most plausible candidate for being the part of the body physically necessary for human personal identity. Aquinas's problem remains without modern solution.

Nevertheless, although neurophysiology cannot tell us which part of his brain is physically necessary for the embodiment of a given man, it does tell us, as I argued earlier, that some of the brain is thus necessary. For the functioning of a given human soul, there has to be a man whose brain contains certain of the matter of

---

[1] *Summa Contra Gentiles*, 4. 81. 12 and 13. (Book IV, translated under the title *On the Truth of the Catholic Faith*, Book IV, by C. J. O'Neill, Image Books, New York, 1957.)

his original brain (but which matter we do not know), similarly arranged. A certain amount of the original brain matter has to be reassembled in a similar arrangement and reactivated by being joined to other brain matter and a body if the soul is to function again. And how likely is it that physical processes will bring about such a reassembly? As the time since death increases, and brain cells and then brain molecules are broken up, burnt by fire, or eaten by worms—it becomes very, very unlikely indeed that chance will reassemble them; or even that human agents can do so for they will not be able to re-identify the atoms involved. (One must, however, be careful here about the possibilities for technology in the twenty-second century. Maybe a brain map could be constructed and a process of labelling constituent atoms devised, which would make possible a reassembly after many years. But the possible development of such a technology seems to me very unlikely.) When the original atoms are reduced to packets of energy, then since these perhaps cannot be individuated, reassembly finally becomes not merely physically very, very improbable, but totally impossible physically. (But the word is 'perhaps'; it is a difficult question in the philosophy of physics whether bursts of energy can be individuated.) I conclude that it is very, very unlikely (and with increasing time virtually impossible) that after death souls will again have reassembled the brain basis which we know makes them function.

Is there any good reason to suppose that the soul continues to function without the brain functioning? Arguments to show that the soul continues to function without the brain functioning may be divided into three groups, involving different amounts of theoretical structure, to reach their conclusions. First, we may consider arguments which purport to show that certain men have survived death, in the sense that their souls have functioned without their brains functioning, directly—i.e. without needing first to establish anything about the nature of the soul or any more systematic metaphysical structure. Arguments of this kind may be called parapsychological arguments.

Arguments from Parapsychology

First, there is the alleged evidence of reincarnation, that souls function in new bodies with new brains on Earth. There are Indian children who claim to remember having lived a certain past life, and whose memory claims coincide with the events of some real past life about which—allegedly—they could not have learnt by what they were told or had read.[2] Now, it is of course open to serious question whether perhaps those Indian children had read or were told or learnt in some other perfectly normal way the details of those past lives. But even if for a few Indian children there was this coincidence between their memory claims and the events of a certain past person's life, without there being any normal cause of the accuracy of their memory claims that would not be enough evidence to show their identity with those persons. For, as I argued in Chapter 9, given the general coincidence of sameness of memory with continuity of brain, we must take continuity of brain as a criterion of identity; and the non-satisfaction of that in the case of the few Indian children (who do not have the same brain matter as the cited past persons), must remain substantial evidence against the supposition that they are those persons.

Next, there is the alleged evidence of spiritualism, that souls function without bodies or with new bodies and brains in another world. Mediums purport to have telepathic communication with dead persons. The evidence that they do is allegedly provided by the knowledge of the details of the dead person's life on Earth (not obtainable by the medium by normal means) which the medium's reports of the telepathic communications reveal. In the reincarnation case there is no doubt that there exists in the present a living conscious person; the debatable question concerns his identity with the past person. In the spiritualism case the crucial issue concerns whether there is a conscious person with whom the medium is in communication.

A serious issue in medium cases, like the similar issue in the supposed reincarnation cases, concerns the source of the mysterious knowledge. Perhaps the medium gets her knowledge from some spy who has done research on the dead person's life. But even if investigation showed clearly that the mediums had gained their knowledge of the past lives of dead person by no normal route, the evidence would still, I suggest, not support the hypothesis of telepathic communication with the dead. For also compatible with the evidence would be the hypothesis that the

[2] For references to the literature, see John Hick, *Death and Eternal Life*, Collins, London, 1976, pp. 373–8.

mediums have clairvoyance—they see directly into the past and acquire their knowledge thus. (Adopting the latter hypothesis would involve supposing either that the mediums were deceiving us about the kind of experiences they were having (apparent two-way traffic with a living person), or that they were deceiving themselves, or that their experiences were illusory.) On the choice between the two hypotheses there seem to me to be two important reasons for preferring the clairvoyance hypothesis. First, there are no cross-checks between mediums about the alleged present experiences of the dead in the afterlife. Mediums never give independently verifiable reports on this. Secondly, their reports about the present alleged experiences of the dead are themselves very banal. Yet one would expect because of the total lack of dependence of the dead on their past bodies, that they would live in a very different world, and that this would emerge in their reports on that world.[3]

Finally, there is the interesting and recently published alleged evidence that souls function while their bodies are out of action. There has been careful analysis of the experiences of those who clinically were as good as dead and then recovered. Such experiences are often called 'near-death experiences'.[4] Fifteen per cent of subjects resuscitated after being in such a condition report strange experiences of one of two kinds. Many of them report the following 'transcendental experiences':

an initial period of distress followed by profound calm and joy; out-of-the-body experiences with the sense of watching resuscitation events from a distance; the sensation of moving rapidly down a tunnel or along a road, accompanied by a loud buzzing or ringing noise or hearing beautiful music; recognising friends and relatives who have died previously; a rapid review of pleasant incidents from throughout the life as a panoramic playback (in perhaps twelve per cent of cases); a sense of approaching a border or frontier and being sent back; and being annoyed or disappointed at having to return from such a pleasant experience—"I tried not to come back", in one patient's words. Some describe frank transcendent experiences and many state that they will never fear death again. Similar

---

[3] On the alleged evidence of spiritualism, see John Hick, op. cit., ch. 7.

[4] There is a brief and well-balanced survey of this evidence in Paul and Linda Badham, *Immortality or Extinction?*, Macmillan, London, 1982, ch. 5. My summary of the evidence is based on this chapter, but I also make use of a very careful and balanced account of a new programme of investigations by Michael B. Sabom, *Recollections of Death*, Harper and Row, New York, 1982.

stories have been reported from the victims of accidents, falls, drowning, anaphylaxis, and cardiac or respiratory arrest.[5]

Resuscitated patients other than those who had transcendental experiences have undergone 'a wide variety of vivid dreams, hallucinations, nightmares and delusions', but some of those who had transcendental experiences also experienced these and sharply distinguished between the two kinds of experience. The 'dreams' were regarded as dreams, and were quickly forgotten; the 'supposed glimpses of a future life' were regarded as real and permanently remembered. These glimpses were reported as having occurred at moments when 'breathing had ceased, the heart had stopped beating, and the patients showed no visible signs of life'. The principle of credulity might suggest that we ought to take such apparent memories seriously, especially in view of the considerable coincidences between them, as evidence that what subjects thought they experienced, they really did. But although the subjects referred these experiences to moments at which the heart had stopped beating, etc., I do not know of any evidence that at these moments their brains had ceased to function. And if the brain was still functioning then, what the evidence would show is not that the soul may function when the brain does not, but only that its perceptual experiences (i.e. sensations and acquisitions of belief about far away places) are not dependent on normal sensory input.

The same conclusion will follow with respect to the considerable but not overwhelming evidence of those resuscitated patients who had experiences of the other strange kind, 'out-of-body-experiences', i.e. being able to view their own bodies and events in the operating theatre from a distance, obtaining thereby information which they would not have been able to obtain by normal means (e.g. having visual experiences of events which they would not have got from use of their eyes, such as views of parts of the theatre hidden from their eyes).[6] This again suggests that the subject's acquisition of information is dependent on some factor quite other than normal sensory input to the brain. But again I know of no evidence that these experiences occurred while the brain was not functioning; and so the available evidence does not

---

[5] *Lancet*, 24 June 1978, quoted in Badham, op. cit.
[6] On this, see Sabom, op. cit., chs. 3, 6, 7, and 8.

support the suggestion that the soul can function without the brain functioning.

My conclusion on parapsychology is that it provides no good evidence that the soul continues to function without the brain to which it is currently connected, functioning.

Arguments for Natural Survival

The second class of arguments purporting to show that the soul survives death purport to show from a consideration of what the soul is like when it functions normally that its nature is such that the failure of the brain to function would make no difference to the operation of the soul. Such arguments verge from very general arguments of what the soul must be like to be conscious at all to arguments which appeal to particular empirical data.

Dualist philosophers of the past have usually affirmed the natural immortality of the soul—that the soul has such a nature, or the laws of nature are such, that (barring suspension of natural laws) it will continue to function forever. There have been a variety of general arguments for the natural immortality of the soul. Each argument has, in my view, its own fallacies; and the fallacies being fairly evident today, there is no need for any extensive discussion of such arguments. (Expositions of the arguments do, incidentally, usually suffer from confusing the existence of the soul with its functioning; wrongly supposing that when it exists, necessarily it will function.)

To illustrate the fallacies of such arguments, I take just one famous argument, put forward by Plato.[7] Plato argues that the soul being an immaterial thing is unextended, and so does not have parts; but the destruction of a thing consists in separating from each other its parts; whence it follows that souls cannot be destroyed and must continue to exist forever.

Now certainly the normal way by which most material objects cease to exist is that they are broken up into parts. The normal end of a table is to be broken up; likewise for chairs, houses, and pens. But this need not be the way in which a material object ceases to exist. Things cease to exist when they lose their essential properties. The essential properties of a table include being solid.

---

[7] *Phaedo*, 78 b–80e. See also, for example, Berkeley: 'We have shown that the soul is indivisible, incorporeal, unextended, and it is consequently incorruptible'— G. Berkeley, *Principles of Human Knowledge*, § 141.

If a table was suddenly liquified, then, even if its constituent molecules remained arranged in the shape of a table by being contained in a table-shaped mould, the table would have ceased to exist. So if even material objects can cease to exist without being broken up into parts, souls surely can cease to exist by some other route than by being broken up into parts.

Nor are the more empirically based arguments of traditional dualists any more successful at showing that the soul has a nature such as to survive death. In *The Analogy of Religion*, Joseph Butler pointed out that many men die of disease, when in full possession of powers of thought; and this, he considered, suggested that weakening of powers of body has no effect at all on many powers of soul:

as it is evident our present powers and capacities of reason, memory, and affection do not depend upon our gross body in the manner in which perception by our organs of sense does; so they do not appear to depend upon it at all in any such manner as to give ground to think that the dissolution of this body will be the destruction of these our present powers of reflection, as it will of our powers of sensation; or to give ground to conclude, even that it will be so much as a suspension of the former.[8]

But, although it is true that weakening of certain bodily faculties does not affect powers of thought, the evidence is manifest that other bodily damage or disease or mere sleep does affect powers of thought. Drugs and alcohol affect clarity of thought, and, as we saw in Chapter 10, there is no reason to suppose that any conscious events occur during periods of deep sleep.

The failure of the above arguments is, I suggest, typical of the failure of dualist arguments to show that the soul has an immortal nature or at any rate a nature such that it is able to go on functioning 'under its own steam'. We need a form of dualism which brings out that the soul does not have a *nature* so as to function on its own.[9]

[8] *The Analogy of Religion*, 1. 1. 3.
[9] Although Aquinas like most other dualists taught that the soul has a natural immortality (see *Summa Theologiae*, Ia. 75. 6), he did claim the powers which its nature gave to a bodiless soul are less than those which it has when embodied, and less even than those which Butler ascribed to it—although understanding and will remain, Aquinas claimed, memory does not. (See *Summa Contra Gentiles*, 2. 81. 11 and 14, translated as *On the Truth of the Catholic Faith*, Book II, *Creation*, by James F. Anderson, Image Books, New York, 1956.)

Is the Soul Naturally Embodied?

If it cannot be shown that the soul has a nature so as to survive death without its connected brain functioning, can it be shown that the soul has a nature such that its functioning is dependent on that of the brain with which it is connected? Can we show that there is a natural law which (i) connects consciousness of a soul with the functioning of some material system, and (ii) connects the consciousness of each soul with the functioning of a particular material system; so that of natural necessity a soul can only function if the brain or other complex system with which it is at some time connected continues to function?

The answer given in Chapter 10 is that this cannot be shown. It has not been shown and probably never can be shown that there is any naturally necessary connection of these kinds between soul and body. All we are ever likely to get is correlations—between this kind of brain-event and that kind of mental event. And in the absence of a theory which explains why a material system of this kind is needed to produce a soul, how this sort of physical change will produce this kind of mental state, how just so much of the brain and no more is needed for the continuity of a certain soul (as opposed to the mere functioning of a soul with similar apparent memories), we have no grounds for saying that souls *cannot* survive the death of their brains. We do not know and are not likely to find out what if any natural necessity governs the functioning of souls.

The situation is simply that the fairly direct kinds of evidence considered so far give no grounds for supposing that anyone has survived death, but we know of no reason to suppose that it is not possible for anyone to survive death. The situation is thus similar to that in many areas of enquiry when no one has yet found a so-and-so but no one has shown that so-and-sos do not exist. Maybe there are living persons on other planets, naturally occurring elements with atomic numbers of over 1,000, or magnetic monopoles; but as yet no one has found them. Someone may argue that failure to find something when you have looked for it is evidence that it does not exist. But that is so only if you would recognize the object when you found it, and if there is a limited region within which the object can exist and you have explored quite a lot of the region. Failure to find oil in the English Channel after you have drilled in most parts of it, or to find the Abominable Snowman if you have explored most of the Himalayas, is indeed evidence that the thing does not exist. But that is hardly the case with souls whose brains have ceased to function. Maybe they are reincarnate in new bodies and brains on Earth but, as they have lost their memories, the evidence of their identity has gone. Or maybe they are where we cannot at present look. They may still function without being embodied (I argued for the coherence of this supposition in Chapter 8) and so there be no place which they occupy. Or if they are re-embodied in another body with another brain, they may be anywhere in this universe or some other. Failure to find souls who have survived death shows no more than that if they do exist, they are not in the very few places where we have looked for them or that if they are, the marks of their identity (e.g. apparent memories of past lives) have been removed. In the absence of any further evidence as to whether souls do survive death we can only remain agnostic and wait until further evidence does turn up.

Evidence of Survival via Metaphysical Theory

There is however a third kind of evidence about whether men survive death which we have not yet considered. This is evidence of a wide ranging character which is most simply explained by a very general metaphysical theory of the world, which has as its consequence that human souls survive death as a result of their nature or as a result of the predictable action of some agent who has the power to bring them to life.

One such theory is the Hindu-Buddhist metaphysic of karma, a deep law of retribution in nature whereby an agent who lives a life thereafter lives another in which he gets the deserts (reward or punishment) for the previous life. (The establishment of such a system would have the consequence that, despite the lack of evidence for this on which I commented in Chapter 10, souls exist before birth; in order to be reborn they must then normally lose much of the character which, I have argued, comes to characterize the soul by the time of death.)

Another such theory is of course Christian theism. The theist has first to argue for the existence of God, a person (in a wide sense) of infinite power, wisdom, goodness, and freedom. He may argue that the existence of God provides the simplest explanation of the existence of the universe, the virtual total regularity of its behaviour in its conformity to natural laws, and various more particular phenomena within the universe. It would then follow that God, being omnipotent, would have the power to give to souls life after death (and if there is no natural law which ties the functioning of a soul to the operation of a brain, God would not need to suspend natural laws in order to do this). The Christian theist will need further to show that God intends to bring souls to function after death. He could show this either by showing that it was an obligation on an omnipotent being to do such a thing, and so that, being good, God would do it; or by showing that God had announced his intention of doing this (e.g. by doing something which God alone could do such as suspending a law of nature, in connection with the work of a prophet as a sign that the prophet who had said that God so intended was to be trusted.)[10]

It will be evident that any argument via metaphysical theory to the survival of death by human souls will have a lengthy and complicated structure. But of course those who produce such arguments are equally concerned about most of the other things which need to be proved on the way. Few people are interested in the existence of God solely for its value in proving life after death. And if I am right in my claim that we cannot show that the soul has a nature such that it survives 'under its own steam', and that we cannot show that it has a nature such that it cannot survive without its sustaining brain, the only kind of argument that can be given is an argument which goes beyond nature, i.e. that shows there is something beyond the natural order embodied in laws of nature, and that the operation of that something is to some extent predictable.

If God did give to souls life after death in a new body or without a body, he would not in any way be violating natural laws—for, if I am right, there are no natural laws which dictate what will happen to the soul after death. The soul doesn't have a nature which has consequences for what will happen to it subsequent to the dissolution of its links to the body.

In the last chapter I argued that the human soul at death had a

[10] I have argued for the existence of God in my *The Existence of God*, Clarendon Press, Oxford, 1979; and I have analysed the structure of an argument to show that God has revealed something through a certain source in my *Faith and Reason*, Clarendon Press, Oxford, 1981, ch. 7. (That chapter elucidates the 'in connection with' of the sentence in the text.)

structure, a system of beliefs and desires which might be expected
to be there to some degree in the soul if that soul were to be
revived. If a man does survive death, he will take his most central
desires and beliefs with him, which is the kind of survival for
which, I suspect, most men hope. In hoping to survive death, a
man hopes not only that subsequent to his death, he will have
experiences and perform actions. He hopes also to take with him a
certain attitude to the world. That attitude certainly does not
always include all aspects of a man's present character. Much, no
doubt, many a man would be happy to dispense with. But it does
include some of his character, and that part just because it is the
part which he desires should continue, is the most central part.

Note that if there does occur a general resurrection of souls with
new bodies in some other world, yet with apparent memories of
their past lives (or a general reincarnation on Earth with such
memories), they would have grounds for reidentifying each other
correctly. For then the general failure of the results of the criterion
of bodily continuity to coincide with those of apparent memory
would by the arguments of Chapter 9 justifiably lead us to
abandon the former criterion and rely entirely on the latter. Not
merely is a general resurrection logically possible but it would be
known by the subjects to have occurred.

Conclusion

The view of the evolved human soul which I have been advocating
may be elucidated by the following analogy. The soul is like a light
bulb and the brain is like an electric light socket. If you plug the
bulb into the socket and turn the current on, the light will shine. If
the socket is damaged or the current turned off, the light will not
shine. So, too, the soul will function (have a mental life) if it is
plugged into a functioning brain. Destroy the brain or cut off the
nutriment supplied by the blood, and the soul will cease to
function, remaining inert. But it can be revived and made to
function again by repairing or reassembling the brain—just as the
light can be made to shine again by repairing the socket or turning
on the current. But now, my analogy breaks down slightly (as all
analogies do—else they would not be analogies). Humans can
repair light sockets. But there is a practical limit to the ability of
humans to repair brains; the bits get lost. Humans can move light
bulbs and put them into entirely different sockets. But no human

knows how to move a soul from one body and plug it into another; nor does any known natural force do this. Yet the task is one involving no contradiction and an omnipotent God could achieve it; or maybe there are other processes which will do so. And just as light bulbs do not have to be plugged into sockets in order to shine (loose wires can be attached to them), maybe there are other ways of getting souls to function than by plugging them into brains. But investigation into the nature of the soul does not reveal those ways. And humans cannot discover what else is needed to get souls to function again, unless they can discover the ultimate force behind nature itself.

APPENDIX

The theory of the evolved human soul which I have been advocating in this book is, I believe, that of the Bible. Both Old and New Testament hold that a man is a thing of flesh and bone. (Because the Jews believed— see Genesis 1—that all material things were good, they could set a high value on man without denying his materiality.) When in the last century BC many Jews came to believe in life after death, and when the Christian religion arose within Judaism affirming life after death, the life which they affirmed was not a natural immortality, but a resurrection—God intervening in history to give to Christ or to all men new bodies and thereby new life.[11] The Nicene Creed affirms belief in 'the resurrection of the body'. Christian theology has always affirmed that the reunion of a soul with a body in the General Resurrection required a divine act. But early in Christian thought there arose the view that the dead exist in an intermediate state of purgatory (or in the case of some souls, heaven or hell) as souls without bodies. This view combined with Plato's view that there was a natural immortality of the soul to yield the view that souls existed in purgatory or elsewhere without bodies under their own natural powers. That view seems to me to be out of line with the Christian emphasis on the embodiedness of men as their normal and divinely intended state,[12] and also to fall foul of the arguments of this chapter. If

---

[11] That the New Testament affirms a resurrection of the dead, body and soul, by divine agency, rather than a natural immortality of the soul is the theme of O. Cullmann, *Immortality of the Soul or Resurrection of the Dead?*, Epworth Press, London, 1958.

[12] Aquinas tried to make provision in his system for the normal embodiedness of men by claiming that the soul separated from its body 'is not a man' (*Summa Theologiae*, Ia. 75. 4). But, although lacking its bodily expression and source of knowledge, the soul is still the subject of action and experience and thus, in my

souls exist in purgatory or elsewhere without their bodies or with totally new bodies, they do so by special divine act, not under their own natural powers.

terminology, a person. Hence, even in Aquinas's system, what we value most about men has a natural immortality; and this seems to jar with the biblical affirmation.

ADDITIONAL NOTES

1 [ch. 4 n. 9]. There has been considerable recent philosophical controversy about whether there is a 'language of thought' (sometimes jokingly called 'Mentalese'). It is not always easy to understand what is at stake here, but what those who advocate this thesis (e.g. J. A. Fodor, *The Language of Thought*, first published 1975, Harvard University Press, Cambridge, Mass., 1979) seem to be urging is that each human is born with an interior language in which he thinks many private 'thoughts'. In order to communicate with others he then learns to translate from Mentalese into some public language, such as English, or vice versa. One problem here is that by 'thought' is often meant 'belief'. But although it is often clear what it is for a combination of symbols uttered or written on a particular occasion, as in a thought (private or public) to be in one language rather than another, it is unclear what it is for a belief to be in a language at all. Cats have many beliefs and yet they can hardly be said to have a language. The interpretation given to organisms having beliefs in a language is that they have beliefs by 'storing sentences'; to each belief there corresponds some inner state which represents it and the 'system of internal representation' is such that 'the sentence-analogs have significant grammatical structure' (Harty H. Field, 'Mental Representation' in (ed.) N. Block, *Readings in Philosophy of Psychology*, Methuen, London, 1981, vol. 2, p. 85), that is, each inner state which represents a belief does so in virtue of having aspects *or* parts which are related to each other as are parts of a sentence—change the aspect and you change the belief in the way that you would change its meaning by replacing one word of a sentence by another. Those who advocate this view normally understand the inner states which represent beliefs to be brain-states, and indeed the representation to be identity-beliefs are brain-states. (I shall argue in Chapter 7 that beliefs are not brain-states, but are caused by them.) But it seems a physiologically rash hypothesis to suppose that the brain operates in this way, and one quite unnecessary in order to express the view that beliefs are brain-states—on this see C. Peacocke, *Sense and Content*, ch. 8, and D. Dennett 'A Cure for the Common Code' in his *Brainstorms*, Harvester, Brighton, 1979. But certainly *unless* beliefs are understood as brain-states, there is no reason for supposing that they are linguistically articulated, until this is done in normal public languages such as English. Again, if by 'thoughts' is meant thoughts in my sense, there is no reason to suppose that they are composed of mental items which have such a structure apart from images of words of normal languages, and little reason to suppose that their brain-causes have such a structure. And against all such hypotheses is the fact on which I commented in the text— that the sort of thoughts and beliefs people have are very much conditioned by the language and practice of their society. Relatively seldom do they seem to have thoughts and beliefs not so expressible; and the beliefs and thoughts of which they are capable grow with their understanding of the language and participation in the practice of their societies. This would be surprising if they had a whole language of thought independent of the public language. All this is not to deny Chomsky's claim that humans have an in-built capacity for learning public language— it is merely to doubt that they have much of a language apart from the public language (which in time they come to use privately). For good discussions of the controversy, see G. Harman 'Language Learning' in Block, op. cit., vol. 2 and 'Language, Thought, and Communication' in (ed.) K. Gunderson, *Language, Mind, and Knowledge, Minnesota Studies in the Philosophy of Science*, vol. 7, University of Minnesota Press, Minneapolis, 1975.

2 [ch. 8 n. 5]. It may be useful, in case anyone suspects the argument of this paragraph of committing some modal fallacy, to set it out in a more formal logical shape. I use the usual logical symbols—'.' means 'and', '$\sim$' means 'not', '$\Diamond$' means 'it is logically possible'.

I then introduce the following definitions:

> p = 'I am a conscious person, and I exist in 1984'
> q = 'my body is destroyed at the end of 1984'
> r = 'I have a soul in 1984'
> s = 'I exist in 1985'
> x ranges over all consistent propositions compatible with $(p.q)$ and describing 1984 states of affairs ('(x)' is to be read in the normal way as 'for all states x . . .').

The Argument may now be set out as follows:

p	. . . . Premiss (1)
$(x) \Diamond (p.q.x.s)$	. . . . Premiss (2)
$\sim \Diamond (p.q.\sim r.s)$	. . . . Premiss (3)

$\therefore$ $\sim r$ is not within the range of x.

But since $\sim r$ describes a state of affairs in 1984, it is not compatible with $(p.q)$. But q can hardly make a difference to whether or not r. So p is incompatible with $\sim r$.

$\therefore r$

The argument is designed to show that r follows from p; and so, more generally, that every conscious person has a soul. Premiss (3) is justified by the quasi-Aristotelian assumption that if I am to continue, some of the stuff out of which I am made has to continue. As I argued in the text, that stuff must be non-bodily stuff. The soul is defined as that non-bodily part whose continuing is essential for my continuing.

Premiss (2) relies on the intuition that whatever else might be the case in 1984, compatible with $(p.q)$, my stream of consciousness could continue thereafter.

If you deny (2) and say that r is a state of affairs not entailed by $(p.q)$, but which has to hold if it is to be possible that s, you run into this difficulty. There may be two people in 1984, Oliver who has a soul, and Fagin, who does not. Both are embodied and conscious, and to all appearances indistinguishable. God (who can do all things logically possible, compatible with how the world is up to now), having forgotten to give Fagin a soul, has, as he annihilates Fagin's body at the end of 1984, no power to continue his stream of thought. Whereas he has the power to continue Oliver's stream of thought. This seems absurd.

3 [ch. 13 n. 5]. There is not as much evidence of such derivability as a brief flip through scientific textbooks might suggest, for a very fundamental reason to which very few physicists draw our attention, but which has been highlighted in a very exciting way by Nancy Cartwright. (*How the Laws of Physics Lie*, Clarendon Press, Oxford, 1983. See especially ch. 6.) In order to derive phenomenological laws from fundamental laws, you need a description of the set-up. In order to get Kepler's laws from Newton's laws you need to describe the initial positions and velocities of the planets; only for certain such initial positions and velocities (and certain more general assumptions) does it follow from Newton's laws that their subsequent behaviour will be that described by Kepler. Cartwright points out that scientists make large simplifying assumptions about the set-up. They have to—for two reasons. There is a limit to the information which in practice they can obtain; and the more information they have, the more difficult the calculations become. So (to take the planetary example, which is far simpler than Cartwright's more contemporary examples), Newton supposes that there is no magnetic or electric attraction between planets, no more distant stars exerting a gravitational attraction on the sun and planets, and a pure vacuum between the planets. Even so, the calculations are impossibly difficult—with or without assistance from any computer. So the scientist simplifies not merely the descriptions of the set-up, but the equations which he is beginning to set down—e.g. he ignores various terms which he supposes will have fairly small values. In Newton's case he ignored the gravitational attractions between the planets themselves, except at certain periods when a massive planet is close to another massive planet. We are still unable to solve the many-body problem and so must make the same simplification.

Now there would be nothing wrong with this process of approximation if we had good evidence as to which approximations we could justifiably make before we set about our calculations. And we might reasonably suppose that to be the case in the Newtonian example—all the independent empirical evidence (e.g. by measurement on Earth) suggests the absence of significant magnetic, electric, etc. attractions. But Cartwright's thesis, illustrated with many contemporary examples, is that what more usually happens is that approximations are made 'bottom up'. The scientist claims to know in advance which are the true fundamental laws, and which are the true phenomenological laws, and then he makes such approximations as will enable him to derive the latter from the former. One beautiful example which she produces (op. cit., pp. 119–23) concerns the derivation from quantum theory of the Lamb shift in the excited state of a single two-level atom. To do this you need to make two crucial approximations, but whether you predict the shift will depend on the order in which you make those approximations, i.e. which one you do first. The calculation was done in 1930 in the way which did not predict the shift. Then the shift was discovered in 1947, and so the calculation was done the other way so as to get the right result.

Now it may well be that Cartwright has exaggerated the plight of modern physics, and that, in general, physicists make approximations which have some plausibility on other grounds. In that case the fact that, given those approximations, we can derive some phenomenological laws from fundamental laws, seems to me to provide evidential support for the claim that the phenomenological laws are consequences of the fundamental ones. However, the support will only be small if there are other equally plausible approximations which do not give these results at all. And there are no doubt cases in which the only grounds for making the approximations in fact made are that the right results follow, in which case there is no evidence for the derivability. We do badly need a general theory of which approximations are plausible and which are not, in order to sort these cases out.

The relevance of all this was to the initially plausible argument in the text saying: we know the fundamental laws of nature which apply to all fundamental particles in simple cases; we have every evidence from the derivability of phenomenological laws to support the claim that they apply in slightly more complicated cases (where there are more particles and ones closer to each other); that suggests that they hold in far more complicated cases; yet all physical events are ones which happen to conglomerations of fundamental particles; hence we have reason for supposing that the fundamental laws govern all matter, and so that there is no more indeterminism in nature than they allow. I have now pointed out that the argument is not as strong as initially it appears since the derivability of the phenomenological laws in the slightly more complicated cases depends on simplifying assumptions, whose justification is sometimes inadequate. There is a great need to sort out, by means of a general theory of approximations, the extent to which such crucial approximations are justified.

INDEX

accuracy of prediction, argument from increasing 236 ff.

Achinstein, P. 47 f.

act descriptions:
 basic, defined 86
 ultimate, defined 87

action by contact 234 f., 241

active events, defined 19

adverbial account of sensation 24

after-life 298–312

ageing 277

agent, defined 5

alcohol 282 f., 306

altruism 218 f., 224–227

Alzheimer's disease 277

analytic/synthetic 209

animal, defined 5

animals:
 mental life of 29, 69, 76, 78 f., 132 f., 174, 180–96, 203–09, 211 ff., 224 f., 231, 252, 261, 262, 296 f.
 synthesized 196 f.

appearance as a criterion of personal identity 163 ff.

appetitive, defined 22

approximation in physics 315 ff.

Aquinas, St Thomas 179 f., 199, 297, 300, 306, 311

Aristotle 153, 180, 297, 300

Armstrong, D. M. 34 f., 38, 42 f., 45, 49

Augustine, St 199, 281

averaging device, defined 245

awareness of mental events 18 f., 23, 31 ff., 96 f., 156 f., 295

Badham, P. and L. 303 f.

Baier, A. 87

basic acts 86 f., 99 f.

bee-dance 207

behaviourism 8, 42 ff., 60

belief 18 ff., 22 f., 34–39, 62 f., 78 f., 81, 83, 97–100, 111 f., 122–40, 147, 152, 156–59, 192 ff., 199, 203–11, 231 ff., 246–97, 313f.
 and action 128 ff.

and probability 124 ff., 266, 270

categorical theory of 136, 286–92

causation of 232–61

continuing mental state 134 ff., 262

-desire sub-systems 292–95

dispositional theory of 123, 135 f., 286–92

evaluative see evaluative belief

Humean theory of 123

involuntary 126 ff.

means–end 122 f., 204

moral see moral belief

passive 126

prominence of 279, 283, 292

relative to alternatives 124 ff.

see also under character and knowledge

Bennett, J. 205 ff., 209

Berkeley, G. 157, 305

biblical view of man 311 f.

blindsight 37 f.

Block, N. 41

blood groups 163 f.

body 7–10, 145–48, 314 f.

bodily criterion of personal identity 165, 172 f., 310
 see also brain criterion

Bond, E. J. 107, 115

brain:
 criterion of personal identity 155, 161–73, 175, 299 f., 302
 disease 275–79
 reactivation after death 299 ff.
 surgery 275–79, 282 f.
 transplantation 9 f., 147–51, 299

Braithwaite, R. B. 123

Brandt, R. 52

Brehm, J. W. 284

Broca's aphasia 276

Butler, J. 168, 306

cannibal, problem of the 300

Cartwright, N. 315 ff.

causal efficacy of mental events 38–41, 82 ff., 100 ff, 110, 136, 192, 288 ff.